MEREDITH OAKES
COLLECTED PLAYS

Meredith Oakes
COLLECTED PLAYS

THE NEIGHBOUR
THE EDITING PROCESS
FAITH
HER MOTHER AND BARTOK
SHADOWMOUTH
GLIDE
THE MIND OF THE MEETING

OBERON BOOKS
LONDON

This collection first published in 2010 by Oberon Books Ltd
521 Caledonian Road, London N7 9RH
Tel: +44 (0) 20 7607 3637 / Fax: +44 (0) 20 7607 3629
e-mail: info@oberonbooks.com
www.oberonbooks.com

The Neighbour first published in 1996
The Editing Process first published in 1996; This edition first published 2010
Faith first published in 1997
Shadowmouth first published in 2006
Her Mother and Bartok first published in 2010
Glide first published in 2010
The Mind of the Meeting first published in 2010

A catalogue record for this book is available from the British Library.

ISBN: 978-1-84002-966-6

Cover design by James Illman

Printed in Great Britain by Marston Book Services Limited, Didcot.

Visit www.oberonbooks.com to read more about all our books and to buy them. You will also find features, author interviews and news of any author events, and you can sign up for e-newsletters so that you're always first to hear about our new releases.

Contents

THE NEIGHBOUR

Characters

JOHN, *a young man*

MARGARET, *his mother*

STEPHI, *a young woman*

JAMES, *the young man she lives with*

LIZ, *James' sister*

SHEILA, *a woman in her fifties*

REG, *Sheila's husband*

MICHAEL, *a young man, James' friend*

Also the offstage voice of CELESTINE

Time: 1990s. Setting: a London council estate.

ACT ONE

SCENE 1

Outside JOHN's council flat. A summer evening.

JOHN is putting something in the dustbin. MARGARET, his mother, comes out.

MARGARET: Are you off out?

JOHN: No.

MARGARET: I thought you was off out.

JOHN: No.

MARGARET: Are you coming in then?

JOHN: In a minute.

MARGARET: What you want to stay out here for?

JOHN: I got a life to lead. Watch out for the door. *(The door is swinging closed.)*

MARGARET: *(Stopping the door from closing.)* Got a key, have you?

JOHN: No.

MARGARET: Neither do I.

JOHN: Don't shut it then.

MARGARET: Are you coming in?

JOHN: Yes, I'm coming in now.

MARGARET: All right. *(She goes in shutting door behind her.)*

JOHN: Mum! *(Sotto voce.)* Fucking vegetable. *(Bangs on the door.)* Mum! *(Gives up, turns away from the door.)* It's a beautiful summer night. You can hear the weeds growing. They're making fertile use of restricted space, like the rest of us. This estate won a design award for witty, compact provision. We've got a red toilet seat. The place is a blank to me. Unreal. No shelter. I believe it was completed five years ago. Before that, the weeds had all the space they wanted. Now they're fighting it out in two hundred garden

11

plots, each the size of a grave but less nourishing. I don't feel lonely out here. In there with her I feel lonely. But I mean to make this my home. The superior man creates, by his very existence, a place of safety. *(JAMES bursts out of the next door house, pursued by STEPHI.)*

JAMES: Get off.

STEPHI: No.

JAMES: Mind my sleeve.

STEPHI: If you go, I'm going back in and cut your clothes to pieces.

JAMES: If you do, I'll get the law on you.

STEPHI: Come back.

JAMES: What for?

STEPHI: I never meant what I said.

JAMES: What you say it for?

STEPHI: I said it to upset you.

JAMES: Yes well it does upset me.

STEPHI: You ain't what I said.

JAMES: Maybe I am.

STEPHI: You ain't.

JAMES: We'll see what I am. We'll see who's the fucking loser. You're the fucking loser. How much you make in a day?

STEPHI: Come inside.

JAMES: You make fuck-all. You work your fucking arse off cleaning up after skinflint fucking yuppies and you make fuck-all, so who are you calling a fucking loser?

STEPHI: Before I'd be what you are, I'd clean sewers.

JAMES: That's how you see me ain't it. Clean fucking sewers. Lick the fuckers clean if you want.

STEPHI: I didn't mean it. I never meant it. It's my temper James.

JAMES: Piss off.

STEPHI: Come back in. Come in eh.

JAMES: What you want a fucking loser for?

STEPHI: Come in. *(A car horn sounds. They look towards it.)* Bitch.

JAMES: *(Calling.)* New motor.

CELESTINE: *(Off.)* I come to take you for a ride.

STEPHI: Where did she get that.

JAMES: Ask her. Maybe she got it off the DHSS.

CELESTINE: *(Off.)* Are you coming?

JAMES: *(To STEPHI.)* Want a ride?

STEPHI: I'd sooner eat nails.

JAMES: Suit yourself. *(To CELESTINE.)* Can I drive?

CELESTINE: *(Off.)* Show us your licence.

JAMES: *(Puts his hand in his pocket.)* I got it in here. *(To STEPHI.)* See you in a minute.

STEPHI: *(As he goes.)* Run it into a wall why don't you.

(JOHN has been trying not to intrude.)

JOHN: Sorry to intrude.

STEPHI: You're welcome.

JOHN: My mum locked me out. Nice to meet you.

STEPHI: Why has it got to be him eh. Why not someone that's got a heart. The point is, I'm a pessimist. He represents my views on life. Settled in all right have you.

JOHN: Yes, we're busy settling in. My mum's a bit confused but aren't we all. Name's John.

STEPHI: Stephanie. Nice meeting you. *(She is about to go in.)*

JOHN: Them newsagents, do you find them obliging?

STEPHI: They'll sell you a paper.

JOHN: Yes I thought they seemed friendly enough. Three of you is there?

STEPHI: That's right.

JOHN: You and him, you got my mum all agog. She's been listening to you fighting through the wall.

STEPHI: I expect you've been having a listen in as well.

JOHN: These walls are paper thin. Shelving is out of the question. *(MARGARET opens the door.)*

MARGARET: Where you been? I been looking all over for you.

STEPHI: *(To JOHN.)* Be seeing you.

MARGARET: Wait a minute, girl, what's your name?

STEPHI: Stephanie.

MARGARET: *(To JOHN.)* Ask her if she wants a cup of tea.

STEPHI: No, it's all right thanks.

MARGARET: *(To JOHN.)* Is she a friend of yours?

JOHN: Yes, we're old friends.

MARGARET: You ought to bring her indoors.

STEPHI: I was just going, thanks all the same.

MARGARET: We ain't been here long.

STEPHI: No.

MARGARET: Nice to get to know people, ain't it. Some people.

STEPHI: Yes.

MARGARET: Not all people.

STEPHI: No.

MARGARET: Not round here.

STEPHI: No.

MARGARET: Do you come from round here?

STEPHI: That's right.

MARGARET: Where do you come from then?

STEPHI: I live next door to you.

MARGARET: Oh.

JOHN: *(To MARGARET.)* So we'll be seeing quite a bit of her.

MARGARET: Yes. Very nice.

JOHN: You can have lots of talks. She can tell you everything goes on around here.

MARGARET: Thanks all the same.

JOHN: That ain't very polite.

MARGARET: Teaching manners you ain't got. *(To STEPHI.)* He talks to me like dirt.

JOHN: Just winding you up, ain't I. I always wind you up.

MARGARET: *(To STEPHI.)* He always winds me up. He thinks I ain't got any feelings, but I have.

STEPHI: Bound to, ain't you.

JOHN: Bound to.

MARGARET: He oughtn't to upset me, ought he, it makes me lose track.

JOHN: What I'll do, I'll make us a cup of tea.

MARGARET: Yes, I'll have a cup of tea.

JOHN: That's right. Stephanie might have a cup of tea as well, stop us misbehaving ourselves.

STEPHI: I ought to get back.

JOHN: He's out enjoying himself, ain't he.

STEPHI: I'll have a cup of tea.

MARGARET: Are you coming in then?

JOHN: Yes, we're coming in, don't shut the bleeding door on us. *(They go in.)*

SCENE 2

Later the same evening, inside the home of JAMES, LIZ and STEPHI.

(LIZ is making a woollen pompom. STEPHI comes in.)

LIZ: I didn't know what to do with your toast.

STEPHI: Did James come in?

LIZ: No. I put it in the bin. Were you wanting it?

STEPHI: No.

LIZ: You could have warmed it up, couldn't you. What a shame. I hope you didn't want it.

(STEPHI is checking the channels on the TV.)

LIZ: Where's James then?

STEPHI: He's your brother, you tell me.

LIZ: I thought you and him was off together somewhere.

STEPHI: No.

LIZ: I thought you and him would have made it up.

(STEPHI goes and checks the answering machine, but there's nothing on it.)

LIZ: Look what I made for Eddy and Freddy. *(Holds up the pompom.)*

STEPHI: Yeah.

LIZ: Do you want to see me give it them? *(Goes to the cage of Eddy and Freddy.)* Hullo Freddy darling, you in your wheel are you? Oh, the little love, he's a little muscle mouse. Where's your friend? Where's Eddy? Look at him, you can see his little mind going round. Eddy? Eddy? Come and see what Liz has got. Something nice and soft for you. Who was that in the car with him? Was that Celestine was it? Oh yes, ain't you a strong little mouse, you can spin that great big wheel all by yourself. Mind you don't catch your tail, that's what happens to little boys that show off. Eddy! I don't know why Eddy won't come out. You won't see James till morning then.

STEPHI: I'd fucking better.

LIZ: He's a law unto himself though, ain't he, you'll never change him. I could never change him. I never had the slightest control. He was such a lovely-looking little boy though. Oh yes Freddy, you're a lovely-looking little boy too, you've got a lovely pink nose and it's ever so pointy. Go and get Eddy for me. Go on. *(To STEPHI.)* I hope Eddy's all right. He might be sick, mightn't he. I ought to take off their roof and see what he's up to. *(STEPHI switches on the TV. LIZ takes the roof off.)* Look at you, you sleepyhead. Don't you want to see what I got for you? Come on, I thought you was supposed to be nocturnal. Here, what you got there. Show Lizzie. Oh! It's a baby! It's a tiny little baby. Fancy that.

STEPHI: What?

LIZ: Eddy ain't a little boy, he's a mother.

(Stephi turns off the TV.)

LIZ: Did you ever see anything so tiny? It looks like it's made of jelly, don't it, like something from the sweet shop. It's like a jelly baby with hands.

(LIZ is reaching into the cage.)

STEPHI: Don't touch it.

LIZ: I'm only going to put it next its mother.

STEPHI: If you touch them the mother rejects them.

LIZ: Eddy won't mind. Eddy's my baby, ain't you darling.

STEPHI: Leave them be.

LIZ: I can't, I'm too excited. Where's it gone, Eddy, where's your little baby? Look behind you, stupid thing.

(LIZ reaches into the cage, then continues watching.)

STEPHI: When he comes through that door I'm off. I'm only waiting to see how much longer he thinks he can be.

LIZ: She's Edwina now. Oh blimey, look at that, will you.

STEPHI: What's the matter?

LIZ: She's eating it. *(STEPHI looks.)* Horrible little creature! Horrible little thing! Eating it! Her own baby!

STEPHI: Put the lid on. *(She does so.)*

LIZ: I shouldn't have touched them, it's against their instincts ain't it. You told me not to touch them. You mustn't disturb them, must you. That's what they say. But it's unnatural, ain't it. I shan't give them that pompom now.

STEPHI: Why not?

LIZ: It'll go straight in the bin.

STEPHI: Well that should bring them to their senses.

LIZ: I suppose you'll say I'm too high strung. *(JAMES enters.)*

JAMES: *(To STEPHI.)* Why didn't you come?

STEPHI: Nice ride was it.

JAMES: What you looking so suspicious for. We drove down into Kent and had a drink. Guess who come in the pub. Marvin. He's living down there with his dad. He come in with a little puppy in a plastic bag with a little blanket and a Farley's rusk, except Marvin ate the rusk.

STEPHI: And?

JAMES: Marvin likes Complan too. It was a very sweet puppy. It had big brown worried eyes, like it was meekly wondering what the fuck it done wrong to end up as Marvin's dog.

STEPHI: What else?

JAMES: And then we drove back.

STEPHI: Then what?

LIZ: I'm off to bed. *(She goes, unnoticed.)*

STEPHI: What did you do?

JAMES: I told you.

STEPHI: You and her.

JAMES: We went back to her place.

(STEPHI goes into the kitchen and comes back with a knife, while JAMES sits down.)

STEPHI: Tell me about it.

JAMES: You've really got a temper on you. We didn't go anywhere.

STEPHI: You just said you did.

JAMES: Well we didn't, all right?

STEPHI: Do you expect me to believe that?

JAMES: All right, I'm lying. What you waiting for?

STEPHI: Don't tempt me.

JAMES: You're so aggressive. I feel totally secure with you. You can murder me any time you want.

STEPHI: You never give me anything I need. You never comfort me.

JAMES: I'll comfort you. Come here.

STEPHI: No.

JAMES: Come on, I'll be getting sleepy soon.

STEPHI: *(Goes across to him.)* You don't understand anything.

JAMES: I know. I'm just a bastard. *(Caressing her. They kiss.)* I'd like to get you a little dog.

STEPHI: What for?

JAMES: I'd like to see it being well treated. I'd like to see you feed it. I'd like to see it chew on your fingers and lick you. Then I'd fuck you.

STEPHI: The dog mightn't like that.

JAMES: Then he'd have to get out, wouldn't he. I'd kick the little fucker out and shut the door. *(While they are embracing, JAMES speaks, unheard by STEPHI.)* I know people, you only got to brush against them and money rubs off. Celestine give me twenty to get her a drink and said keep the change. I can make a hundred in a night just by sitting in the right company in the right place. I like to feel money circulating, you can float on it. You get high on it. When I got to come off it, everything frustrates me and I become restless and irritable. I got to take it out on someone because I got too much energy and I'm very touchy. Stephi always accepts whatever I do. At times that annoys me and I get encouraged to take it further. It's just my curiosity. I'm very curious, but unfortunately she's got very few secrets.

STEPHI: Oh James, what you doing to me.

JAMES: You're so beautiful. You're so delicate. Celestine's a camel beside you.

STEPHI: Is she? Am I better?

JAMES: Yes. *(Kisses her.)* You like me don't you.

STEPHI: Yes.

JAMES: Why?

STEPHI: I love you.

JAMES: What for? Stop fooling around.

STEPHI: No.

JAMES: What's wrong with you Stephi?

STEPHI: Eh?

JAMES: How can you like a black rotten heart?

STEPHI: You ain't got a black rotten heart.

JAMES: You been telling me I do.

STEPHI: I never said that.

JAMES: Like when you look at me, you see this invisible stain.

STEPHI: I only criticize you because you mean too much to me.

JAMES: So what happens if I ain't bad? You might not like me then. So you're good, is what you think, but to please you I got to be a bad boy. People are strange.

STEPHI: You're the strange one. *(Kisses his chest.)*

JAMES: Fuck off! What you bite me for?

STEPHI: I never.

JAMES: You bit my heart.

STEPHI: Don't be stupid, James, I never bit you at all. If I bit you, where's the mark?

JAMES: Devils leave no mark. They suck your heart out with a straw.

STEPHI: I ain't a devil.

JAMES: I never said you was.

STEPHI: What you talking about?

JAMES: Nothing.

STEPHI: Do you know what you just said?

JAMES: Let's go to bed, I'm knackered.

STEPHI: Are you all right?

JAMES: No, I told you, I'm fucking knackered.

SCENE 3

A week later, around midday.

MICHAEL is sitting in a tree near the road. He has a large sports bag. JAMES walks up.

JAMES: Mike?

MICHAEL: Hullo James.

JAMES: You're in a tree. What's the point of it Michael?

MICHAEL: Waiting for the milk float. Late, ain't it. It's a disgrace.

JAMES: Why aren't you waiting for it in your home?

MICHAEL: I couldn't rob it if I was in my home.

JAMES: Why has that tree got no leaves? You ain't hidden. You're visible. Ain't you got nothing better to do?

MICHAEL: No I fucking ain't.

JAMES: Go down the pub.

MICHAEL: Pub's a fucking shithole.

JAMES: Go down the shop.

MICHAEL: Shop's a fucking rip-off.

JAMES: Go and see your mum.

MICHAEL: Mum's a fucking slag.

JAMES: Go and see your sister.

MICHAEL: She's fucking with my dad.

JAMES: Planning to raid the milk float, are you? Ambush it, will you?

MICHAEL: I'm working it out.

JAMES: Rich pickings there.

MICHAEL: I only need the yoghurts.

JAMES: Are you a health freak?

(MICHAEL is climbing down. He opens his sports bag and takes out a bedding plant which has been uprooted.)

JAMES: That's a pretty flower.

MICHAEL: How many of these have I got?

JAMES: I couldn't really say Michael.

MICHAEL: Forty-two.

JAMES: That's a lot, ain't it.

MICHAEL: When I get them yoghurt pots, I can plant them in and knock them out next Sunday down the market. Two fifty a piece.

JAMES: Where did you get them.

MICHAEL: I been for a walk in the park. The security down there is a joke.

JAMES: The point is, they don't envisage somebody like you. *(SHEILA enters.)*

SHEILA: It's no use giving him flowers, Michael, he'll never appreciate you the way I do. You're looking well today, the pair of you. I do like this warm weather, it's so much more modern.

JAMES: It gives me a headache. You got anything for a headache?

SHEILA: I ain't a fucking witch.

JAMES: Go on, you got everything in that bag.

SHEILA: How would you know what I got in my bag? *(She starts to search.)*

JAMES: Could you get the attention of a milkman?

SHEILA: I can't even get the attention of my husband. Here you are. Open wide. *(She feeds him a pill.)*

JAMES: Got any more?

SHEILA: You're like a bleeding baby bird. *(She feeds him another.)*

JAMES: Could you chat him up?

SHEILA: What for?

JAMES: Michael's short of a pint, ain't you Michael.

SHEILA: Why don't I buy him one?

JAMES: No. Tacky.

MICHAEL: Wait up. Here he is.

JAMES: *(To SHEILA.)* Keep him talking across the road.

(SHEILA goes. They watch.)

JAMES: What you going to put them in?

(MICHAEL empties the plants out of his sports bag and goes off stage to rob the milk float. Returns a moment later with the bag full of yoghurts.)

JAMES: You're an artist, man. You are so nonchalant. You walked up to that milk like a worker to his machine. You packed that up like you was being paid for it.

MICHAEL: It's fresh here.

JAMES: It's the suspense that made me fart, Michael. Reading the labels, a master stroke.

MICHAEL: I only like the pineapple. I ain't making much on this, all right?

JAMES: Three-way split. Definite.

MICHAEL: Up your arse. *(SHEILA returns.)*

SHEILA: Oh James I felt such a fool. "Where's Canford Street," I says. "You're in it," he says. End of conversation. "Oh," says I, "fancy that, what a stroke of luck". Then lo and behold he says to me, "I feel lucky too". He wants to meet me. He says I got good bones. Don't tell Reg. I wouldn't have good bones after that.

JAMES: I'm good for you, see. I take you out of yourself. I enable you to make new friends.

(Meanwhile MICHAEL has taken off his shirt, and is putting the plants into it and tying it up.)

SHEILA: Did you manage, Michael? Good lord, what's he doing.

JAMES: *(Takes one of the flowers, breaks off the root, gives her the top.)* Who knows. Come on. *(They all leave.)*

SCENE 4

Outside John's house the same afternoon.

JOHN is using stripping fluid on a piece of wooden furniture, and scraping off the old varnish.

JOHN: Dear Stephanie. So this is love. What was I like before I met you last week? I've forgotten. I was a closed book but now I like to think I have a reader. What is the book about? Trust. If you feel differently, it is better to find out straight away, that is why I am writing you this letter. Only a fool would stay in a burning house rather than jump out the window. Only a fool would sit outside the kitchen smelling the food but never daring to eat any in case it poisons him. Since last week, I finally hope I belong in the world though up till now I have always felt like a stranger. Shit what a wank. Start again. Dear Stephanie...

(LIZ has entered, holding a dress.)

LIZ: Excuse me. You know nail varnish, well I spilled it on this dress. I just caught sight of you from out the window, and I thought I'd come and ask you. Could you shift it?

JOHN: Pleased to meet you.

LIZ: I'm Liz. I rubbed it with remover but all I did was spread it. I tried methylated spirits but I might as well have been using lemonade. So then I did leave it in Coca Cola for a while. I got some petrol and poured it over, and then a friend of mine suggested I soak it overnight in a paste of sugar, salt and vinegar with a touch of cayenne, but I think they was having me on.

JOHN: The stuff I've got here, your dress might shrivel up altogether.

LIZ: Really?

JOHN: A woman come up to me, her husband had been spray painting the car but he was a bit shortsighted and pointed it at her instead. She asked me to remove it from her dress. Before I knew what was happening she'd got hold of the bottle and was dabbing it on. Next thing, her dress fell off her in rags.

LIZ: It never.

JOHN: She was running round here bollock naked not long before you came down. It's a wonder you didn't see her from your window.

LIZ: I didn't see anything like that.

JOHN: You can't have been looking properly.

LIZ: I was though. *(Pause.)* The use I've had out of this dress, it wouldn't matter anyway. It's my brother, see, he wants me to smarten myself up, go out and that. That's the reason I bought it. I don't much enjoy going out. I generally get sick to my stomach when I go out.

JOHN: What does your boyfriend say about that?

LIZ: I ain't got a boyfriend.

JOHN: Go on, I don't believe you.

LIZ: I have had, but it takes getting used to, don't it. He wanted to get married but I didn't think I could face it, not having my own room and that.

JOHN: No place to hide eh.

LIZ: You know James, you must have seen James, my brother, James thinks I'm not all there. I've always been the responsible one. I'm ten years older, see, I was the one that brought him up really. I never developed, he took over where I left off. It's not my fault, is it. There's no call for him to go on about it, is there. I shouldn't be talking to you, you're busy ain't you.

JOHN: I'm sorry about the dress.

LIZ: You ought to call round one of these days. See how the other half lives.

JOHN: Yes, it's always interesting, ain't it. Mind how you go now.

LIZ: Goodbye then.

JOHN: Goodbye. *(Continues to work.)* Dear Stephanie. Well. A new friend. Am I demented writing to you? Please will you

25

find a way to reassure me. *(Stops work.)* So far as I can see, the person you are currently linked with stays in bed most of the day. In the evening you are generally out. Why don't you come round and see me? He won't like it if you leave him. All in all he is plainly difficult. *(Starts work.)* There must definitely be satisfaction to be got out of kicking people around in the way he seems to like, but there is also satisfaction in being more careful where one puts one's feet, and in my view this is what the superior man ought to prefer. Self-restraint. However, we all have to tread on someone some time.

(SHEILA enters, with the flower that JAMES gave her.)

SHEILA: You'll poison yourself with that. Sorry love, did I give you a shock did I? I was only saying to my husband, I wonder when the new people are going to show themselves, I've hardly set eyes on them. I'm Sheila from number nineteen.

JOHN: John.

SHEILA: And what are you up to, John?

JOHN: Doing a bit of stripping.

SHEILA: It's ever such nice wood. Worn smooth. Antique is it, like me. I hate to think what you must have paid for it.

JOHN: Once this has passed through my hands I couldn't afford it. A man I know sells them see, I clean them up for him.

SHEILA: Creative. Lovely.

JOHN: Indoors with that stripping fluid it's enough to make you puke.

SHEILA: You need a nice big space with somewhere to put all your equipment. My husband works on cars at the moment, he does it up the road, I won't have him under my feet. There he is, he's just coming down. Big, ain't he. Big and wayward. Not for the faint-hearted.

(REG appears.)

SHEILA: Come here and meet John.

REG: *(Wiping his hands.)* Look at that. Blood. I must have took a piece out of my finger.

JOHN: I hope it's not serious.

REG: Ask yourself this. What is serious?

SHEILA: He once had his ear bit off in a fight and he never noticed until they saw it lying on the floor.

REG: Here. See this scar on my neck?

JOHN: My goodness yes.

REG: Four years ago I had this growth troubling me. I got sick of waiting to see them in casualty so I come home here and took it off with a chisel.

SHEILA: The doctor said he ought to have been a sculptor.

REG: Tell him how I proposed to you.

SHEILA: Propose. He never proposed. The first time I went out with him he took out this knife and cut the knickers off me.

JOHN: Those were romantic days.

SHEILA: You got your mother with you, is that right?

JOHN: Yes.

SHEILA: I seen her on the doorstep talking to herself, bless her.

JOHN: That's her.

SHEILA: Change upsets them, don't it. What is it exactly? She ain't that old.

JOHN: No, not that old.

SHEILA: What a shame. What exactly do they say it is?

JOHN: Nothing definite, nothing anyone ought to put a name to. Often as not she's all right.

SHEILA: The people before you died out. (To REG.) He wouldn't leave the house, would he.

REG: Never left the house.

SHEILA: She did all the to-ing and fro-ing. He never even went to her funeral.

REG: He was afraid of his own shadow. Well. Think about it. A man's own shadow is a frightening thing.

SHEILA: We could never get close to them really. Any night you want to come in for a drink, or a Sunday afternoon you know, our door is always open.

JOHN: Thank you very much.

REG: Better go indoors and get washed up.

JOHN: That's a nasty cut.

REG: I'll crush some garlic on it, pour on a bit of vodka, soon be good as new. *(He goes.)*

SHEILA: Nice to meet you.

JOHN: Mind how you go. *(She goes.)* Dear Stephanie. Are they friends of yours?

SCENE 5

Later the same afternoon, outside John's house. The piece of furniture is gone.

JAMES arrives, calling to MICHAEL who is offstage.

JAMES: Hey Mike!

MICHAEL: What you want?

JAMES: Think it over.

MICHAEL: What?

JAMES: Three ways man!

MICHAEL: Piss off!

JAMES: All right, you and me.

MICHAEL: Dip your balls in batter!

JAMES: Watch yourself!

> *(Picks up half a brick, throws it at MICHAEL who is still offstage.)*

MICHAEL: Accurate throw James. *(Throws the brick back. JAMES dodges.)*

JAMES: *(Throws the brick back.)* Stand still you fucker!

(MICHAEL throws the brick back. JAMES dodges and the brick goes through the glass in Margaret's front door. MARGARET emerges.)

MARGARET: You come here! *(JAMES looks towards MICHAEL but he has run away.)* Did you throw that?

JAMES: No.

MARGARET: Yes you did.

JAMES: No I fucking didn't.

MARGARET: My son will be back in a minute.

JAMES: That's nice.

(He turns to go. MARGARET catches hold of him.)

MARGARET: What about my hall? You ought to see in there. You ought to pick that up. You ought to walk on that in your bare feet, see what it's like for others. Who's going to fix my glass? Anyone can get in there, it's not safe. I'm going to get the law on you.

JAMES: I ain't done nothing, you old fungus.

MARGARET: You near frightened me out of my wits. I can't keep track when I'm upset. They'll never fix that, will they. My son says to me, two weeks we been here, are you happy, and I says no, this sink's blocked, and he says, we'll get someone in to fix it, and I says no we won't, they'll never bleeding come. They never will.

JAMES: That's because you disgust them. I'm going now.

MARGARET: *(She is still holding him.)* No you ain't.

JAMES: I'd like to feed you to some animal, get every last scrap cleared away. *(He tries to get free.)*

MARGARET: You ain't even apologized. You ain't even said you're sorry.

JAMES: *(Pushes her so that she falls.)* Get off.

(At this moment, JOHN arrives.)

JOHN: Fucking hell. *(Grabs JAMES.)* What you push my mother for?

JAMES: I never pushed her.

JOHN: Bollocks.

JAMES: I was walking away. What's up with her, she don't seem right in the head.

JOHN: So what you push her for?

JAMES: I'm sorry she fell over. All right? You ought to keep her somewhere out of harm's way.

JOHN: I'll put you somewhere out of harm's way.

JAMES: Are you starting? Are you starting? Come on then, have a taste. Have a try.

(They are beginning to fight. REG, who has been working on a car nearby, walks in, picks JAMES up and holds him midair.)

REG: Explain yourself.

JAMES: I never...

REG: Shut up.

JAMES: Calm down Reg.

REG: Do you want me to deck you?

JAMES: No I don't.

MARGARET: There was no call for that, was there. There was no call for what he done to me.

REG: None at all. I seen it.

JAMES: Something come over me. I thought she was my mum.

REG: Eh?

JAMES: Let me go, fuck you. I thought I was seeing things. I thought she was my mum come back to get me.

REG: *(Letting go.)* Tell me, James, why would you want to throw down your mum on a concrete path?

MARGARET: I'm not to be upset. Am I John.

JOHN: Go indoors mum, have a lie down.

MARGARET: I ought to take one of them pills.

JOHN: You go in, I'll be in in a minute.

MARGARET: I ought to telephone to the police.

REG: Don't worry love, we'll take care of it. Won't we John.

MARGARET: They'll never come about that window. We shall have to board that up.

JOHN: What window?

JAMES: I never broke no fucking window.

REG: *(To JAMES.)* Where's your wallet? *(JAMES gives it to him.)* It's thicker than a fucking dictionary.

JAMES: That ain't mine, I got to hand it on.

REG: Hand it on less a hundred. *(He takes money out and gives it to JOHN.)*

JAMES: Don't do that, man, you're getting me in shit.

REG: Shut your face.

JAMES: You'll get my fucking legs broken.

REG: You ought to have thought of that sooner.

JAMES: I never smashed no fucking window. I give you my word.

REG: I'm losing patience with you. This is John, tell him you apologize.

JAMES: I'm sorry about your mum.

JOHN: Yeah.

REG: What you want to do, John, you want to take it further?

JOHN: No use crying over spilt milk, is there. We're all neighbours here.

REG: You're a philosopher. James could learn from you.

JOHN: I ought to go and see how she is.

REG: Good night then John.

JOHN: Good night. Thank you. *(He goes in.)*

JAMES: If I come up a hundred short I'm dead. Who do you think it's for.

REG: I don't want to know.

JAMES: You're a good friend, Reg. My friend.

REG: I am your friend.

JAMES: You think all you got to do is call yourself my friend
and you can shit on me to your heart's content.

REG: What's a hundred these days.

JAMES: You think I'm working for people who can't count.

REG: Perish the thought, you're too choosy ain't you.

JAMES: Fuck you.

REG: Here's fifty. You'll have to raise the other half by your
own efforts. Sell one of your trainers.

JAMES: The man's a cunt.

REG: Eh?

JAMES: He didn't have to take it, did he.

REG: I give it him.

JAMES: It's too much anyhow. He could fix another couple of
windows with that. I could go and bust them for him now.

REG: You owe that man a debt of gratitude. You're fortunate
his disposition is so pleasant.

JAMES: I don't trust any cunt that's pleasant. I don't trust any
cunt that forgives me what I done to them. What must they
be feeling, they must be all twisted up inside.

REG: John is a man who prefers to let bygones be bygones.

JAMES: So you think I made no impression.

REG: You made an impression James. I hope that poor
woman's all right. I'm going down the pub in a minute,
come and help me pack up.

(REG goes. JAMES remains behind for a moment.)

JAMES: When someone finds fault with me, it interrupts my
inner life. Therefore I become violently angry. Technically
they might be in the right, in which case I might not enjoy
my revenge. But if they're in the wrong, I definitely will.
I had to get that woman off me. Being old is catching,
you don't want to let it touch you. Each time it touches
you, you lose a bit more immunity, you lose another life.
They'll have a grudge against me now. The fact is, when

32

you wrong someone, you ought to get on and finish the job. It's a shame to leave damaged people wandering round. They're dangerous and they're ugly. *(He goes.)*

SCENE 6

Reg and Sheila's home the following Sunday afternoon.

STEPHI is lying face down on the floor and SHEILA has her foot on STEPHI's back. JAMES and MICHAEL are drinking

STEPHI: *(To herself.)* Sundays with Sheila. They think the sun shines out of her. She gives herself out like prizes, rationed though, she's never at a loss. Some women must be differently made. I ain't got no interest in men I can get the better of. She's got an interest in getting the better of men she ain't even got any interest in.

SHEILA: Hands by your sides. Relax yourself. A structural engineer taught me this.

STEPHI: What you going to do? *(SHEILA starts to walk along her back.)* Shit!

SHEILA: What's wrong with you?

STEPHI: You'll put my back out.

SHEILA: I'm putting it in, love. Any pain you feel, it means you've got something that isn't where it ought to be. When I'm finished you'll have it all in the right place.

STEPHI: Where's that, Australia?

JAMES: Sheila.

SHEILA: Yes?

JAMES: Michael's got a back problem.

MICHAEL: Fuck off.

SHEILA: Have you, love?

JAMES: He doesn't like to talk about it.

SHEILA: You don't need to talk, Michael, get down on the floor.

MICHAEL: Thanks very much, it's all right thank you.

SHEILA: Lie down love.

(MICHAEL obeys. SHEILA abandons STEPHI and starts to walk on MICHAEL's back.)

JAMES: *(To STEPHI.)* She's finished with you, she's got an urgent case.

SHEILA: Goodness, Michael, what a lot of lumps you got.

JAMES: You ought to see the other side.

SHEILA: I can feel every knob in your spine. Relax, Michael, I'm massaging you with my toes. I'll make you sore if you're stiff. Pretend the floor is made of rubber.

MICHAEL: Oh.

SHEILA: What's the matter?

JAMES: He can't feel it. *(Rubs his foot violently on the base of MICHAEL'S spine.)*

MICHAEL: Christ! Get off!

(He grabs JAMES by the ankle, pulls him to the ground and they start to wrestle, dislodging SHEILA.)

JAMES: You're over-reacting Michael. You're acting on impulse... *(REG enters with a dish of squid salad.)*

REG: Calamari. Who's having some? Stephi my love, you want feeding up, you got nothing there a man can get his hands on.

STEPHI: What is it?

REG: Calamari. Squid.

STEPHI: I'm not eating that.

REG: Ask yourself this. Why do you fear foreign food? "I'm not eating that," she says, "I ain't letting anything past my lips that ain't English".

STEPHI: Disgusting animals they are, all them legs.

REG: What's wrong with their legs? White and tasty, washed by the sea. Look at that. The English, if there ain't a nursery rhyme about it, they won't eat it. The English don't want to be adults. *(He eats.)*

(Doorbell. SHEILA goes to answer it. REG offers the dish to MICHAEL, who dubiously eats a piece of squid.)

SHEILA: *(Letting JOHN in.)* Come on in love, ain't that nice that you decided to come along. He brought me a six-pack. Ain't you a man of the world, not like this other rubbish. *(To the others.)* I expect you know John.

REG: John will eat calamari. John is a man of vision.

JOHN: That's right. If I see it, I eat it.

JAMES: Why does he smell of air freshener? What did you put on yourself, John? Was it Airwick?

JOHN: Disinfectant. In case I met you.

JAMES: It don't smell like disinfectant. It smells overpoweringly sweet, like the stuff in the little plastic holder that people leave on the back of the toilet to disguise the smell of shit.

REG: Come and sit down, John. Ignore the banter.

JAMES: Reg wants to hug you, cos he's a hugging man.

REG: Are you going to keep a civil tongue in your head? Or am I going to push you through the wall?

JAMES: You're masterful Reg. You're a godsend to us young ones. Ain't you got any friends your own age?

REG: You can piss off out of here.

JAMES: Yeah. You can patronize someone else. I see right through you. Stephi?

STEPHI: Off you go then.

JAMES: Suit yourself. Michael?

SHEILA: Michael's going to stay and tell me all about his back.

JAMES: Michael?

MICHAEL: Catch you later, man.

JAMES: Fuck you too. *(He goes.)*

REG: If he'd have been my son, he wouldn't have lived to grow up and embarrass me.

JOHN: I ought to have picked a different time.

REG: How can anyone excuse behaviour like that? That's the problem I'm facing. Eh Stephi?

STEPHI: I'm sorry he was so rude. I don't know what possessed him.

JOHN: Didn't he tell you we'd met before?

REG: The less said about that the better.

SHEILA: Me and Reg don't like nastiness. We're too old for it. The thing with James is to give him space. Let him rave. I would never oppose him directly, no. Little by little I would seem to agree with him while gradually bringing in a different point of view. The object is, to lead him on to think that he might have been being just that little bit hotheaded. He'll never admit to it mind. He's a little terror. He oughtn't to be let loose.

REG: James needs a rock. I would never cut myself off. Because he needs to understand that a man has got a soul, and a soul is a thing that never changes. You turn to it and it's always there. Physical strength is a pale image of the strength in a soul. He thinks we're soft.

SHEILA: Not me, he don't.

REG: He thinks we're fucking soft. I'm not enamoured of going round frightening people. I don't enjoy it. I've been bodyguard, rent collector and avenger. I've hurt people physically. I know how to set fires so it looks as if they sprang up by magic. I can make a fuse box sing. Most of life's problems are very simple. If someone causes you offence, adjust their piping with a monkey wrench. Or block their sewer with a brick. Calamari, John?

JOHN: Oh. Thank you.

REG: Michael?

MICHAEL: Got to go to the bog. *(He goes.)*

STEPHI: Ain't you got anything civilized to eat? Packet of crisps?

REG: God in heaven, Stephanie, I'll find you a biscuit. *(He goes to the kitchen.)*

SHEILA: He don't know where they are. *(She follows him.)*

JOHN: I ain't seen you.

STEPHI: I'm out cleaning most days.

JOHN: Where's that?

STEPHI: Round Elgin Road. James don't like it. That's why I do it.

JOHN: What else will you do that James don't like?

STEPHI: That's a funny question.

JOHN: Women in your situation will generally look to their own best interests.

STEPHI: What's wrong with my situation?

JOHN: Your situation is shit.

STEPHI: You got a right to your opinion.

JOHN: No, I didn't mean that. What I meant was...

(SHEILA comes in with a packet of biscuits. REG and MICHAEL also appear.)

SHEILA: *(Throwing the biscuits to STEPHI.)* Catch, love.

REG: Arm wrestle, John. Over here.

JOHN: Not on your life.

SHEILA: Did you see on the telly last night about American women's false tits? The surgeon has to use his full strength to get one of them in. Who would have thought a woman's chest could put up so much resistance? Come and sit down, Michael, tell us your views.

MICHAEL: They ought to invent something natural. *(He sits.)*

SCENE 7

John's house.

(JOHN comes through his front door into his sitting room, which contains items of furniture that he has been working on.)

JOHN: Fool! Amateur! Turd! I made a complete fucking fool of myself. She was well impressed. She wouldn't have minded at all if I'd seeped out through the floor. "You got a right to your opinion". Bitch! On the other hand. On the other hand. What was that about "James don't like it". There's a message there. I ought to think about that. She's telling me something there. She ain't aware of it, that's all. Next time I see her, I'll be ready. Next time I see her, she'd better watch out. Oh fuck. I made a total bollocks of it. Kami-fucking-kaze. *(Starts to work, sanding wood.)* Her James didn't stay long. He can't forgive me for his own fucking bad behaviour. There must be another side to him. The cunt must be lovable in some way. Otherwise they all love him for being a cunt, don't they. Which is absurd. It's unfortunate that I upset him, though. He's right next door. I feel like I'm a mouse with a cat outside. No matter how big a mouse is, it sees things from the mouse's point of view. What does the superior man do in such a case? Blot out the negative, be twice as positive. The fact is, he's a potential friend. We got mutual dislike in common.

MARGARET: *(Entering.)* You're back are you?

JOHN: Yes.

MARGARET: I didn't know you was back.

JOHN: No.

MARGARET: Are you doing that sanding now?

JOHN: That's right.

MARGARET: Nasty dust it makes.

JOHN: I'll clean it up later.

MARGARET: Sawdust over everything. Look at the couch beside you. That will get down into the fabric. You'll never get rid of that. That will eat its way down.

JOHN: I'll hoover it up when I'm finished.

MARGARET: I can hardly move in here for your mess. I can hardly turn round. You ought not to take up so much space.

JOHN: Got to be active, haven't I.

MARGARET: When you was a boy you used to keep to your room.

JOHN: Yes, quite right, you kept me contained.

MARGARET: When you was a baby you was tiny.

JOHN: I got to make a living.

MARGARET: You ought to have more consideration.

JOHN: I can't leave you, see.

MARGARET: That's what you say. You say I can't manage.

JOHN: You're all right.

MARGARET: I can't, can I.

JOHN: You manage.

MARGARET: I ain't been eating right. I ain't been looked after.

JOHN: I look after you. You're all right. You was always a bit forgetful. Nobody's fault, is it.

MARGARET: Raising you brought me to this.

JOHN: And me. Nothing wrong with it, is there. I look after you, don't I.

MARGARET: I want the telly switched on.

JOHN: Switch it on then.

MARGARET: I can't hear it with your racket.

JOHN: Switch it on, I'll be finished in a minute.

MARGARET: Never mind.

(MARGARET sits in silence while JOHN continues to work.)

JOHN: *(Stops.)* Fuck this.

MARGARET: You watch your mouth.

JOHN: I don't mean to make you unhappy.

MARGARET: You can't help it, can you.

JOHN: No.

MARGARET: You going to switch it on then? *(JOHN switches on the television.)*

39

SCENE 8

Next day.

MICHAEL carries a bag of newspapers, and is putting some through James' door. JAMES comes out

JAMES: I thought it was you.

MICHAEL: Paper.

JAMES: Call that a paper.

MICHAEL: I'll be off then.

JAMES: *(Extracting papers from the door.)* South East Gazette.
   Five copies. *(Drops four on the ground.)* That bag's getting
   lighter by the minute. Why don't you deliver us some
   more *(Takes a handful of papers out of Michael's bag, drops
   them.)* No point pushing them through all them letterboxes,
   it only shreds them.

MICHAEL: I thought you wouldn't be pleased to see me.

JAMES: But you brought me a paper. What you do that for?
   What are your stars?

MICHAEL: Virgo.

JAMES: *(Looking for the astrology column.)* Virgos are critical.
   They fasten on others' weaknesses. Here you go.
   "Professional colleagues will want to bounce ideas off you,
   and you'll have plenty to say in return." You are definitely
   a Virgo, are you?

MICHAEL: Eh?

JAMES: "Spend Wednesday with the love of your life." Who's
   the love of your life, Michael?

MICHAEL: Marilyn Monroe.

JAMES: It says here, spend Wednesday with her "and there will
   be some exciting surprises". Like finding out she's got bits
   of blue-tack stuck to the back of her. "Call me if you want
   to know more. Julian Trent." Fucked if I will, you squeezy-
   faced little chiseller. *(He drops the paper on the ground.)*

MICHAEL: Better get on.

JAMES: If you want.

MICHAEL: You ain't offended then.

JAMES: Who's offended. If anyone's offended, it's you.

MICHAEL: That's all right.

JAMES: Thank you. What did I do?

MICHAEL: Nothing.

JAMES: If I done nothing, why do you say, "that's all right"? I done something, right? What did I do?

MICHAEL: I never said you done anything.

JAMES: Yes you did.

MICHAEL: I never said nothing.

JAMES: Like you never said nothing yesterday. You let me walk out of there on my own.

MICHAEL: We all got a choice.

JAMES: You made your choice, didn't you.

MICHAEL: Reg is my friend.

JAMES: Reg ought to know better.

MICHAEL: Leave Reg out of it. Reg is like a father to you. Reg can't do enough for you. He's a great man. He's a teacher. Everything I've learned is down to Reg.

JAMES: Well that's a feather in his cap.

MICHAEL: Yeah, it is.

JAMES: So you're loyal to Reg then.

MICHAEL: A man without loyalty is no better than a devil.

JAMES: It's a shame you ain't loyal to me.

MICHAEL: I ought to smash you for that.

JAMES: No point crying about it. Maybe we're changing, going our separate ways.

MICHAEL: Don't talk to me like a stranger. It's a liberty. We're close, man.

JAMES: What's close?

MICHAEL: We got energy between us. I would never deny energy. I would never turn my back on my friend. I'd defend you the same as if I was defending myself.

JAMES: I can manage, thanks all the same.

MICHAEL: Just don't accuse me, all right?

JAMES: What you think of John then. All have a good time did you?

MICHAEL: He's all right.

JAMES: Did you see the way he looks for a little joke. Like he sees it scurrying past, a little joke running across the floor. He's got to catch it and pop it in the conversation. You see his eyes get wild and nervous. Will he get it. Should he make a lunge for it. Rate him, do you?

MICHAEL: I hadn't thought about it.

JAMES: I wonder if he's still looking for them little jokes when he's at home. Searching desperately, alone with his mum. "John, John, I've trod in something. Get it off my shoe." "Certainly. Christ, it's a little joke. You've squashed it. Never mind, can't afford to waste it, I'll clean it off and it will do for Michael." I forgot. You never met her. You're the friend that chucked a fucking brick through the fucking window and left me to take your fucking heat.

MICHAEL: You're too fucking slow.

JAMES: Slow. She come out the door like she was on a fucking spring. Like a fucking cuckoo clock. She was hanging on to my clothes, I couldn't get rid of her...

(MARGARET emerges from her house pushing or carrying a piece of John's furniture. She is talking to herself. She leaves it outside and goes in to fetch some more.)

JAMES: Well. That's exhibit A.

MICHAEL: She's inspired.

JAMES: John strips down furniture, don't he. That's because he wants to better himself. He don't want to remain among the understains.

42

(MARGARET comes out with another piece of furniture.)

MICHAEL: She don't know we're here.

MARGARET *(To JAMES and MICHAEL.)* I can't be doing with it indoors. I ain't got room to swing a cat. He's got a grandfather in there.

JAMES: You'll be telling me he's got a father next.

MARGARET: It's too heavy. I can't shift it. Will you shift it for me?

JAMES: Shift what, darling?

MARGARET: Shift it out here.

JAMES: Oh I'll shift it. Any place you like.

MARGARET: I want it all out here and out from under my feet.

JAMES: Course you do.

MARGARET: Come on then.

JAMES: What's your son going to say?

MARGARET: He's got no right. He's taking up too much space.

JAMES: Yeah. He is.

MARGARET: *(Leading them into the house.)* He's making me tired half to death.

(JAMES and MICHAEL emerge carrying a grandfather clock, which they put with the other items. MARGARET speaks through the door just before she closes it.)

MARGARET: Much obliged.

JAMES: That's all right. *(Sotto voce.)* Now go and have a look for your mind, when's the last time you had it?

MARGARET: Good boys, good boys. *(She shuts the door.)*

MICHAEL: Stuff won't last five minutes out here.

JAMES: You're right

(JAMES picks up a newspaper from the ground, crumples it, starts to stack paper round the furniture.)

MICHAEL: What you doing?

JAMES: You give me an idea all of a sudden.

MICHAEL: Wait up.

JAMES: Don't want it nicked, do we.

MICHAEL: This is a bad idea. It's mindless.

JAMES: Yeah, I thought you'd like it. Come on, it's as dry as tinder. It'll go up lovely. Magic.

MICHAEL: It's worth hundreds, man.

JAMES: You want to nick it, don't you.

MICHAEL: Yeah.

JAMES: Don't be so bourgeois.

MICHAEL: Antiques, ain't it.

JAMES: People ought to tread that wormy depressing old crud underfoot, get some self-respect. *(Takes out his cigarette lighter.)* Come on, we ain't got all day. *(MICHAEL collects papers to add to the pile. JAMES lights his cigarette lighter.)*

ACT TWO

SCENE 1

Tuesday morning in the flat of JAMES, STEPHI and LIZ.

LIZ is eating breakfast. JAMES comes in from a bedroom

JAMES: Fucking quiet, you are. I been lying in bed hearing you being fucking quiet. That fucking drawer. You been sliding it in and out like you was putting it under a fucking microscope. How many times do you have to open the fucking thing to get a fucking spoon. And when you got it, what the fuck do you do with it. Why do you have to stroke it round the bottom of your fucking cup without moving the fucking coffee. Can't you fucking stir it.

LIZ: You got sleep in the corners of your eyes.

JAMES: This place stinks.

LIZ: Don't you want a tissue?

JAMES: Your vermin are stinking us out.

LIZ: I give them a dusting down with talcum powder yesterday. Go and smell them if you like, it's mimosa. *(Silence.)* I found two of your fag ends in the nest with them.

JAMES: Naughty little mice.

LIZ: They don't know tobacco's poison, do they.

JAMES: If it's poison, why don't the bastards die. They're the master race. They'll be here a million years from now, when all of us are fucking fossil fuel.

LIZ: Someone was asking for you last night.

JAMES: Yes.

LIZ: He seemed very upset.

JAMES: Yes.

LIZ: He said he was intending to call the police. He said his mind was made up. I said he should do whatever he thinks is best. I hope you won't be annoyed.

JAMES: Bollocks. You hope I will be annoyed, and I am fucking annoyed, so you've got what you wanted, ain't you.

LIZ: Did you help the woman next door carry out some furniture yesterday?

JAMES: He's talking to the pigs, is he.

LIZ: Only someone set light to it.

JAMES: What a shame.

LIZ: I wonder what made you the way you are. I used to pray to God to take you away and bring me a little sister.

JAMES: Straight to the pigs. The man's a zero.

LIZ: Your games was never constructive.

JAMES: What's your opinion then. You assume I put a fucking match to it.

LIZ: If they put you in prison, mind you don't do away with yourself in your cell. A lot of young men have wound up in the papers on account of that.

JAMES: What proof has he got. He's got no more proof than you. You'll never know the truth and you don't want to know the truth. You know what you want to know.

LIZ: They get so desperate, there was one that dug the veins out of his wrist with his dinner fork. They only give them spoons now.

JAMES: You hate me.

LIZ: But it's too easy, ain't it. I mean to say, if them officers don't like you for any reason. Three against one, what chance would somebody have. They're all trained in self defence.

JAMES: So if the pigs was to come asking after me, what would you say.

LIZ: They've got no reason to ask me.

JAMES: Wanting to know my alibi.

LIZ: I'd say I didn't know.

JAMES: Would you.

LIZ: What else would I say.

JAMES: If I was to get nicked, there are people who'd be worried. Know what I mean.

LIZ: No.

JAMES: People I work with sometimes. You wouldn't take to them. They might think I was telling tales, see.

LIZ: You ain't got no tales to tell. You're only their errand boy.

JAMES: You know a lot about it.

LIZ: That's what Reg says.

JAMES: What Reg says don't interest me. Reg is a geriatric sniffing round the hole where his life used to be. If they was to think I was telling tales, you might find them calling. They might take it out on you, see, thinking it would upset me.

LIZ: They wouldn't think it would upset you if they knew you.

JAMES: All I'm saying is, be loyal. Be my sister. Then you got no worries. If the pigs ask you, tell them I was here. That sorts it.

LIZ: You want me to tell a lie for you.

JAMES: Please.

LIZ: What will you give me.

JAMES: How much do you want.

LIZ: Oh I don't want money. No.

JAMES: What you want.

LIZ: You think of something. I can't think.

JAMES: Oh for fuck's sake. Do you want a dress?

LIZ: I don't think so. You're always trying to dress me up, ain't you, making out you're ashamed of me.

JAMES: Do you want a watch?

LIZ: I got a watch. I don't need two watches, do I.

JAMES: How does anyone know what you need.

LIZ: I don't have needs. You're the one that has needs.

(STEPHI and SHEILA arrive.)

SHEILA: Frowsting here, look at you James. Why don't you come to the pool with us next Tuesday. It uses a whole different set of muscles, don't it Steph.

STEPHI: I couldn't walk up the bleeding steps.

SHEILA: He's lovely though, ain't he. I'd like to clone him. I want one just like him to take home with me. How are you Liz, all right.

LIZ: Yes thank you.

JAMES: It's early. I should be in bed.

SHEILA: Ain't you going to have a coffee.

JAMES: No, it would only keep me awake.

(He goes.)

SHEILA: *(To LIZ.)* What about you. Why don't you come swimming one of these days.

LIZ: I wouldn't like that. I wouldn't like to make a spectacle of myself.

SHEILA: Not much chance of that is there?

LIZ: You never know what's in that water, do you.

STEPHI: Yeah, you might get pregnant, Liz.

SHEILA: No she wouldn't, they sterilize it, don't they.

LIZ: I'd never be able to put my face in.

SHEILA: Some people say it's boring. It is. It's very, very boring. But that's the challenge, ain't it, to find the excitement within the boredom. Some days I wake up and I really don't want to go. But I persuade myself, because I can always get the better of myself, I've had that much practice on other people. You get down there and you get in the water and start trogging up and down, and your body don't want to join in, it's like hauling yourself through wet concrete, which of course some people might enjoy. Anyway, you keep going and after a while you loosen up, and then you begin to feel the benefit. Because there's something about being in the water, scientists have proved that it releases the ecstasy in your brain. All you got to do is keep on with them rhythmic movements and chemicals are created that uplift you, take away your pain, and put you in touch with your inner source of happiness. It's so easy to lose that.

STEPHI: There was this man kept brushing up against me.

SHEILA: I got a frog kick like a mule.

STEPHI: Guess who give me a letter yesterday. He come up to me at the bus stop. John. He says to me, "how do you spell your name". So I told him and he says, "Then this must be for you", gives me this letter he's written and walks off. He's off his trolley.

LIZ: What did it say.

STEPHI: It said, "Dear Stephanie. You know the rest. John".

SHEILA: Not much of a letter. He wants you to write it for him, does he.

STEPHI: He was making up to me at your house.

SHEILA: On Sunday. He never had the chance.

STEPHI: You saw to that.

LIZ: It's time I was off.

SHEILA: You'd think he'd have more sense.

LIZ: If you give them the wrong impression and they think they can do what they like, then you've only got yourself to blame I always think. Not that I'm an expert. I'll be back this evening.

(She goes.)

STEPHI: She drives me mental. She picks at you like a little child picking at its plate. In the kitchen she's disgusting, she slops around with a wet cloth and leaves it lying anywhere. Wherever she's been, there's tissues dropped like tears from the heavens. She stuffs them down the furniture. She stuffs them in her clothes and they spring out at you. She's always trying to tell me what James likes. James don't like his toast that dark. James won't use a 60-watt light bulb. James gets pains in his feet. I could tell her what brings them on. He won't move out of here, see, he reckons she ought to move, he don't want to lose this place. But she can't move, can she. All her tissues are here. Stuffed into the cracks.

SHEILA: Yes, she's put down roots, bless her.

STEPHI: It's a wonder James ain't worse.

SHEILA: He come round yesterday, did he tell you that? He apologized on account of what happened Sunday. So I says to him, it's Reg you ought to be apologizing to, and he says, "Fuck that, I know what side my bread's buttered". He does too. Reg don't understand that he and James aren't the same age. James is older, the little devil. He plays Reg along, I can see him doing it, and he bleeding well knows I can.

STEPHI: You don't want to indulge him on my account.

SHEILA: I don't indulge him. That's just what I don't do. You got to let them know where they stand.

STEPHI: Most people have got a memory that connects everything up. That's where James is superior. He don't make the connections. He's got no way of knowing what anyone means to him. He's supernatural.

SHEILA: Is he?

STEPHI: He can promise you anything, because he don't keep his promises. He floats.

SHEILA: Does he.

STEPHI: He's moody. He can't lie still at night. He grinds his teeth. Nobody unnatural can really be happy, can they. They might be ahead of the game but they won't be happy, will they.

SHEILA: No.

STEPHI: I want to make him happy. Then he'll know what the rest of us have got to go through.

SHEILA: Yes, good for you love.

(The doorbell. STEPHI goes. Comes back in.)

STEPHI: James! It's the police to see you.

SCENE 2

Tuesday evening. A pub.

(MICHAEL is sitting at a table with LIZ. Telephone some distance away.)

LIZ: It's ever so nice of Reg.

MICHAEL: Yeah.

LIZ: You find out who your friends are.

MICHAEL: Yeah. Soon be here.

LIZ: Do you think so? Only I ought to get back soon, I'll be missing my programme. It's only on of a Tuesday. Although I missed it last week. The reason was, I lost my hairbrush. There's nothing more frustrating, is there.

MICHAEL: No.

LIZ: Not that I needed it, but you know how it is, once a thing goes missing you can't rest until you find it, can you. It's the thin end of the wedge. I turned the house upside down. I couldn't remember the last time I'd used it, my mind was an absolute blank. Panic will do that, won't it.

MICHAEL: Yeah, definitely.

LIZ: The worst of it is, I began to get this itching in my scalp, until soon I was ready to pull out all my hairs one by one. That wouldn't have solved anything, would it.

MICHAEL: You wouldn't need a hairbrush then.

LIZ: I hope everything's gone smoothly down the nick, don't you.

MICHAEL: Bound to.

LIZ: Yes I expect you're right. How's your mum keeping?

MICHAEL: She's in Rio.

LIZ: Oh lovely. Been to see her, have you.

MICHAEL: Yeah.

LIZ: It must be lovely there, is it? Subtropical. I imagine the life is very different there.

MICHAEL: Yeah. She give me some sun glasses.

LIZ: That's my drink finished.

MICHAEL: You want another.

LIZ: Just a single if you don't mind.

(MICHAEL gets up, goes to the phone, waves to LIZ to show that he'll be getting the drinks in a moment. He dials. Listens. Breathes heavily. Hangs up. Waits. Dials again.)

MICHAEL: *(In a disguised voice, not heard by LIZ.)* Where you been all this time. I been trying urgently to reach you... A friend. Listen. I got some advice for you. You didn't ought to leave your mother on her own. She's liable to get frightened out of her wits. You don't want that, do you... Don't threaten me. I got a message to tell you... No it ain't James. It's a friend of James. James has got a lot of friends. How could it be James. No-one knows better than you where James is. You put him there. The pigs come for him this morning, didn't they. You'll be seeing him soon enough. They won't detain him long. Ain't you feeling well. You didn't ought to be. If I was you I'd be shitting myself. This is the message. It's from James. He says to tell you he once knew a guy that grassed. Are you listening. This is important. He wants you to know what they done to this guy. They took him for a ride in the country and hammered a six-inch nail in his neck, but unfortunately he made so much noise they had to split his head open with a shovel, and they said when his brains come out they smelled disgusting, a real traitor smell...

(JOHN has hung up. MICHAEL puts down the phone and goes off to get the drinks as REG, STEPHI, SHEILA and JAMES arrive and join LIZ.)

REG: End of a perfect day. James is buying.

STEPHI: I will. What you having Sheil?

SHEILA: My name is Sheila, my drink is tequila.

JAMES: *(To STEPHI.)* Sit down.

LIZ: Michael's looking after me, thanks all the same.

(JAMES goes off to buy drinks.)

REG: *(To LIZ.)* They never even booked him. He was coming out the door by the time we got down there. I had the bail money in my hand.

LIZ: Fancy them taking him down there if they wasn't intending to book him. You'd think they'd have more sense, wouldn't you.

STEPHI: Would you have rather they locked him up?

REG: Don't be sensitive girl, she never meant it like that.

LIZ: I did though.

REG: We're here to celebrate. Ours not to reason why.

STEPHI: Well, he's free, ain't he.

REG: Free as air, and as fragrant.

LIZ: There's nothing they can do, is there.

SHEILA: James is a lucky boy.

REG: I can't think why that John didn't come to me.

SHEILA: Out of order, going public like that. James will resent that.

STEPHI: He might have resented getting his stuff torched.

SHEILA: That's not the point, is it. We all get problems.

REG: But we don't go giving out names.

STEPHI: I might.

REG: I put up with a lot from you Stephanie. You talk a lot of cobblers. But you're James's friend so we keep our mouths shut. If only you could pay us the same compliment. You're a nice-looking girl except you talk shit. You understand fuck-all about how mankind lives. You girls, you're living in a different world. You sit up in the stands waving a handkerchief, you don't want to know what it's like on the field. Why does a man fuck a woman? I'll tell you. Because he wants her to know what he knows. He wants to pass it on. But a girl like you just don't get the message. You got a hard heart, Stephanie. All you want to do is sit in judgment.

SHEILA: I expect it was only intended as a bit of fun.

REG: Once the pigs get hold of you, you never know what people are going to think you told them. Plus, you never know what you're going to tell them.

SHEILA: James knows what to tell them.

REG: Fucking right. Every fucking thing he ever fucking knew, and if anyone was to say, that ain't fucking much, he'd say, wait up, I got more, and he'd compose the entire thousand fucking nights for them cunts, not forgetting the one extra fucker.

SHEILA: Fine friend you are.

REG: We do our friends no favours by muddled thinking.

SHEILA: Some of us know how to think without moving our lips.

REG: Some of us wouldn't move our lips if our arse was on fire.

STEPHI: James ain't weak.

REG: He's weak as piss. He's so weak it's a form of strength.

SHEILA: *(To REG.)* You're saying, everything you stand for, James don't give a toss for it.

REG: That's right.

SHEILA: He don't give a toss for you.

REG: Nor you.

SHEILA: But you can't keep your distance.

REG: My distance. Bleeding Christ on high. Ask yourself this. What is my distance? Who's to say what my distance is? Anyone telling me what my distance is better be fucking sure what their own distance is, because it seems to me their distance is not so much fact as fantasy. And fantasy is all some people have got. Where's my beer?

LIZ: That John has only stored up trouble for himself. I hope he knows what he done.

(JAMES and MICHAEL come back with the drinks.)

JAMES: Who?

SHEILA: It's a shame they didn't charge you love, I been planning your campaign. "Free James. He was only arson about".

JAMES: Who was you talking about? Judas?

STEPHI: You don't even know it was him. It could have been his mum that said.

JAMES: Oh definitely. Keep an open mind. It's important to you.

STEPHI: I will.

JAMES: Think the best of him. Why not. Think the worst of me. You do, don't you. Tell the world what a cunt I am. Be perfectly honest.

STEPHI: I am.

JAMES: That's right. Blacken my name.

REG: No-one's blackening anybody's name. We love you, James. We come here to share with you. You don't want to be downhearted. You got friends looking out for you. Ain't he, Michael.

MICHAEL: Yeah.

REG: And you and your friends are going to get rat-arsed, because that's what friends are for. Alcohol is a solvent. It solves. It goes through your system like petrol, cutting out the tarnish and leaving it as shiny, bright and clean as the day you were born. Soon you'll be lit up inside like a colourful juke box, and music will come out. Won't it Michael.

MICHAEL: *(To James.)* To vengeance eh?

SHEILA: *(A toast.)* To liberty.

(They drink. JOHN appears at the door of the pub. Stares at them. JAMES speaks, aside.)

JAMES: He seems upset. The way they're staring at him I'm not surprised. I don't think he'll come back in this pub for a while. Even he must be getting the feeling he's about to trip over someone's feet with his head. Such a lot to learn, where's he supposed to begin. They don't want you, John.

You got bad presentation. They look at you, they see a
man that's easily damaged. That's the last thing they want
to be reminded of, that people are easily damaged. Because
they're people. I ain't a person. I'm less than a person and
more than a person. I'm a cutting edge. Because metal
is not so easily damaged. Never mind who told me that.
What I get told in here *(Strokes his temple.)* is nobody's
business but mine and them that tells me. *(JOHN leaves.)*

SHEILA: Ain't it embarrassing. He ought to know better than
to come in here.

MICHAEL: Insensitive cunt.

JAMES: He just realized, he came without his little joke. He'll
have to go back for it.

SCENE 3

*Outside John and Margaret's door. A fortnight later. Graffiti. Their
dustbin has been emptied on the doorstep. JOHN comes out, speaking to
MARGARET who is somewhere behind him*

JOHN: Come on. I got your cardigan. *(Sees the mess on the
doorstep. Hastily clears it up.)* They got them little bakewells
in that shop.

MARGARET. *(From inside.)* They make them too sweet. They
didn't ought to make them as sweet as that. *(She appears.)*
Have I got my purse?

JOHN: You got it in your bag.

MARGARET: *(Starts going through her bag.)* Hold these.

JOHN: What you want all these safety pins for.

MARGARET: Hold on to my hand lotion. I ain't got any lipstick
on. *(She is taking her lipstick out of her bag.)*

JOHN: Yes you have.

MARGARET: Have I got it on? Where's my mirror? *(Finds
a mirror, looks in it.)* Fancy that. I put my lipstick on and
forgot my tooth.

JOHN: You don't need your tooth. Who you going to bite? It's
broad daylight.

MARGARET: There's the phone. Ain't you going to answer it?

JOHN: No.

MARGARET: What, is it them again? You ought to get the police on them. You ought not to let it go on.

JOHN: I don't know who it is, do I.

MARGARET: Them phone calls have been going on and on.

JOHN: Twelve days and twelve nights.

MARGARET: Did I find my purse?

JOHN: Yes.

MARGARET: No I never. You're imagining things.

JOHN: Come on. I ain't going to wait all day.

MARGARET: Don't rush me. I get confused if I'm rushed.

JOHN: We'll get some of them bakewells, won't we.

MARGARET: You can if you want. They're too sweet for me. Who's going to look after the house?

JOHN: Can't stay here all the time, can we. We can't stay in that house for the rest of our lives.

MARGARET: Someone ought to look after it. You go on down the shop. Buy yourself something nice. Wait a minute and I'll get you a pound. *(Rummages.)*

JOHN: I don't want a pound mum. I want you to come down the shop with me. You need a change of scene. If you ain't coming, I ain't going.

MARGARET: Who's going to get the shopping then?

JOHN: No-one.

MARGARET: Don't you defy me.

JOHN: You'll have to do without. Are you coming?

MARGARET: I'll go hungry, thank you.

JOHN: You will.

MARGARET: I know I will. Nobody cares, do they.

JOHN: You ain't been out the door for the last ten days. Have you. You're afraid to come out the door.

MARGARET: I been out.

JOHN: Where?

MARGARET: To the shop.

JOHN: What did you buy?

MARGARET: All the necessities.

JOHN: Where are they?

MARGARET: Get more if you ain't satisfied.

JOHN: If you been out, you can come out now, can't you.

MARGARET: I can come out when I want.

JOHN: Show me. Come out here.

MARGARET: What for.

JOHN: Show me if you can.

MARGARET: I ain't a performing seal.

JOHN: What you want from the shop?

MARGARET: I don't know. You better get some of them little bakewells.

JOHN: Nice and sweet, are they.

MARGARET: Too sweet.

JOHN: How many shall I get?

MARGARET: Get us a couple of packets while you're there.

JOHN: One thing.

MARGARET: Yes? What you want?

JOHN: Step out here before I go. Show me you can step out here. Then I'll go down the shop for you.

MARGARET: What's the point of that? There's no point to it.

JOHN: Do it to please me.

MARGARET: What you going to do?

JOHN: Nothing.

MARGARET: I don't do things for no reason.

JOHN: Show me you ain't afraid to come out.

MARGARET: I've got nothing to be afraid of. I done nothing to be ashamed of. It's you that's brought all this trouble on our heads. They told me that on the phone. *(She goes in, slamming the door.)*

JOHN: She forgets everything except who to blame. Nobody's life is perfect. I can't do more. I can't even make her smile. I can't even flirt with her, bullshit her, raise her spirits. I'd have to raise my own. Despair is the ultimate sin. The superior man will fend it off. I'll get her them little cakes. They pissed through the letterbox last night. I wish I'd heard them. Madame Guillotine. Then I'd burn the door. Burn everything they've touched. Burn the house. Basically it ain't the house's fault. Burn myself. I don't want to catch them. I don't want to know who they are, or how many they are. What's the difference. People are all much the same. So long as I don't see them, no permanent harm is done. In days to come, when all this is forgotten, I might get to know them. It will be forgotten. I'm capable of forgetting it now. My mind can slip away to where I'm sitting in the pub with them. Reg is there, telling us how to manufacture explosives, and Sheila's getting too close, and Stephi's there looking nice. It'll never happen. I feel like they've seen my insides. I feel like some disgusting freak of nature.

(STEPHI arrives carrying bags of shopping, on the way to her door.)

JOHN: Are you going to walk right past?

STEPHI: I didn't see you there.

JOHN: I didn't know I blended in so well.

STEPHI: I got to go.

JOHN: You seem embarrassed.

STEPHI: I got my reasons ain't I?

JOHN: I been wishing I could talk to you.

STEPHI: I'm sorry about what's happened.

JOHN: I been getting phone calls in the middle of the night. You know what I mean? Two skips I never ordered come to my door last week.

STEPHI: I'm sorry.

JOHN: And fourteen speciality pizzas.

STEPHI: I don't hold with it.

JOHN: I've had some very unusual post.

STEPHI: People don't know when to stop.

JOHN: Nobody speaks to me. Strangers look away from me. Everybody knows just one thing about me, which is that I'm to be avoided. You're part of it. I still can't believe it.

STEPHI: Not really.

JOHN: One look from you and I'd be revived. I'd wake up out of this as if I was in heaven. How can you refuse to give me something I need so much? You aren't what you seem. You're some kind of cold-hearted puppet made to deceive me. You're so lifelike and tender-looking, you must have been made by the devil himself. Don't go.

STEPHI: I got to get inside with these bags.

JOHN: Put them down. Give them to me.

STEPHI: I got to go. There's nothing I can do.

JOHN: You been shopping for his food. It's heavy. I'll take it to the door for you.

STEPHI: I can manage.

JOHN: I ain't jealous. You want to feed him, I'll help you. I'd spoon it in his mouth if it meant I could be near you. *(REG and JAMES emerge through STEPHI's front door.)*

STEPHI: Hullo Reg.

REG: Hullo Steph.

JAMES: You planning to come in? *(STEPHI goes in through the door, watched by the others.)* I'll be back in a minute, all right? *(Shuts the door. Meanwhile JOHN has been trying to unlock his front door.)* Trying to get it in are you?

JOHN: Go and fuck yourself.

JAMES: What's your problem?

(JOHN gets through his door and shuts it.)

JAMES: What's he playing at, talking to her. What's he playing at. I ain't going to stand for that.

REG: Then you'll have to call him out. Explain your feelings. Half a broken bottle in the face can generally be relied upon to put Cupid to flight.

JAMES: I can't understand her.

REG: A plank with a couple of nails sticking out can often be found lying conveniently to hand. In no way is the man who picks up such a plank in the heat of the moment guilty of intent.

JAMES: She knows my feelings. She done wrong to let him speak to her.

REG: A heavy spanner, or a hammer normally used for bashing out the rims of tyres, can easily enter into a combat of this sort when feelings are running high and normal restraint and good manners have been cast aside. The simplest weapon is often the most effective.

JAMES: Oh shut it you goon.

REG: It's better than ringing on the fucking doorbell and hiding round the corner. That's your level.

JAMES: You want to see my head bashed in?

REG: Can't stand here dreaming all day. Are you coming to help me sort this motor?

JAMES: Might as well. *(They leave.)*

SCENE 4

Evening of the same day.

STEPHI is sitting in the yard of her house, at the back.

STEPHI: So I spoke with who I shouldn't. I got a mind of my own, haven't I. The black looks I got. He looked ready to throw me across the street. Why don't he come back. Not late, though, is it. It ain't late enough to start feeling like I will do later. I'm enjoying the sunset. No point suffering in advance, is there. James. It ain't jealousy. Any excuse to punish me. If someone was begging at his feet he'd punish them twice over for embarrassing him. If they wasn't, he'd punish them twice over for being proud. He's been gone six hours. I ain't going to mind until it becomes absolutely necessary. I ought to put it off as long as possible. Each time, I ought to put it off a bit longer. Finally I'd give it up. I'd remain in harmony with myself and with nature, even if he never came back the whole night long.

(LIZ enters with a boiling kettle.)

LIZ: How can you sit there without your shoes on? The ants will get up your legs.

STEPHI: They can and welcome.

LIZ: What they do, they undermine the paving. They dig it out underneath. One day, it will simply tip down. *(She pours boiling water on the ground.)* I don't like ants, I'm sorry to say.

STEPHI: It's so warm and peaceful, you didn't ought to kill them at a time like this.

LIZ: Ants don't stop for sentiment. If I was to do this every day for a year they'd still be marching up from under there. They don't all die at once. Sly creatures. *(Pours some more water.)*

STEPHI: I thought you was an animal lover.

LIZ: To them that deserve it I am.

STEPHI: I'm glad you ain't God.

LIZ: If I was God, I'd make nicer insects. *(JAMES comes in.)*

JAMES: Anybody ask for me?

STEPHI: No.

JAMES: Anybody telephone?

STEPHI: No.

(JAMES goes in, switches on the answering machine. A message from CELESTINE.)

CELESTINE: This fucking ansaphone. Where are you James? Just a minute while I light my cigarette. Shit. Nearly dropped the lighter in my lap. That would be a big mistake. It's that hot down there, it'd go up in flames. That ain't the reason I'm phoning. I seen Oliver. Oliver says he ain't got nothing for you because Richard, Terry and Patrick are all in custody. He don't want you coming round. I told him no way could you be to blame, all right? It's three o'clock in the morning and I wish you was here. If the wrong person hears this it's your own fucking fault. Answer the fucking phone next time.

JAMES: *(Switches off the machine and comes back into the yard.)* What you looking at. *(Silence.)* Did you know that was on there?

LIZ: No.

JAMES: Stupid time to phone.

LIZ: Did you shop them James?

JAMES: Is there anything to eat?

STEPHI: You germ.

JAMES: I'm sorry she phoned, all right. What am I supposed to do.

STEPHI: Did you shop them?

JAMES: What's it to you?

STEPHI: I'm interested to know what you're capable of.

JAMES: Interested.

STEPHI: Yes, you're the most interesting person I've ever met.

JAMES: You're far more interested in me than I am in you. But then, what's there to know about you?

STEPHI: Don't rack your brains.

JAMES: Do you think I feel jealous? I don't. That's how predictable you are. I see you with someone else, it don't bother me.

STEPHI: Good. I'll bear that in mind.

JAMES: Next time you're talking to your friend next door, remember to thank him for destroying my credibility. I'm skint, ain't I. I'm unemployed. I'm going to have to live off you from now on, and you can't even afford to keep me in this hairstyle. What you being so quiet for? Tired are you. You ought to get a better job. Since you been out cleaning your hands are like alligator paws. They ain't soft like they used to be.

STEPHI: No. And they'll harden to stone and wear away to dust before you'll speak to me kindly.

JAMES: This ain't the first time that things have gone wrong for me. But I'm lucky. My enemies go down and I survive. You want to know what I'm capable of. I'm capable of anything. What you want me to do? You want a demonstration. What you doing with the kettle, Liz? Give it here. Come on, give it, it ain't yours. Now watch this, Steph. I'm going to throw it on you, look. *(Makes as if to throw it. LIZ screams.)* Don't you trust me? What you take me for? You got a high opinion of me, ain't you. I can't make you out. You're living every day with someone who puts you in fear. It's unbalanced.

(JOHN puts his head over the fence that divides his garden from theirs.)

JAMES: What's your problem?

JOHN: I got no problem.

JAMES: You think so.

JOHN: Why did she scream? *(To STEPHI.)* Is he threatening you?

JAMES: What's it to you?

JOHN: *(Climbs in over the fence as LIZ hurries out.)* Be sensible.

JAMES: *(Taking out a knife, gripping JOHN and threatening him with it.)* You're trespassing.

JOHN: *(Alarmed.)* The weak have recourse to weapons, but the superior man uses no shield.

JAMES: You're an absolute dick.

JOHN: The strong man gives way when the weak are inflexible. The weak not uncommonly appear to have the upper hand.

JAMES: You're an unbelievable arsehole.

JOHN: The strong understand the weak, the weak fail to understand the strong. We come into this world looking for friends.

JAMES: Nobody wants to be your friend. You're like a newborn baby. You ought to be left outside to die. Nobody wants to change your nappy. Nobody wants to feed you. You got the brains of a calf. What you want a friend for? We're born alone and we die alone. Especially some.

(LIZ returns with REG, SHEILA and MICHAEL.)

SHEILA: Summer at last. The great outdoors.

REG: Watch yourself James. If I was him I'd have had that knife off you by now.

(JAMES looks at JOHN. REG disarms him.)

JAMES: You animal, you hurt my hand.

REG: I never even touched you. The man with the knife in his hand needs eyes in the four sides of his head, like the seraphim of the Old Testament.

LIZ: *(Conversationally, to JOHN.)* I'm glad we weren't too late.

JAMES: What you all looking at? You know me, I like to fool about. I like a joke, don't I.

JOHN: You evil little cunt. You little twister.

REG: When we want your views we'll ask for them.

MICHAEL: But we ain't going to want them.

JOHN: One of you pissed through my door last night. What pervert done that?

MICHAEL: I never pissed through no fucking door.

JAMES: Nobody pissed through no fucking door. Somebody don't like you.

JOHN: Are you all in this? How can you stand for it? Aren't you ashamed? Yes, you're ashamed, and you don't like being ashamed, and you don't like being reminded you're ashamed, so you can't stand the sight of me. It's perfectly logical. Where will it end? Petrol through the door, put a match in. Ain't you got any pity? My mother hides in there all day, she puts her clothes on then she gets back into bed. She won't have the curtains open. It's like a fucking funeral parlour with her lying on her back in there. How many people are doing it? Is it two or three? Is it the whole street? I'm cut off and I'm shut in. I'm like a prisoner. The mind of the prisoner tries to travel out through the building, but it's too weak to reach the outside wall. All of a sudden it's as if he's in his tomb.

LIZ: I feel sick to my stomach.

SHEILA: She's too high strung, bless her.

MICHAEL: *(To LIZ.)* Do you want a mint?

SHEILA: She ought to go inside.

LIZ: No I'll stay here if you don't mind. I'll have a mint.

REG: *(To JOHN.)* You ain't doing no good here. There's nothing to be gained by histrionics.

JAMES: He's in my garden.

REG: *(To JOHN.)* Take yourself off.

JOHN: What am I going to do?

JAMES: If you don't get off my premises I'm going to call the cops.

JOHN: Stephi? What am I going to do?

JAMES: Yeah. Ask her.

REG: A fair fight. Man to man and toe to the breadbasket. In mediaeval times, barehanded men could fight to the death. They weren't in such a hurry in those days.

SHEILA: I seen kangaroos do it on TV.

(MARGARET appears at a window of her house, looking into the yard.)

MARGARET: Who's there, is it him? What's he doing there? I been looking up and down the house for you. Are you coming in now?

JOHN: In a minute.

MARGARET: Who's that you're talking to?

JOHN: You remember Stephi.

MARGARET: Hullo love. How you been keeping?

STEPHI: Well, thank you.

MARGARET: I ain't seen you, have I?

JOHN: You ain't been out.

MARGARET: I ain't been going about much. You better not ask me why. Don't want to tell the world, do I. You can't be too careful.

STEPHI: No.

MARGARET: I ain't been very well.

STEPHI: Ain't you?

MARGARET: I've had an accident. I must have been upset, mustn't I. I didn't know where he'd got to. I been trying to wipe it up. It's embarrassing, ain't it.

JAMES: *(Sotto voce.)* So we'd best keep it to ourselves.

MARGARET: You don't mind, do you.

STEPHI: No.

MARGARET: I don't know what come over me. We've had some trouble you know. You'd never believe what goes on, would you. There's people round here that are not quite human.

MICHAEL: *(Sotto voce.)* That's cause they're muppets.

MARGARET: I'm sorry if I don't come down and meet your friends. I washed my things out. I got fresh on. He only needs to come and do the carpet.

JOHN: I'll be there in a minute.

MARGARET: I don't want it to smell.

STEPHI: No.

MARGARET: Good night, love. Nice talking to you.

STEPHI: Goodnight Margaret.

ALL: *(Except JOHN.)* Goodnight Margaret. *(MARGARET goes.)*

MICHAEL: Go and wipe it up John.

JAMES: You don't want it to smell.

MICHAEL: You ought to rub her nose in it, teach her not to do it again.

SHEILA: Shut it, Michael.

JOHN: *(To JAMES.)* What do you want from me?

JAMES: I don't want nothing from you.

JOHN: I got to live. Ain't I?

JAMES: What you asking me for?

JOHN: Because I don't fucking know.

JAMES: Why don't you put it to the test. You know what I done once? I tried to hang myself off the branch of a tree, but it broke and I found myself sitting on the ground alive. Since then I got no worries. I made the offer but it wasn't accepted. I do what I like since then. I think I'm going to live to be a hundred. Have you got a head for spirits?

JOHN: No.

JMES: I got a bottle of vodka in there. *(To LIZ.)* Go and fetch it. *(She goes.)* I believe in chance, it's what I live by. I respect it like a god. Most people hide from it, they build up a wall. They think, if they take care and lead a sensible life, they'll be spared. They get punished by chance for wanting to do a deal. *(LIZ reappears.)* Some people can drink a bottle of vodka straight down, and they're laughing. Other people fall down dead.

JOHN: I'll drink it for this reason. I'll drink it to prove you can trust me.

JAMES: What you want me to trust you for? I don't trust nobody. I don't trust myself.

JOHN: I'll drink it if it means you'll let me be.

JAMES: It ain't me. I got people that want to do things to please me.

JOHN: Would they stop then?

JAMES: They might.

JOHN: The man who drinks poison and lives becomes a superior man.

JAMES: Right then. *(Hands him the vodka.)* Afterwards we'll bear no grudge.

JOHN: I'll drink to that. *(He drinks the whole bottle while the others watch.)* Time to go home.

JAMES: Mind how you go.

(JOHN goes out through the front of the house.)

JAMES: Stupid fucker. He done it. Did you see that? As obedient as a little child. I felt sorry for the poor bewildered cunt. I almost found myself saying, "look, John, you don't have to do this, we love you, course we do." I can't believe it. Eager. What a twat.

LIZ: It'll be on your conscience if that don't agree with him, won't it. You'll never live that down.

MICHAEL: Bollocks. It's euthanasia.

SHEILA: I got such a thirst on me. You got any more of them bottles, James? I could go a whole one and all.

STEPHI: Good-natured, ain't you Sheila. I've never seen you anything but good-natured. That's because you got the finer feelings of a fucking rhinoceros.

SHEILA: I thought you said you didn't fancy him.

REG: You and your friends been giving him a hard time, ain't you James. It's a shame, in my opinion, that you ain't a fighter.

JAMES: You split old punchbag. You moralizing lump of shit. You think I'm the son you never had, you bender. You always want to patronize me. You're always making out you understand me. You understand nothing about me. If you was to understand one fucking thing about me, that would be the thing I'd change. Because all a failure understands is failure. You failed thug. You're carved in concrete. I'd rather be dead. I can move, see. I can fly. You're slow. I'm quick. You're stiff. I'm flexible. You're limited. I'm unlimited. If you don't like what I done, why didn't you stop me. You was there. Not one of you raised your voice. I heard fuck-all of a fucking word from any of you.

LIZ: You've always had your own way.

JAMES: That's because I'm surrounded by weakness. One shake and you'd all fall off me like fleas.

SHEILA: Get us a drink Michael. I refuse to be slagged off any more unless I got a drink in my hand.

REG: *(To JAMES.)* A man's honour was at stake. The onlookers' hands was tied.

STEPHI: *(To REG.)* He don't mean it. He goes a bit mental. He needs loyalty.

REG: One day girl, I'll teach you what's needed and what ain't.

JAMES: *(To STEPHI.)* I see you move your lips, but your voice comes out from between your fucking legs.

(JOHN, already very drunk, appears at the fence.)

JOHN: No James, no mate, don't speak to her like that. You don't mean it. *(To STEPHI.)* He don't mean it.

JAMES: Ain't you dead yet?

JOHN: No.

JAMES: Well fuck off and don't come back till you are.

JOHN: I come to tell you. I understood everything. I come through my front door and that vodka hit me. I was sitting down on the floor, and at that moment I understood everything. Everything. I can't remember it.

JAMES: What a shame.

JOHN: I was sitting there, not sad and not happy. Because emotion, what is it? Powerful engines were massaging the inside of my head. Engines or butterflies, powerful butterflies. The roar of their wings seemed to set me apart, on an island, and then I heard, very faintly, human voices. This reminded me of you. Because I'm fond of you. That's ridiculous, ain't it. How can this be? *(He climbs into the yard.)* Everyone we know is part of us. You are part of me. I am part of you. *(He sits down, dropping his wallet out of his pocket. He picks it up, opens it, shows a picture to SHEILA.)* Battersea Park.

SHEILA: Is it? Yes, I can see the grass. And the trees.

JOHN: *(Pointing to the photo.)* Who's this then?

SHEILA: It's never you, is it?

JOHN: Who's that I'm with?

SHEILA: Your mum and dad, is it?

JOHN: My auntie.

SHEILA: *(Takes a closer look.)* Let's see.

JOHN: She's dead.

SHEILA: She's never.

JOHN: Yes, unfortunately. She only took me there the once.

SHEILA: What was her name?

JOHN: Annie.

MICHAEL: Knock knock. Who's there. Annie. Annie who. Annie never went there again.

SHEILA: She wasn't Annie Palmer, was she?

JOHN: That's right.

SHEILA: You mean to say she's Annie Palmer?

JOHN: Yes.

SHEILA: My sister was a friend of Annie Palmer's cousin Linda. You remember Linda, Reg.

REG: She had a mole.

SHEILA: No she didn't, that was Elizabeth. Linda married the youngest Bodoni boy. There was three of them, Giulio, Maurizio and Terence.

MICHAEL: My dad had a partner Maurizio Bodoni.

SHEILA: He never, did he?

MICHAEL: He done a runner.

SHEILA: Well he would, wouldn't he. Too fast to live, he was. He would have whipped the rug from under a dervish. Did you ever hear what he done to Graham Frith?

MICHAEL: Who's Graham Frith.

LIZ: Graham Frith used to visit our mum.

SHEILA: Now ain't that extraordinary.

JAMES: Not really. Show me the man that didn't visit our mum.

SHEILA: It gives you a sense of a greater pattern. His wife was Jane. She used to be Jane Raynor.

(MARGARET appears at the fence.)

MARGARET: Jane Raynor was half sister to my husband. Did you know Jane?

SHEILA: She was an angel.

MARGARET: She was a saint.

SHEILA: Couldn't do enough for you.

MARGARET: Nothing was ever a trouble.

SHEILA: Tragic, weren't it.

MARGARET: Oh, it were tragic.

SHEILA: Still, it was better really.

MARGARET: It were a mercy really.

SHEILA: Come round tomorrow love, eh? You know where I live don't you. Just the other side. John'll tell you. Come round in the morning, we can have a talk.

(JOHN falls to the ground.)

SHEILA: Your boy's had a drink too many.

MARGARET: Always something, ain't there.

SHEILA: Don't worry, love, let him sleep it off.

MARGARET: No point in worrying. The doctor give me some pills to calm me down.

SHEILA: Lovely.

MARGARET: I ought to take one, oughtn't I.

SHEILA: You do what you want, bless you.

MARGARET: I'll go in and take one. Be seeing you then.

SHEILA: Churra, love.

(REG has been looking at JOHN.)

REG: He's croaked.

JAMES: That's all I need.

REG: He's lost all his tone, see.

MICHAEL: I never seen a dead man before. Show us his eyes, Reg.

STEPHI: Why don't you get down and have a good look. Count his teeth while you're about it.

JAMES: What are we going to do?

REG: Get on the phone, Shiel, get a doctor.

SHEILA: What you want to drag me in for?

JAMES: What's a doctor going to do, vaccinate him?

REG: *(To SHEILA.)* We knew about James.

SHEILA: Knowing is no reason to suffer.

JAMES: I want him shifted out of here.

SHEILA: We've done enough for you. We've made enough exceptions for you. Shame you never made no exception for us.

REG: He shouldn't have died.

JAMES: That's why you've got to help me.

SHEILA: We don't got to do anything. We deserved better from you. You owed it to us to keep us out of your childishness.

REG: He needn't have died. The odds were against it.

SHEILA: That's where James has let us down. That's his gratitude. I'm off.

STEPHI: I'm getting the doctor.

JAMES: Wait up. What you going to tell them?

REG: We felt no malice towards anyone. Therefore this shouldn't have happened.

SHEILA: Come on, or we'll be witnesses.

(They leave.)

JAMES: *(To STEPHI.)* What you going to tell them?

LIZ: He looks so lifelike, don't he.

STEPHI: I'll say we was having a drink.

JAMES: Where are the glasses then? Get some glasses,

STEPHI: Stop acting like you killed him. *(She goes.)*

MICHAEL: I got to take a video back. They'll be shutting up shop.

JAMES: Ain't you going to stay with me?

MICHAEL: We all got to stand on our own two feet some time.

JAMES: But Michael, this ain't the time.

MICHAEL: Your feet are out of my hands. *(He goes.)*

LIZ: You never seem to keep your friends. *(JAMES turns and hits her. She retreats into the house.)*

JAMES: *(To the corpse.)* Nobody cares you're dead. So don't come crying to me. You got your mouth jammed open. *(Attempts to shut it.)* You're getting very cold. Look at that. You got one ear bigger than the other. *(Holds them both.)* The left one is half as big again. It didn't notice, though. People don't look that close, do they. Not when you're alive. I could look at you all over, you wouldn't care now, would you. I'm sorry you're dead, all right. You'll hold this against me permanently, won't you. I got a stomach ache. You're giving me a stomach ache. I ought to have kept my distance.

JOHN'S VOICE: Are you sorry then?

JAMES: Don't make out you're talking to me. I ain't a madman.

JOHN'S VOICE: But I am talking to you, you can hear me clear as a bell.

JAMES: I ain't listening. I can't hear nothing, all right? It's very quiet, actually, tonight. I can hear them washing up five doors away.

JOHN'S VOICE: Yes, it's a nice night.

JAMES: Don't speak to me, fuck you. Get away.

JOHN'S VOICE: I can't.

JAMES: Yes you can. I'm going to help you. I'm going to sit here, very quiet, and relax my body, first the feet and legs, then working my way up until I reach the hair of my head. When I'm completely relaxed, you will disengage.

JOHN'S VOICE: You think you're in control, but you ain't. I died without anybody crying for me. I'm lonely. I never set out to be your enemy. I wanted to be your friend. I wasn't good enough, was I.

JAMES: You want me to apologize, I'll apologize. I'm sorry I had that attitude.

(STEPHI comes out into the yard.)

STEPHI: Who you talking to?

JOHN'S VOICE: Tell her.

JAMES: *(Furtive.)* No, get fucked.

STEPHI: James?

JAMES: Did you get through to the doctor?

STEPHI: They'll call back.

JOHN'S VOICE: Typical. Just as well I ain't dying.

JAMES: What do you expect? The surgery's closed.

JOHN'S VOICE AND STEPHI: That's when these things always happen.

JAMES: Eh?

STEPHI: Are you all right?

JOHN'S VOICE: Tell her, tell her.

JAMES: Why shouldn't I be?

JOHN'S VOICE: Don't try to pretend I don't exist.

JAMES: Shut it or you'll get me put away.

STEPHI: What you think I am.

JAMES: Not you for fuck's sake.

JOHN'S VOICE: Tell her.

STEPHI: You're upset. You don't need to fight it. It means you're good if you're upset. It means you're sorry. That why I would never betray you, because you're good.

JOHN'S VOICE: You and I know better, don't we.

JAMES: *(Kicks JOHN's corpse.)* Stupid wanker.

STEPHI: James!

JAMES: Fuck off! *(To JOHN's corpse.)* Taking liberties are you? Think you're special because you're fucking dead. *(Kicks and attacks JOHN's corpse. STEPHI runs off.)* Think you've finally cracked it. This is what I think of you. You're a loser. The eternal fucking loser. *(Stands exhausted. Silence.)* He's fucked off. I thought he'd never take the hint. That would be the end, I mean it. I wouldn't go through life with him dossing about in my brain like he was in bed up there. I'd top myself rather than put up with that. I do let some of them in. If they're kind and want to tell me things I need to know. I never used to get them, they waited till I was ready, and then they come and told me about the people of the future, that will survive when the rest can't breathe in the air any more. Because the world is rotten. The people of the future will look like anybody else but they got a second way of breathing. When the air finally goes black and the world is like a festering sore, the second breathers will be the only ones left, because they can breathe poison and thrive on it like the sweetest air. I been told this because I'm a second breather. They come and tell me things to my advantage. And if I get the other kind, that only want to rubbish me and take away my secrets, I don't let them in. I'm always in control of what gets talked about in my mind and of who's listening. That's why if Stephi ever starts in about me needing the doctor I know for a fact she's talking bollocks. It's getting cooler now. I feel cool.

JOHN'S VOICE: You're a cunt, James. You treated me like a cunt.

JAMES: Ah. God.

JOHN'S VOICE: I was weak and helpless. I was unwanted. You'd do anything rather than be like that.

JAMES: God won't you fuck off.

JOHN'S VOICE: It's your greatest fear. Why did you choose that fear? Because it's your destiny.

JAMES: Bollocks.

JOHN'S VOICE: Why is it your destiny? Because you're different. You're heartless. Who wants you, James? Weak people want you, people you can fool. There's nothing to you. You're empty inside.

JAMES: I ain't listening to you.

JOHN'S VOICE: When people find you out, you'll be left to perish. You're weak. That's why you can hear me. You ain't got the inner strength.

JAMES: Try me.

JOHN'S VOICE: I will try you. I'll always try you. Just wait till people start to hear you answering me back. Stephi's probably on the phone right now, phoning for the doctor.

JAMES: Don't give me that bullshit.

JOHN'S VOICE: Lie down, James.

JAMES: Get stuffed.

JOHN'S VOICE: It's a hard world for a weak boy. Always fighting, always pretending. No-one loves you because no-one knows you. And if they did know you, they wouldn't love you. Because you don't deserve it. Lie down with me, I'm the one that understands you.

JAMES: Never.

JOHN'S VOICE: Lie down. It's natural. You been under a lot of pressure. Lie down close to me and I won't talk. I'll let you alone.

JAMES: You won't talk.

JOHN'S VOICE: I'll give you a break. I'm sorry for you. You never was sorry for me.

JAMES: You swear you won't talk.

JOHN'S VOICE: I swear.

JAMES: I'll lie down for a bit.

JOHN'S VOICE: Clear your head.

JAMES: I'll lie down.

JOHN'S VOICE: We'll be company for each other. *(JAMES lies down. MARGARET appears at a window.)*

MARGARET: What they doing down there. I wouldn't lay down there. They'll catch their death. Everything to live for, and all they can do is lay about down there. John? Are you coming in?

THE END

THE EDITING PROCESS

Characters

WILLIAM, *nearly 60, editor of Footnotes in History*

PEGGY, 50s

TED, 29

ELEANOR, 22

LIONEL, 39, *general manager of the parent publishing company*

TAMARA DEL FUEGO, 29

CHRIS, 26

MILES MOORE, 33

Setting: a London publishing company in the
1990s

ACT ONE

SCENE 1

A newish, empty high-rise office with telephones on the floor. (CHRIS is painting the woodwork. MILES MOORE, agitated, stands holding a diskette.)

MILES: I'm sorry. I can't wait any longer *(CHRIS continues painting)*. Could you give this to the editor, please. When he comes in. *(He puts the diskette on the floor and leaves. A phone starts ringing. CHRIS ignores it. After a while WILLIAM enters and answers the phone.)*

WILLIAM: Footnotes in History... What?... What magazine? *(ELEANOR walks in)*... Sounds Hard magazine? No this is not Sounds Hard magazine... Yesterday. Well, they might have been here yesterday, but they're not here now. We are Footnotes in History. *(WILLIAM puts the phone down. He addresses ELEANOR.)* Yes?

ELEANOR: Is this Footnotes in History?

WILLIAM: Yes.

ELEANOR: Then I think I must be working here.

WILLIAM: Is that so. Where are you from?

ELEANOR: Bungee Jumpers Hotline.

WILLIAM: Are you a bungee jumper?

ELEANOR: I've done it. You know. Like everyone.

WILLIAM: Everyone.

ELEANOR: It's just a word.

WILLIAM: Just a word. Have you been working long in publishing?

ELEANOR: Oh yes. Six months.

WILLIAM: As you probably know, Footnotes in History is the world's leading journal of historical biography.

ELEANOR: Oh. Really. Well, I'm really looking forward to working on it.

WILLIAM: Do you know anything about historical biography?

ELEANOR: No. That's why I'm looking forward to it

WILLIAM: Yes. Our previous publisher was Blezzard. Have you heard of Blezzard? No? Well, this company has bought the distinguished old firm of Blezzard in its entirety.

ELEANOR: We're always doing that, always buying things. Half the time we just throw them away.

WILLIAM: I was in Russell Mews for twenty years, it will take a little time to get one's bearings in Acton. Do you know of a good fish restaurant?

ELEANOR: I generally bring a pot noodle.

WILLIAM: Yes, a pot noodle. But I welcome the change. Blezzard is extinct. The last monstera deliciosa has departed, the last cardigan. Now that we've come here, we must take Footnotes in History forward. American distribution, do you see what I mean. Heritage is much in demand in some places. *(To CHRIS.)* Could we open a window?

CHRIS: What for.

WILLIAM: Isn't the smell of paint troubling you?

CHRIS: I'm OK thanks.

WILLIAM: Nonetheless could you open a window please.

CHRIS: Sorry, I can't do that.

WILLIAM: I must have a window open.

CHRIS: You can't open these windows.

WILLIAM: *(Goes to a window, tries to open it.)* It's locked. Why do they lock them? Do people jump? *(To ELEANOR.)* Do you bungee jump out of here? *(To CHRIS.)* Who has the keys?

CHRIS: There are no keys.

ELEANOR: No-one can open them, it spoils the air conditioning.

WILLIAM: They didn't tell me. They should have told me. I should have known. But of course. Air conditioning. Of course it is. Has anyone ever sent you a postcard from the

Mexican town of Guanajuato? or perhaps you've been there yourself, they keep rows of dessicated corpses leaning up against the wall like so many dried umbrellas, and the cause of it is air conditioning. Subjected to air conditioning for any length of time, one's skin shrinks so it won't cover one, and then it cracks, and one's brain, which in times of plenty was nourished by a thousand streams swarming with messages, becomes a desert marked by the tracks of dead watercourses, like the planet Mars. Never mind. I'll get used to it.

(PEGGY enters. Office furniture will be carried in from now on.)

PEGGY: *(To WILLIAM.)* Isn't it stuffy in here. Why don't you open a window?

WILLIAM: Thanks Peggy, good idea, thank you. *(PEGGY disappears.)* My secretary.

ELEANOR: Yes.

WILLIAM: In addition there is Ted. Ted is the assistant editor. You are the editorial assistant.

ELEANOR: I met him when he came in yesterday.

WILLIAM: Yesterday? Ted came in?

ELEANOR: He came in yesterday. He's nice, isn't he.

WILLIAM: Ted. Ted nice. Yes. Ted's not very good.

ELEANOR: I was showing him the systems.

WILLIAM: Ted asked you to show him the systems.

ELEANOR: I'm keen to help. If there's a way.

WILLIAM: Help Ted.

ELEANOR: I'll show them to you.

WILLIAM: If Ted wouldn't mind.

ELEANOR: You're not offended.

WILLIAM: We're surrounded by this magnificent technology, aren't we, whose powerful rays may soon mutate us into superbeings as well as facilitating the editing process. *(PEGGY comes in.)*

PEGGY: For God's sake, William, the tea chests.

WILLIAM: I can't think about the tea chests now.

PEGGY: Then when?

WILLIAM: I can't think about when.

PEGGY: When *can* you think about when?

WILLIAM: How are you Peggy? Are you coping?

PEGGY: Coping. Of course I'm *coping.*

WILLIAM: You're coping with the tea chests, are you.

PEGGY: They're your tea chests, William. They're all yours. Goodbye.

WILLIAM: Peggy, where are you going.

PEGGY: I'm resigning, what do you think.

WILLIAM: *(Putting himself between her and the way out.)* Don't resign. Please. Not at the moment. Tell me about the tea chests.

PEGGY: Well. If you're interested.

WILLIAM: I am.

PEGGY: Come and see.

WILLIAM: May I?

PEGGY: They're gone.

WILLIAM: But I was so looking forward to seeing them.

PEGGY: There's been some stupid mistake.

WILLIAM: *(With venom.)* Where's Ted? *(They all leave except CHRIS.)*

SCENE 2

The same office a few days later. Morning. Furniture and computers are more or less in place. ELEANOR, PEGGY.

ELEANOR: They give people their salary cheque and it's postdated.

PEGGY: I'm surprised you put up with it.

ELEANOR: Oh it hasn't happened to me.

PEGGY: So you're quite fortunate really.

ELEANOR: Yes it's different when you're someone's niece.

PEGGY: I'm sure it is.

ELEANOR: Yes. I don't get paid. It's very competitive these days.

PEGGY: Yes, I expect everyone wants to be someone's niece these days.

ELEANOR: My mother keeps saying it will lead to a position.

PEGGY: What position had you in mind?

ELEANOR: I don't know, I have to find myself.

PEGGY: Yes you'll definitely have to find yourself if you want to put yourself in a position.

ELEANOR: But you have to be excited about it, don't you, because unless you're excited they don't give you the job.

PEGGY: Do you have any interests at all?

ELEANOR: I'm sort of excited about art, but other people are excited about it who can actually do it. So I'm hoping to become excited about something that isn't so exciting.

PEGGY: You'll rotate will you. You'll move on.

ELEANOR: I want to do what people want, but it's difficult isn't it, because I don't understand what it is.

PEGGY: My family never expected me to wind up in publishing, but here I am, I've always been drawn to the bohemian side. My sister works in textile rental.

(TED enters.)

Good morning Ted. Did you have a difficult journey?

TED: No, thank you for asking, it was absolutely no problem. But thank you. *(He is settling at his desk, switching on his computer, starting to work.)*

PEGGY: Well of course we begin to worry when you're late.

TED: Why's that, Peggy, do you miss me?

PEGGY: It's not me, Ted, the world needs you.

TED: Is William in?

PEGGY: It isn't a competition.

TED: I didn't know what to have for breakfast this morning.

PEGGY: Did you not?

TED: No I didn't want any cereal.

PEGGY: So what did you do?

TED: I had a bit of jelly.

PEGGY: A bit of jelly. And was it nice?

TED: It was very nice, thank you, and then I had an egg.

PEGGY: Good for you. Good for him, Eleanor, don't you think?

TED: Eleanor, who's your uncle?

ELEANOR: Oh I don't know.

TED: Her uncle's on the board.

ELEANOR: I don't know him.

PEGGY: Eleanor, you must know your uncle.

ELEANOR: I know who he is. I mean, he's in the family, that's why I don't know him, anyway it's probably just as well, or I don't think he'd have given me this job.

PEGGY: Surely that's not true.

ELEANOR: I'm hopeless though, aren't I.

PEGGY: You're willing, dear.

TED: Does William know about your uncle? He'll love it, he'll start commissioning articles from all your important relatives, he loves being on the phone to people like that, talking to Lady Aphasia yesterday, he was drawing little coronets all down the side of someone's manuscript, what a tosser, hullo William.

(WILLIAM enters. Silence. WILLIAM sits at his desk. Silence for a while.)

TED: *(He's editing an article on screen.)* What does this mean. "His not unenviable solitude." What does she mean.

WILLIAM: What's the matter, Ted.

TED: Why can't the woman write what she means.

WILLIAM: What do you think she means?

TED: Well, it's quite obvious what she means.

WILLIAM: It's obvious, is it.

TED: Yes I think so. I think it's obvious.

WILLIAM: That's all right then.

TED: No, my point is, she makes it difficult to understand what she means, it just so happens that I do.

WILLIAM: Ah.

TED: But that's not good enough, is it.

WILLIAM: I don't know, Ted, if you can understand what she means I would have thought most people would.

TED: I mean to say, what difference is there exactly between "his not unenviable solitude" and "his enviable solitude"? I'm going to change it.

WILLIAM: Ted.

TED: Yo?

WILLIAM: Don't change it.

TED: Don't you see, the meaning is exactly the same.

WILLIAM: No it isn't.

TED: In what way?

WILLIAM: There are two shades of meaning.

TED: If there are two shades of meaning, why can't I see them?

WILLIAM: Because you're thick, Ted.

TED: You think so. I think you should take a good look at your Footnotes in History, it's as vibrant and exciting as a self-addressed envelope, why can't I be despised by someone serious. What am I doing here, well, it's obvious what I'm doing here. I'm being taught the meaning of despair, and what I want to know is, once I've totally resigned myself to being a self-satisfied garrulous prat like you, how am I going to find any reason to carry on?

WILLIAM: Power, Ted, power.

(LIONEL and TAMARA enter.)

LIONEL: And here we have Footnotes in History.

TAMARA: Right.

LIONEL: Don't mind us, we couldn't keep away, could we Tamara. We're very impressed by the work you do, don't you hate being impressed, Tamara?

TAMARA: No I love it, it's a shot in the arm Lionel.

LIONEL: It gets up my nose Tamara.

TAMARA: Lionel, you find it impossible to say yes.

LIONEL: Do I?

TAMARA: You never say yes to me.

WILLIAM: I don't think we've met.

LIONEL: William, this is Tamara del Fuego.

WILLIAM: I beg your pardon?

LIONEL: Our corporate image consultant.

WILLIAM: Our what.

LIONEL: She's been brought in to help us understand how wonderful we really are.

TAMARA: It's a huge task.

LIONEL: She's absolutely instinctive William, she takes one look at you and you're solved, she can put a Rubik's cube in order by the action of her eyes alone. She'll be helping us to know each other better. Your name is William. *(Turns to TED.)* And what shall we call you?

WILLIAM: *(To TAMARA.)* Should I show you something?

TAMARA: That would be amazing.

LIONEL: *(Looking at TED.)* Or if there's any input your staff can help us with.

TED: We have an exciting future.

WILLIAM: This is Ted.

TED: I've got some ideas.

WILLIAM: I'm sure he does.

TED: I like to think of us as a heritage publication with potential on the American market.

LIONEL: I'm interested.

WILLIAM: I, on the other hand, am appalled to hear Footnotes in History described as a heritage publication, and believe that to launch it on the American market would be fatal to our character and integrity.

PEGGY: *(To LIONEL and TAMARA.)* Would you like a cup of coffee?

TAMARA: Are you going to make one?

PEGGY: Yes, I am.

TAMARA: No thanks.

PEGGY: Have I said something wrong.

LIONEL: She thinks you're a victim, love, I'll put the kettle on.

TED: I will.

WILLIAM: I shall. Oh do sit down, Peggy, and stop being so bloody obsequious.

PEGGY: Is that an order, William?

WILLIAM: Yes and have some coffee! *(He puts the kettle on, and organizes mugs etc.)* Who else wants one.

TED: I'll have one if you like.

WILLIAM: Eleanor?

PEGGY: We've only got four mugs, William.

TED: Don't worry about me, then.

WILLIAM: No, Ted, have one, do.

ELEANOR: I don't want one, honestly.

TED: What about Peggy then?

WILLIAM: Don't be tiresome, Ted, have a cup of coffee.

PEGGY: I'll wait till everyone's gone.

LIONEL: Ted, what is Footnotes in History actually about?

WILLIAM: It consists of biographical articles about historical figures and is therefore a tool of historical research in addition to being a jolly good read. You've seen the copies I gave you.

LIONEL: I think reading is amazing. Tamara, don't you think reading is amazing.

TAMARA: Reading is blinding.

WILLIAM: How many spoonfuls should I put in?

LIONEL: I like mine strong.

TED: Black as night, hot as hell and sweet as a woman's kiss.

WILLIAM: Are you fond of strong coffee, Ted?

TED: It can't be strong enough for me.

WILLIAM: Can't it? *(He puts a great many spoonfuls of coffee into Ted's cup and pours the water on.)* Sugar? *(He tips in half the bag, stirs the coffee and gives it to TED.)*

TED: You don't seriously expect me to drink that.

WILLIAM: I shall be very much offended if you don't. You said, in the hearing of all present, that it couldn't be strong enough for you.

TED: Perhaps it isn't strong enough for me and that's why I'd rather not drink it.

WILLIAM: That's easily remedied, here, I'll put in more.

TED: Don't bother.

WILLIAM: Then you'll drink it as it is, will you? because failing to do so would be very rude and embarrassing to our visitors. *(TED takes a sip. WILLIAM stares at him. He takes another sip.)*

PEGGY: Our visitors haven't got any coffee, William.

TAMARA: I don't drink coffee, it overstimulates me.

LIONEL: *(To TED.)* Might I have a piece of paper? *(TED gives him one and he puts it on TED's desk and writes on it.)* In case you need my extension.

TAMARA: *(Taking out a notepad and writing on it.)* I'm fully accessible. *(Tears out the page and puts it on TED's desk. TAMARA and LIONEL leave.)*

PEGGY: Well. I don't know about anyone else, but I think I'll have a coffee. *(She sets about making it.)*

WILLIAM: *(To audience.)* Death first visits us as children hiding in our beds from the night. At that time Death is to us a huge, fantastic shadow, like the shadow of a monster on the wall, and we wriggle like bait caught on a little hook of existence, trying to curl up and hide in our own warmth. But Death passes by and leaves us less fearful, and the next time he visits, we find that we have been growing while he has diminished, and so he keeps diminishing and fading, until at last he's a mere tedious caller, an undesirable relative, an embarrassing bore, an ambitious mediocre colleague. The less he frightens us, the more he tires us, until at last we can hardly be bothered to resist him: and if we do resist him, it's only because we still have our pride, and don't want to be seen dead with him.

PEGGY: Coffee, anyone?

WILLIAM: *(Angry.)* No thank you. *(He goes.)*

TED: Why does William hate me? The point of hatred is to be baffling I suppose. To let a person know why would spoil it.

PEGGY: Do you think so?

TED: The point of hatred is to bring you face to face with chaos and eternal night. No matter how much I hate him in return, it's never going to be as good because he's so obviously earned it.

PEGGY: William has devoted his life to Footnotes in History. But you always seem to know better.

TED: I can't help that, can I.

PEGGY: You seem to imagine you could do as well as he does.

TED: Are you suggesting I'm after William's job?

PEGGY: Well. Aren't you?

TED: Do you really think I'd –

PEGGY: I do.

TED: I'm not that desperate, thank you. I'm a scholar! Everything comes second to my biography of Guizot. Unfortunately, in the absence of any proper financial support, I have to depend for my livelihood on a pompous complacent old bully, working for this snotty, half-baked magazine, on which I'm forced to squander my best energies until such time as I'm recognised.

PEGGY: We recognise you, Ted.

TED: You think so.

PEGGY: You think you're too good for your job, so you're bad at it.

TED: In your opinion.

PEGGY: Not only mine.

TED: I'd like to see William try to get along without me.

PEGGY: He might like that too.

TED: I do the work here. He just telephones.

PEGGY: William believes in his job, so people believe in William. I believe in William.

TED: *(Looks at the pieces of paper that have been left on his desk.)* I'm not going to quarrel with you. I don't need to. I have a life. Eleanor.

ELEANOR: Yo?

TED: What are you doing tonight?

ELEANOR: Nothing.

TED: Perhaps we could have a drink.

ELEANOR: Why?

TED: If you're not doing anything.

ELEANOR: I don't really think that's a good enough reason.

SCENE 3

The photocopying room. CHRIS is making a great many copies of a single item. TED enters, carrying a sheet of paper. CHRIS is willing to let him take over the machine.

CHRIS: Be my guest.

TED: I'll wait, honestly.

CHRIS: Suit yourself. *(He carries on photocopying.)*

TED: You're busy.

CHRIS: *(Ready to yield his position.)* Here.

TED: No honestly I'll wait, it's something to do, isn't it. *(He waits. CHRIS looks at him anxiously.)* No, carry on. *(CHRIS carries on, then looks at him anxiously again.)* You're good.

CHRIS: Finishing up now.

TED: Take your time.

(CHRIS goes. TED makes no attempt to use the machine. He puts his piece of paper in the bin, and waits. LIONEL enters and locks the room from the inside.)

LIONEL: Hi.

TED: Hi. Look, I -

LIONEL: I've terminated three magazines today, my productivity is amazing.

TED: I owe it to you to make something clear.

LIONEL: You don't owe me anything as boring as that.

TED: I mean, I'm really glad to meet and have a talk.

LIONEL: The publisher had Footnotes in History on this week's death list. I talked him out of it.

TED: But you've only just bought us. We haven't even published an issue.

LIONEL: People's self-expression is of very little interest to the publisher.

TED: Footnotes in History is a hundred and fifteen years old.

LIONEL: That's why it doesn't have much sex appeal. Unlike some of its staff. Did you like my note?

TED: Yes very friendly.

LIONEL: What did I write?

TED: You wrote, "You didn't get lips like those sucking oranges".

LIONEL: Well. Did you?

TED: I was a bit surprised. I don't think most people would regard me as particularly attractive.

LIONEL: Don't worry. I have a gift for enjoyment.

TED: It's just, I don't think I can really satisfy your expectations.

LIONEL: I'm used to that.

TED: So I hope you don't think I've brought you here under false pretences, but I was really very glad of the opportunity to have a talk with you.

LIONEL: There's the question of your staffing as well, because you have to admit that four of you is excessive.

TED: At Blezzard we were three. Though Eleanor's invaluable, I mean.

LIONEL: Don't worry about Eleanor. She's the only one that's really safe. Where do you live?

TED: Nowhere nice.

LIONEL: I live somewhere nice.

TED: I suppose I was wanting to talk to you about William.

LIONEL: William.

TED: I mean, what will become of him.

LIONEL: Do you care?

TED: I don't think William's in touch.

LIONEL: I want to have sex with you.

TED: Maybe so. But what about William?

LIONEL: I don't want to have sex with William.

TED: Does William have a future in this organisation?

LIONEL: I think you're exploiting me.

TED: You don't mind, do you?

LIONEL: No no, it's what I'm here for.

TED: Yes. William. I mean, I mention the words "American distribution". All at once I'm talking to Mad King George. "Colonies. Traitors. Not a single magazine must fall into American hands." It's funny, because American distribution was William's idea in the first place.

LIONEL: That's why you stole it.

TED: Yes. I realize I'm throwing myself on your good nature.

LIONEL: Couldn't you throw yourself on something a little less flimsy?

TED: It's just that I haven't, um. Not since, um, school.

LIONEL: Fine with me.

TED: No really, if it makes a difference, I'll have a go.

LIONEL: You'll have a go. Decent of you, Ted.

TED: That's all right.

LIONEL: *(To audience.)* I'm tired. I hate being tired. I'm doing this to prove I'm not tired, which I am. As for my work. The publisher is a man who has fads. This publishing company's a fad, he made his money in sunbeds. Last year his fad was management training and he sent me off for a week's survival in Scotland. Twenty-four middle management abseiling down a Scottish cliff. A perilous descent, like their future careers. The course was run on military lines. Never apologize, never explain, kill people. Our activities were exhausting and pointless, no-one was told what anyone was doing and there were no decent shops for miles. I definitely found it relevant to my work. It's a shame about my survival team of six. The course was devised to make us form an effective unit based on trust and we did, but I'm the only one left now, I've sacked the rest.

SCENE 4

Back at the office, early morning.

(PEGGY and CHRIS. CHRIS is mending the electric kettle.)

PEGGY: Stupid of me. I switched it on and it was empty. There was tension in the air and I just pressed the button. It's such a confusing place. So many publications, all about everything, opera, motorbikes, lacemaking, air freight, body-building, and all on top of each other. How does anyone manage to think?

CHRIS: What you want to think for?

PEGGY: Publishing and thinking go together, don't you think?

CHRIS: Not here they don't.

PEGGY: Then why did this company of yours buy a magazine like ours?

CHRIS: By mistake, probably.

PEGGY: It's good of you, helping like this. He won't drink the coffee machine coffee, he likes an instant coffee in his own mug, at Blezzard a kettle was provided. I've brought this one from home.

CHRIS: What's your magazine about?

PEGGY: It's historical biography, I'm not an expert, I'm here on a casual basis, I've been on a casual basis for fifteen years.

CHRIS: Right.

PEGGY: It's astonishing what there is to know about history, if one chooses to... I think I just enjoy the fact there are people who choose to... What would life be, without people like that, who have a sense of direction. But of course, Blezzard was nothing like this. One was completely central. And the moulded ceilings, I miss the moulded ceilings above...

CHRIS: Here. It's fixed.

PEGGY: Thank you.

(CHRIS is leaving. ELEANOR, coming in, encounters him.)

CHRIS: Smile. *(He goes out.)*

PEGGY: Good morning Eleanor, I've opened the post.

ELEANOR: What shall I do then?

PEGGY: I should relax, Eleanor. *(MILES MOORE comes in.)*

MILES: I think you have a diskette of mine.

PEGGY: What's your name?

MILES: Miles Moore.

PEGGY: Is it something we commissioned?

MILES: It's a monograph about the poet Fitch.

PEGGY: Eleanor, have we seen his monograph about the poet Fitch?

MILES: Could it have got lost in the post, do you think?

PEGGY: It's not impossible, is it.

MILES: Yes it is, actually. It is actually impossible. I delivered it to this room with my own hands. So how could it have got lost in the post?

PEGGY: If you delivered it to this room with your own hands, then you were the last person to see it. If this were a murder case, the finger of suspicion would be pointing firmly at you.

MILES: There was nobody here. There was nothing.

PEGGY: And tell me, was the door locked from the inside?

MILES: I thought, what is this place?

PEGGY: We recently moved here from Blezzard.

MILES: And in that short time you've succeeded in losing my diskette.

PEGGY: Have you seen his diskette, Eleanor?

ELEANOR: Perhaps William has it.

PEGGY: If William's got it, he'll have lost it.

MILES: Why should a writer have to subject himself to this?

PEGGY: To what?

MILES: Publication! *(WILLIAM enters.)*

WILLIAM: Ted not here?

PEGGY: William, this is Mr Miles Moore, a writer.

WILLIAM: Hullo.

PEGGY: He's missing an article.

WILLIAM: Just the one?

MILES: *(Smiling.)* Hullo.

WILLIAM: How very brave of you to have come here in person.

MILES: *(Smiling.)* I sent you a monograph about the poet Fitch.

WILLIAM: Did we commission it?

MILES: We spoke on the telephone. I'm not expecting a fee.

WILLIAM: I'm afraid we can take no responsibility for unsolicited articles.

MILES: *(Smiling.)* Of course not, they must be a terrible bore.

WILLIAM: They are.

MILES: So you have no recollection of a monograph about the poet Fitch.

WILLIAM: Yes. I've read it.

MILES: The wetlands poet.

WILLIAM: Yes.

MILES: I think you'll agree that Fitch is a major find. A voice from the marsh.

WILLIAM: Major, you say. Well documented.

MILES: Well documented, yes.

WILLIAM: By people of repute.

MILES: Absolutely. There are critical studies by Savage, and essays by -

WILLIAM: Because we're not so terribly interested in subjects that are well documented.

MILES: Of course there's been nothing at all since 1931.

WILLIAM: That whole group has received rather a lot of exposure. We recently published five thousand words about Folwell.

MILES: But Folwell is famous.

WILLIAM: More famous than Fitch.

MILES: Folwell is far more famous than Fitch.

WILLIAM: So Fitch is quite obscure.

MILES: Yes. Obscure. My discovery.

WILLIAM: Deeply obscure.

MILES: Yes.

WILLIAM: Then could you tell me, please, why I should publish your woeful article about a deeply obscure and stupid poet who seems to have spent his mercifully short life scuttling about in reed beds like some coot?

MILES: You're wasting my time. *(He goes.)*

PEGGY: I've got the kettle fixed, William.

WILLIAM: Oh have you? I've been rather enjoying that coffee from the machine.

(LIONEL enters.)

LIONEL: William. Could we meet in here. Someone's using my desk.

PEGGY: Eleanor and I shall buy a poinsettia. One must keep in touch with the seasons.

(PEGGY and ELEANOR leave.)

WILLIAM: Thank you for coming. I have some proposals.

LIONEL: So have I. You're overmanned.

WILLIAM: You mean Ted.

LIONEL: Not Ted.

WILLIAM: Not Ted.

LIONEL: We feel that Footnotes in History is a prestige product and we're determined to find the money to ensure that it remains as uncommercial as ever.

WILLIAM: Oh good.

LIONEL: So how are we to cut the cost of production.

WILLIAM: Eleanor is unpaid. We're very fond of Eleanor.

LIONEL: Yes, of course, and so we feel that Eleanor, who as you rightly observe is on a trainee salary, should take over the functions of Peggy.

WILLIAM: Peggy!

LIONEL: With the saving that would make, there's every likelihood Footnotes in History can remain on the team for the next six months at least.

WILLIAM: I beg your pardon.

LIONEL: We wouldn't have to axe it.

WILLIAM: Axe it.

LIONEL: If Peggy goes.

WILLIAM: You've been so enthusiastic about Footnotes in History. How can you axe us if you're so enthusiastic?

LIONEL: It's the power of positive thinking.

WILLIAM: Peggy's been with me for fifteen years!

LIONEL: Don't agonize over it, William, because you know you're going to wind up doing it. I've seen a lot of this kind of thing, and I find the way people agonize is rather boring, given that they always wind up doing it. *(PEGGY comes in, with the kettle.)*

PEGGY: Sorry, I've just filled the kettle, I thought I'd pop it in and you could make yourselves a cup of coffee.

WILLIAM: Thank you, not now.

PEGGY: I'll switch it on shall I. *(She switches on the kettle. Blackout.)* Oh my poor kettle.

SCENE 5

Continued blackout. TAMARA and TED are having sex in the photocopying room.

TED: Oh my God, it's gone completely black before my eyes.

TAMARA: Ted, the lights are fused. *(Secondary lights come up.)* See?

TED: Yes. I see. Sorry. It's all right, I'll be OK in a minute.

TAMARA: Don't worry about it.

TED: Remember what you told me about?

TAMARA: What did I tell you about?

TED: Oysters.

TAMARA: What about them?

TED: I've got some in my pocket.

TAMARA: In your pocket? That's a bit of a weird place.

TED: Frankly I don't think it's half as weird as the place you told me about.

TAMARA: Show us. *(TED takes out a tin of smoked oysters.)* Ted.

TED: Yo?

TAMARA: They're smoked oysters, Ted.

TED: Yes I know, we're a long way from the sea here.

TAMARA: I'm not doing it with preservatives.

TED: Well then. Are you hungry? *(He takes out a can opener and starts to open the oysters.)* How was the meeting?

TAMARA: I told them about Veronica.

TED: Who's Veronica?

TAMARA: I told him, anything this big, it has to be Veronica. She'll do it for fifty grand, she's a colour consultant.

TED: Sometimes, when you say something, I suddenly feel as if I'm looking at the world through a glass of water and it's all gone sideways. It's amazing how my tiny magazine has a role to play in your huge sphere of projects.

TAMARA: Your magazine? Yours?

TED: Because I thought we agreed, something will have to be done about William.

TAMARA: Do you want us to get rid of William and make you the editor?

TED: Only it's what you said. You said he's academic.

TAMARA: Tell me about this book you're writing.

TED: Oh it's not so much of a book. It's more of a profile. It's more of a personal map of the ambitions and the erotic conflicts within a Belgian historian.

SCENE 6

Somewhere in the building, CHRIS is mending wires. LIONEL passes.

LIONEL: Will it take much longer?

CHRIS: It'll take a long time.

LIONEL: Why is that?

CHRIS: Because you don't pay what it costs.

LIONEL: Are you trying to hold this company to ransom? You're sacked. *(CHRIS gathers his things and leaves. LIONEL continues on his way.)*

SCENE 7

The office. Lunchtime. WILLIAM alone. TAMARA enters.

TAMARA: William I didn't get back to you, I'll phone you and we can arrange to speak.

WILLIAM: We're speaking now.

TAMARA: You're right. We are. Well. Obviously we need to change the perception, so a relaunch. All right? Have you met the in-house designers? Don't. I've contacted a very good outside outfit, they're so innovative William they're practically mutants.

WILLIAM: So it isn't true what I've been told, that we're going to be closed down.

TAMARA: You're being relaunched.

WILLIAM: We're being relaunched. Not closed down.

TAMARA: Why not both.

WILLIAM: But seriously, I'm feeling quite upset, Lionel seems to be saying that in the interests of modernisation, Peggy should go.

TAMARA: Peggy. Is that what he says.

WILLIAM: Why. Who else.

(PEGGY enters, with her lunch and the tin of smoked oysters.)

PEGGY: *(Speaking to WILLIAM.)* A open tin of smoked oysters, in the photocopying room. People are disgusting. *(She settles at her desk.)*

TAMARA: I'm optimistic, William.

WILLIAM: Why?

TAMARA: It's what I'm paid for. Do you think you could spare Ted?

WILLIAM: Ted? Oh yes, I think so. I think we can spare Ted.

TAMARA: Good. I'll be working with him on development.

WILLIAM: You'll be working with Ted?

TAMARA: He tells me you haven't a lot for him to do.

WILLIAM: I don't understand.

TAMARA: Ted understands. *(She leaves.)*

WILLIAM: My heart. The old can never agitate the young as much as they agitate us. However much we try to agitate them, they don't have the additional agitation of knowing that being agitated is probably going to kill them.

PEGGY: Why did that woman say Ted understands?

WILLIAM: I don't know.

PEGGY: Although, to give Ted his due -

WILLIAM: Let's not.

PEGGY: - he's conscientious. He'll worry all day about a comma. If something doesn't make sense to him, he'll change it and change it till it does.

WILLIAM: And then it doesn't make sense to anyone else.

PEGGY: I don't think you ought to be complacent William. What did she mean? She made it sound as if they're trying to get rid of you. Doesn't anybody know who you are? What's the matter, William.

WILLIAM: There's nothing the matter that your sympathy can't make worse.

PEGGY: Because surely they can see, however marginal it might be, Footnotes in History is you.

WILLIAM: Peggy, do you like this place?

PEGGY: That's not what's important, William.

WILLIAM: It must be difficult for you, travelling here every day.

PEGGY: Travel and see the world.

WILLIAM: How old are you? Aren't you tired?

PEGGY: If you go on talking like that, I'll think you don't want me here... Do you not want me here?

WILLIAM: I just thought you might not want to be here.

PEGGY: Well. I do. So long as I can help. Why. Is my work not satisfactory?

WILLIAM: Naturally not, it never has been.

PEGGY: Is that how you really feel.

WILLIAM: Look, it doesn't mean I –

PEGGY: Iit's perfectly all right. Thanks for your honesty. I resign. *(She stands up and starts clearing her desk.)* If that's what you want. *(Continues clearing her desk.)* And after fifteen years I'm sure you do know what you want. *(She goes to the door.)* I've never in my whole life known what I wanted. It's vulgar in a woman. And in a man.*(She waits, but there's no response.)* Goodbye. *(She's going out.)*

WILLIAM: Peggy!

PEGGY: *(Coming back in.)* Make up your mind.

WILLIAM: Come back.

PEGGY: *(Silence.)* I'm stupid, I know I am. I imagine, do you see, that I'm of use to you.

WILLIAM: You are of use to me.

PEGGY: I just don't know any more. Everything's different here.

WILLIAM: You've got your nice flat.

PEGGY: My nice flat.

WILLIAM: Your nice flat where I brought you all your books in boxes, I thought at the time how extremely nice it was.

PEGGY: I've been in my nice flat for four years and seven months and those books are still in their boxes. Everything's still in its boxes. *(Starts to cry.)*

WILLIAM: Do you not like your flat?

PEGGY: Boxes in the rooms and in the hall. I dust them. If anyone saw the way I live, they'd think I was mad. I shouldn't have divorced him. But what could I do? I'd always given him what he asked for, and that's what he asked for. No wife could have been more conscientious. I should have demanded a reference. Excuse me a minute.

(PEGGY off. ELEANOR in.)

WILLIAM: Eleanor, have you and your uncle ever discussed this publication?

ELEANOR: I never see my uncle. My uncle used to shut my mother in the dressing up box, sit on it and fart.

WILLIAM: These family traditions. The dressing up box.

ELEANOR: Before they got married, my father drove his Austin up to the front of the house to visit my mother and my uncle put a potato in the exhaust.

WILLIAM: The house. Where was the house?

ELEANOR: It doesn't matter. It belongs to my uncle.

WILLIAM: How can a girl like you be so unhappy?

ELEANOR: Yes I know I can't be as unhappy as someone like you.

WILLIAM: Am I unhappy? I'm the editor.

ELEANOR: Yes but, once you used to be a child.

WILLIAM: Even supposing I was, it's rude to draw attention to people's origins. Unless they're yours.

ELEANOR: If the child you used to be were to come and look at you now, what would he think of you?

WILLIAM: I expect he'd find me rather comical. Children do find adults rather comical, rather crude I think, rather a caricature. Adulthood is an acquired taste. Once we've acquired the taste of adulthood, we forget how nasty, perverse, leathery and coarse any bit of it used to seem. To a child, I'd be a gross fleshy monster who spends his days doing unnatural things that neither make me dream nor make me laugh, or if I laugh it's the lurid laugh of a monster. A child can't conceive of numb laborious creatures like us that can live without elation.

ELEANOR: I'm nowhere near as unhappy as you.

WILLIAM: Then why don't you smile?

ELEANOR: I'm not unhappy enough to smile when I don't want to. *(She stands up.)*

WILLIAM: Eleanor.

ELEANOR: What.

WILLIAM: I wish you'd invite me.

ELEANOR: Where?

WILLIAM: Back in time to where you are. Perhaps if you take my hand.

ELEANOR: Would you like a coffee? *(ELEANOR hurries from the room. WILLIAM sits for a moment, then looks around for Peggy. He calls experimentally.)*

WILLIAM: Peggy? (He leaves the room to look for her.)

(After a moment, TED comes in with LIONEL.)

TED: You've been avoiding me. I feel I've been used.

LIONEL: Perhaps you have.

TED: But I haven't been used enough!

LIONEL: Look, I'm terribly busy.

TED: That's it. You need a deputy.

LIONEL: Do I.

TED: What am I to you. Just a cheap thrill.

LIONEL: I wouldn't say that.

TED: Then prove me wrong. Make me your deputy.

LIONEL: Why?

TED: Because you've told me yourself, publications are being terminated all the time here, so what I really need is to become a part of the permanent management structure, and then my position would be more secure. Wouldn't it.

LIONEL: What you need isn't really the point.

TED: It is to me. It's true that I'm first and foremost a scholar. But scholars will only be respected if they're seen to hold their own in the market place. I know a lot about Guizot's views on the development of the monarchy in Europe. Are you saying my knowledge is irrelevant?

LIONEL: Yes.

TED: Guizot has some interesting things to say about periods in history when selfish forces are let loose and when egotism prevails, either through ignorance and brutality or through corruption. At such times society, plunged into conflicts of personal will, and unable to summon any will to the common good, passionately desires strong guidance by a sovereign, so as soon as any institution displaying sovereign characteristics appears, people flock to it, Guizot says, like condemned men seeking sanctuary in a church. I think we can agree that a company such as this one is a sovereign institution. A company such as this one is a bulwark against social collapse. I'd make it my aim to promote company loyalty. Tamara's already using me in a management capacity.

LIONEL: The woman's a swamp, go in there and there'll be nothing left of you but your fountain pen. And it won't write.

TED: You've no reason to feel jealous. *(Puts his hands on LIONEL's waist.)* I could do it right here. You think I'm joking.

LIONEL: *(Trying to retreat.)* No, you're serious I'm afraid.

TED: But it's so good. It's so good when you feel you just can't stop, it gives you faith in something beyond. Oh God. The computer. What's wrong with the computer? What's this doing here? *(Lifts the tin of smoked oysters, puts it down again. Presses buttons, panicking. Smoke rises from the computer.)*

SCENE 8

The office later that afternoon. ELEANOR, PEGGY, WILLIAM, TED. CHRIS clearing up mess on the floor.

WILLIAM: I simply asked, in the most reasonable way, how it happened.

PEGGY: In all the years I've worked for you, I've never before been accused of sabotage.

WILLIAM: I can't think why not.

(TAMARA enters.)

TAMARA: Everything all right in here? Congratulations William. You've cost this company more than I have. But hey, who's counting. Here's your new masthead, doesn't that instantly say to you, heritage, the remake, it's a mock-up, obviously, the editor's name goes here, we can put that in later in order to avoid any uncertainty.

WILLIAM: What uncertainty?

(TAMARA off.)

PEGGY: I wasn't aware you valued my contribution so highly.

WILLIAM: Circuits have been thrown into confusion.

PEGGY: Your circuits have.

WILLIAM: The damage commenced with oil from a tin of smoked oysters.

PEGGY: I'm only doing my best, William.

WILLIAM: That's the problem.

ELEANOR: That's not fair.

PEGGY: Nice of you Eleanor, to be fair to me. I'm glad you're able to be fair. I'm glad you have the leisure to think about being fair. Is that what you do all day, as you're sitting there? Really it's as if you were sitting there in your nightdress when it's broad daylight in here, you remind me of some sort of painting, lilies in a pond, and I suppose the lilies would be thinking, would they, some sort of liquid thoughts they'd have, sitting there in their nightdress in their pond, leaving a normally active and practical person feeling that there's simply no point.

WILLIAM: Nobody wishes to condemn anyone.

PEGGY: Speak for yourself, William.

WILLIAM: I simply felt it would be useful to establish how the thing could have come about, in order to avoid a repetition in the future.

TED: I don't think a repetition is likely.

WILLIAM: It isn't a question of guilt.

PEGGY: What's it a question of?

WILLIAM: It isn't a question of blame. I have personally taken the blame.

PEGGY: But William, the blame is mine.

WILLIAM: The blame is not yours, the blame is mine.

PEGGY: Perhaps we should offer the blame to the room at large. Does anybody else want the blame? Well then! I resign. *(Silence. PEGGY is grabbing her things from her desk.)* That's it. I'm going. Do you hear me.

WILLIAM: I hear you.

PEGGY: I'll go then.

WILLIAM: All right.

PEGGY: You'll manage without me I'm sure. You've already adapted so well.

ACT TWO

SCENE 1

Some weeks later. Early morning

MILES: From marigolded marsh I came

       Into the mighty city

       No sunny sedge, no sweet fleabane

       I found, no lilies pretty

       Through streets of stone the people pressed

       A hard and hurtling throng

       That plucked no reeds, and pulled no cress

       And heard no plover's song

SCENE 2

ELEANOR and WILLIAM in the office. WILLIAM is on the phone.

WILLIAM: Lord Quarto please... *(To ELEANOR.)* You don't understand. She was always resigning. I could never rely on that woman, not in fifteen years' continual dependance.

ELEANOR: Why did she always resign?

WILLIAM: To make me ask her back.

ELEANOR: But this time, you didn't ask her back.

WILLIAM: Hullo? Lord Quarto? Hullo, it's William here... William at Footnotes in History... Thank you, yes it is a good issue, isn't it, the first of many with this company, I hope, I'm told the publisher's pleased, do you know him at all?... No I've not met him yet. I thought your piece for us was splendid, so deceptively simple ... Thin? absolutely not, quite the reverse I assure you... No I don't mean thick, of course not... maybe so, but off the top of a head like yours is better than off the bottom of many a, anyway you liked the issue... Yes I like to feel that with the advantage of maturity in this modern company we can be a sort of old head on young shoulders... ha ha, very good,

Frankenstein's monster, very good. I wonder, do you know anything about a woman called Tamara del Fuego, she's a marketing consultant, I don't suppose you'd have met her... no... I think she's dishonest...Very good, that's what they're paid for, very good, but seriously I think she may be taking this company for a great deal of money, and unfortunately I have a young assistant who seems to be involved *(TED enters.)* Hullo Ted. My young assistant Ted has just walked in, he's been working on the most exciting schemes, haven't you Ted, with this wonderful new marketing consultant, Tamara del Fuego, he's tremendously involved with her I believe, and I'm sure they'll transform this company beyond recognition, beyond recognition... Oh would you? Discreetly? Yes that's very kind, yes exactly, help them on their way. Thank you... Thank you... Goodbye. How are you Ted.

TED: Very well, thank you, William. Who was that?

WILLIAM: You don't know him.

(Silence. All work. ELEANOR eventually falls asleep.)

TED: Eleanor, what's this word supposed to be? Eleanor? Earth calling Eleanor. *(She wakes up.)* Where were you last night?

ELEANOR: Karate.

TED: Are you learning self-defence?

ELEANOR: Not really.

TED: Good, is it, what you're subbing?

WILLIAM: Eleanor is subbing a piece entitled, Impressions in London Clay, Pissarro in Norwood.

ELEANOR: It's very interesting, it's just, interesting things are boring sometimes.

TED: I hesitate to say this, but if it's boring why are we printing it?

WILLIAM: Most things are boring, Ted.

TED: We're not short are we?

WILLIAM: No, we're not short, thank you Ted.

TED: April I'm talking about.

WILLIAM: Yes Ted, thank you, April.

TED: Uh-*huh.*

WILLIAM: Yes?

TED: Because I've just commissioned an article from Hopkins Hudson for April.

WILLIAM: Sorry. You've commissioned.

TED: For April.

WILLIAM: Sorry. You've commissioned.

TED: Sorry. For April.

WILLIAM: For April.

TED: It has to be April, that's when his book comes out.

WILLIAM: You don't commission, Ted. I commission.

TED: Well. I'm sorry.

WILLIAM: You'll have to explain there's been a mistake.

TED: It's difficult.

WILLIAM: You must telephone at once.

TED: I can't.

WILLIAM: You're mad. Why did I never see it. It explains so much.

TED: I'm not mad, William.

WILLIAM: Don't worry, I'll take care of everything. Have you got his telephone number in your book? Have you got a little book?

TED: Yes I've got a little book.

WILLIAM: Have you got his telephone number in it?

TED: Yes.

WILLIAM: Show me. *(Smiles.)*

TED: William, I'm not mad and I can't withdraw the commission.

WILLIAM: Fine, just give me the book!

TED: I made the commission at the direct request of the publisher.

WILLIAM: That's impossible. I've never met the publisher.

TED: The publisher asked me to commission his friend Hopkins Hudson.

WILLIAM: Where did you meet the publisher?

TED: So perhaps we should add some pages.

WILLIAM: Where did you meet him.

TED: At a party.

WILLIAM: You.

TED: So perhaps Pissarro in Norwood could be held over until May.

WILLIAM: At a party. What sort of party? What sort of publisher would meet you at a party? and you're asking me to hold over material commissioned and accepted for publication by me as editor, to hold it over in favour of material springing from some publisher you met at a party, but I shall protect my material, that is what I'm here for, to guarantee the survival and propagation of my material, that is what survival means, so you see, this is a matter of life and death. You must telephone immediately, Ted, immediately. Where's the number? *(He rushes over to Ted's desk and throws things around, looking for the number.)* Where's your little book? What have you done with your little book? Look in your pocket. *(He's forcibly going through TED's pockets.)* Stand up. *(He grabs hold of TED and tries to force him to stand. He slaps TED's face. TAMARA comes in.)*

TAMARA: Ted, the publisher wants to see you.

TED: *(To WILLIAM.)* Sorry. Got to go.

(TED and TAMARA leave together.)

WILLIAM: So, Eleanor. Pissarro in Norwood. It's a fascinating piece.

ELEANOR: Yes.

WILLIAM: They've sent us a picture showing Streatham High Road as it was in 1882. One can almost see oneself standing there in the dust of a passing carriage.

ELEANOR: Yes almost.

WILLIAM: People are unaware of Pissarro having been there.

ELEANOR: The dust might have made him invisible.

WILLIAM: Ted has been spending money. I wonder if your uncle has discussed any of this.

ELEANOR: I haven't seen my uncle.

WILLIAM: Do you think you could possibly arrange for me to have a talk with your uncle, do you think you could possibly signal to your uncle that -

ELEANOR: I can't signal to my uncle. I'm invisible to my uncle. I hate my uncle. He despises us. He despises mummy. He's got granny's corner cupboard, it was the only thing in my grandparents' house that mummy really wanted. Granny said it was going to be mummy's, but when they got back to the house after the funeral, mummy discovered it was gone. Afterwards she saw it in his flat. He couldn't care less about me. The only reason I've got this job is, we haven't got the corner cupboard. Excuse me, I have to wash my hands.

(ELEANOR goes.)

WILLIAM: What would it be like to be redundant? After a lifetime spent trying to silence the inner voice that said one always was. We're obsessed with finding a function for ourselves, and as soon as we find one, we're replaceable. Because any function we can carry out can be carried out by another. *(TED enters.)*

TED: I've just had a strange meeting with the publisher, William.

WILLIAM: Surely not. You were getting on so well.

TED: He says there are questions, financial questions, about my work with Tamara. Do you know where this is coming from? I think you do. And I just want to ask you why you want to pull down everything we've been working so hard to put in place. Until today I was welcomed into this organization, I was made to feel I have something to contribute to this organization, you never made me feel that, you wouldn't know how, because this magazine is frankly all you care about, and that's why you don't belong here.

WILLIAM: I'm sorry, Ted, you're having this trouble. I suppose they don't know you as I do. And now they've found you out.

SCENE 3

MILES: I sang to them of shimmering strand

Of pond and mud and mere

Of ditch and drain and waterland

They did not stop to hear

SCENE 4

The gents. TED and LIONEL.

TED: You must think I'm stupid. (Silence.) Sorry, I know you don't think I'm stupid, it's just my paranoia. (Silence.) Sorry, of course I'm not paranoid, it's just they're after me.

LIONEL: You must distance yourself from Tamara.

TED: But without Tamara I'm nothing.

LIONEL: That's true.

TED: How can I be so ungrateful?

LIONEL: You'll find a way.

TED: Tamara doesn't understand you. She says you're very supportive of her and she finds it very confusing and she can't defend herself.

LIONEL: What?

TED: Because you refuse to take advantage.

LIONEL: Women are mad.

TED: She and I have talked about this quite openly. Does that surprise you? But instead of feeling threatened by this feeling she has about you, not that I'm saying you've encouraged her, that's the trouble, you haven't, well, instead of feeling threatened as some men would, I welcome it.

LIONEL: Nice of you. Ted. Try and concentrate.

TED: I mean, you don't mind. You and I, we don't mind. We're not a problem. Not a serious problem. (Very infatuated.) Until Tamara, I didn't know what a serious problem was.

LIONEL: Well now you do.

TED: I'm so depressed. I'm so anxious. I'll be out of a job. I'll be back where I was a year ago, sleeping till noon every day, not enjoying it, sleeping that guilty half-numb sleep that steals your life away, and in my dreams I'll see buildings like this one with hundreds of windows lit up day and night, where the electricity holds all the people together. And if you're not part of it you're dark, and the sheets you're wrapped in are sheets of lead. If you're not part of it you can't signal.

LIONEL: Tell the Board she misled you.

TED: What do you care. What does Tamara care? All she thinks about is you! I'd carry her shoes in my teeth if she wanted.

LIONEL: She's got her own teeth.

TED: She doesn't love me! And I work so hard for this company. She's letting the company down!

(TAMARA bursts in. TED addresses her.)

TED: You're dead! (Puts his hand over his mouth.)

TAMARA: (To TED.) What will you tell the Board?

LIONEL: There's a sign on the door that says "men". Is that what attracted you?

TED: (To TAMARA.) I'll tell them I stand by everything you've done.

TAMARA: Everything I've done. All by myself.

TED: I didn't know what was happening.

TAMARA: Of course you knew.

TED: I knew, but I didn't understand.

TAMARA: Well. You wouldn't.

TED: How can you speak to me like that and expect me to stand up for you.

TAMARA: I don't. You never have, not for more than thirty seconds.

(She walks out. TED sinks to the floor.)

SCENE 5

The office later the same day. ELEANOR at work. WILLIAM returns happy after a long lunch, hangs up his coat.

WILLIAM: Messages?

ELEANOR: No.

WILLIAM: What of it? I've been eating lunch with people messages come from. (Goes to the door, pauses.) Ted not back?

ELEANOR: He's been called to a meeting of the Board.

WILLIAM: I hope he's not in trouble. I'll go and see.

(WILLIAM goes. TED comes in..)

TED: I told them she's a phenomenon. I tried to explain to them this blind loyalty she inspired in me. That's true isn't it?

ELEANOR: Blind yes. Loyal no.

TED: All it amounts to is a couple of countersignatures for payments she said were needed. And I believed her. Was I a fool?

ELEANOR: *(Silence.)*

TED: What does your uncle think?

ELEANOR: Look! I'm no relation of my uncle's!

TED: Couldn't you talk to him?

ELEANOR: That would be totally meaningless!

TED: Nothing anyone does is meaningless. Everyone's important. Well anyway, you are. You can help me. I know you may think I'm contemptible. Well, I am. I'll happily admit to being everything you think I am, and worse.

ELEANOR: Go on then.

TED: All right. When Peggy resigned, it was me who crashed the system. I was trying to get something fixed and it all went wrong, and afterwards I didn't say.

ELEANOR: Ted, how could you, that's awful.

TED: Yes, I'm awful, I'm spineless and weak, that's why I need you. Please will you talk to your uncle.

ELEANOR: I'm nothing to do with my uncle! I don't know why people keep drawing attention to my uncle as if he were some part of my body that everyone can see except me. If I could see where it was I'd cut it off!

TED: If I lose this job I'll have to live at home, which spells the end of my manhood. God. The sofa. God. The sticky table mats with pictures of cathedrals. It will all be over in a minute. That's what the doctor used to say when he gave me my jabs. Didn't he understand, it was that minute I was worried about. There I was, a boy, an entire little universe of wellbeing, and in that minute, a terrible sting was going to come and convulse the little universe, and the boy that was left would not be the boy from before. That happy boy would be extinct. I'll never make it, I'll continue as a blockhead with strained features and a nervous laugh, I'll be humble, I'll say stupid things, I'll think stupid thoughts, my mind will be paralyzed, I'll never finish my biography of Guizot, I'll never be able to move away from home ever again. *(He rocks back and forth with his head in his hands. MILES MOORE comes in with a diskette.)*

MILES: *(To ELEANOR.)* I've found a new facet.

ELEANOR: I beg your pardon?

MILES: I've found a new facet of Fitch.

ELEANOR: We're rather busy just now.

MILES: This is an editorial matter.

ELEANOR: We're rather too busy for editorial matters.

MILES: That makes no sense. Is this, or is it not, a magazine? Are you, or are you not, working on it?

TED: I don't know!

MILES: I've unearthed a further body of Fitch's poems.

ELEANOR: Perhaps you should be speaking to the police.

MILES: He wrote them in despair of ever being published.

ELEANOR: I suppose you must know how he felt.

MILES: I've rewritten my article. You'll find there are extensive revisions, I'll take the other one back if I may.

ELEANOR: Your article on Fitch.

MILES: Yes, if you could be so kind as to give me the other one back. Your editor expressed an interest in publishing the piece if you remember.

ELEANOR: No, I don't.

MILES: Even if you don't, could you please give it back. My diskette.

ELEANOR: I haven't got it.

MILES: Yes you have.

ELEANOR: No I haven't.

MILES: Then where is it?

ELEANOR: I haven't got it, I don't want it, I don't give a toss about the poet Fitch. As far as I'm concerned he can go and jump in the lake.

MILES: Not the lake. The marsh.

ELEANOR: I'll have a really good look and post it back if we find it.

MILES: What if you don't find it?

ELEANOR: If I don't find it, nothing will happen.

MILES: If that piece were to be published in its unrevised form I have to warn you, I'd take it as a deliberate attempt to make me a laughing stock.

ELEANOR: I'm not aware of any plan to publish it.

MILES: Oh you're not.

ELEANOR: No.

MILES: So he's discussed it.

ELEANOR: No.

MILES: Rather than bring it to a publisher, a writer should encase his work in concrete, sink it under the sea, or launch it into the sun.

ELEANOR: Yes, perhaps you should try that.

MILES: Let me make it clear what I intend to do. If my original diskette fails to arrive at my address by post within the next four days, I shall take out an injunction. I shall prevent any mention of the poet Fitch in your magazine ever.

ELEANOR: Would you really.

MILES: Yes I'm afraid I would.

ELEANOR: Oh dear how dreadful.

MILES: Please would you make sure he gets this. *(Hands her a diskette.)* This is the revised version.

ELEANOR: Thank you.

MILES: Yes. Yes I think I mentioned before, I'm not expecting a fee. *(He leaves. WILLIAM and LIONEL come in by the other door.)*

WILLIAM: Well Ted.

TED: Hullo.

LIONEL: Hullo Ted.

TED: Hullo.

WILLIAM: *(To LIONEL.)* I'd very much like the Board to see this. It's a series of one-hour programmes, with myself on camera as editor discussing historical figures from the magazine, featuring the cover in the opening credits. I think it's quite exciting.

LIONEL: Well done, William.

WILLIAM: I think this is more to the point than colour schemes don't you? I think this is more to the point than American distribution.

TED: Is it definite?

WILLIAM: What's this, Ted? Lessons in prudence? It's a proposal.

TED: Have they earmarked the budget?

WILLIAM: What do you care for budgets?

TED: They have, have they?

WILLIAM: That would be premature, first comes what they call the development, meaning my initial idea must be developed.

TED: What's their development budget?

WILLIAM: I beg your pardon?

LIONEL: What are they proposing to spend on development?

WILLIAM: No no, that's not how it's done.

TED: Yes it is.

LIONEL: They'd normally have a budget for development, William.

TED: If they're serious.

WILLIAM: They're a small independent company, and they'd naturally be looking to us to assist them with money for development in the first instance.

TED: Not serious.

WILLIAM: *(To LIONEL.)* So naturally I said I was sure it could be arranged.

LIONEL: A small independent outfit.

TED: Oh dear.

LIONEL: Shut up, Ted.

WILLIAM: Three thousand pounds.

LIONEL: Normally I'd say no chance.

WILLIAM: Such a relatively small sum, for such enormous potential benefit.

LIONEL: Of course you saved us a bit, the way you managed Peggy, we didn't have to find a redundancy payment for Peggy so perhaps we could find this.

TED: Yes, well done, William.

WILLIAM: I assure you, Peggy resigned of her own free will.

LIONEL: And very fortunate.

TED: You didn't tell her about the redundancy, did you. You let her go.

WILLIAM: And what would you have done?

TED: Me? The same.

WILLIAM: Yes.

(WILLIAM, thoughtful and disturbed, puts his face in his hands. Telephone.)

ELEANOR: Footnotes in History. *(Hands the phone to LIONEL.)*

LIONEL: Me.. Really.. Really.. Really.. Really. I told you so. *(Puts down the receiver.)* Ted, the owner's very impressed by your handling of the Board. He's making you co-editor.

TED: Oh I couldn't.

WILLIAM: *(To LIONEL.)* He couldn't.

LIONEL: *(To TED.)* Shall I tell them you refuse?

TED: Oh I couldn't refuse. But what if people think the change is just cosmetic? I'm trying to envisage the masthead.

(WILLIAM rushes from the room.)

SCENE 6

Reception, same afternoon

MILES: Oh heedless, hectic, heaving herd

So heartless and so harsh

What care you for the little birds

That warble in the marsh?

What -

(CHRIS is seized upon by WILLIAM coming from the entrance doors..)

WILLIAM: I have to get out of the building.

CHRIS: *(Pointing in the direction WILLIAM has just come from.)* That way.

WILLIAM: The doors are locked! Why are they locked? Could you come and unlock them please.

CHRIS: No, I can't.

WILLIAM: Why not?

CHRIS: Because they're not locked.

WILLIAM: I've tried them. I've hurled myself.

CHRIS: Did you push them?

WILLIAM: Of course I pushed them!

CHRIS: You're supposed to pull them.

WILLIAM: I see. Perhaps you're right.

CHRIS: Oh no I wouldn't swear to it. There's this word on the door, it says P-U-L-L, but I'm not literary.

(WILLIAM, about to flee in the direction of the doors, sees TAMARA entering through them with a big spiked plant.)

WILLIAM: Save me from that woman. *(He hides behind CHRIS. TAMARA enters and places her plant. CHRIS, protecting WILLIAM, keeps himself turned towards TAMARA.)*

TAMARA: This is where people come in.

CHRIS: And go out.

TAMARA: I want plants in here that really speak. I want plants that really say something.

CHRIS: Like what.

TAMARA: Plants that make your eyes move faster. I want plants that make you think you've hallucinated them.

CHRIS: I've got some plants in my flat will make you think that, and they wouldn't be wrong.

TAMARA: How much an ounce?

(LIONEL enters, not from the entrance doors. Seeing TAMARA, he tries to retreat unnoticed.)

TAMARA: Lionel. *(She leaves in pursuit.)*

MILES: What do you care, puffed up with pride
      And plunged in city strife
      For the marsh crake that sings beside

The lost lagoons of life?

WILLIAM: That man. Do I know him? What's his job?

CHRIS: He's been carrying those papers around.

WILLIAM: What papers?

CHRIS: Redundancies probably.

WILLIAM: What?

(MILES is approaching. WILLIAM hides behind CHRIS again. CHRIS keeps himself turned towards MILES. MILES is trying to look behind CHRIS, so CHRIS has to keep turning. Eventually MILES is standing between CHRIS and the entrance doors. WILLIAM leaves the shelter of CHRIS and hides behind the plant. MILES finds there is no-one behind CHRIS..)

MILES: The man who was here. Where did he go?

CHRIS: Maybe up. Maybe down. You never know in this place.

(CHRIS leaves. MILES stands thinking by the entrance doors. Then he approaches the plant..)

WILLIAM: *(Hidden behind the plant.)* Bugger off.

(LIONEL enters with TAMARA in pursuit. They pay no attention to anyone. WILLIAM bursts from behind the plant and flees. MILES goes in pursuit of WILLIAM..)

TAMARA: Amazing meeting, Lionel.

LIONEL: You know it isn't personal.

TAMARA: How could it be personal? You're not a person.

LIONEL: I'd better get back there.

TAMARA: The meeting's over.

LIONEL: Then I'll find another one. *(He's leaving.)*

TAMARA: My contract's been extended.

LIONEL: That's impossible.

TAMARA: Yes, the owner's asking the impossible. Why not? I can offer him that. I offered him the impossible straight after you left, and he was ecstatic. He wants to know why you're not ecstatic.

LIONEL: I'm sorry I spoke against you at the meeting, but our friendship is on a different plane.

TAMARA: Lionel, that plane has left.

LIONEL: I was surprised by Ted, I didn't think he'd let you down you like that.

TAMARA: No, it was quite against everything I know of Ted because basically he's a loyal and very sweet person, but when I realised he'd done it on your advice, well then of course it was obvious what had happened, because you're Satan.

(TAMARA off. LIONEL off..)

SCENE 7

The gents. WILLIAM enters and hides in a cubicle. MILES enters, looks, sees WILLIAM's feet under the door.

MILES: Please read this.

(He posts the paper under the door. WILLIAM opens the door. He has the paper in his hand..)

WILLIAM: This is what I think of your redundancy.

(He puts the paper into the toilet and flushes. MILES dives and retrieves the paper. He reads from it..)

MILES: Go then, you fashionable fools

    You brutes and dupes and plotters

    Heed not the bright eyes in the pools

    The voles, the newts, the otters

    Go on the way that -

WILLIAM: Just sack me, will you. Forget the verse.

MILES: This verse has already been forgotten. It's a previously undiscovered poem by Fitch.

WILLIAM: Who are you.

MILES: My name is Miles Moore.

WILLIAM: Are you a contributor?

MILES: Well. If you say so.

WILLIAM: So you're nothing to do with anything.

MILES: Please read this poem.

WILLIAM: Perhaps when it's dried out. Or you could take it to my assistant, I mean to my co-editor. Co-editor. Excuse me.

(WILLIAM rushes from the gents..)

MILES: Go on the way that madness lies

> Far from forgotten fen
>
> One day the shining mud will rise
>
> And swallow you again

SCENE 8

LIONEL, WILLIAM.

WILLIAM: Please understand. Footnotes in History isn't just any magazine.

LIONEL: No. It's an exceptionally insignificant one. Now, William -

WILLIAM: Of course it's not mainstream. I wouldn't want it to be mainstream.

LIONEL: Good. William -

WILLIAM: It focusses instead on the marginal things that complicate the picture and generate uncertainty.

LIONEL: Just what we all need, I'm sure.

WILLIAM: Yes. Because living with uncertainty is the mark of a civilised mind. And true uncertainty comes from being exactly informed. In exact language. Which brings me to Ted.

LIONEL: Right. William, I'd just like to say –

WILLIAM: Ted can't edit. Ted thinks "access" is a verb. I can't work with him. Not as co-editor. As if we were the same. Don't you see, he has to go.

LIONEL: William, I understand.

WILLIAM: Do you?

LIONEL: I do.

WILLIAM: It's me or him. I've already passed a memo to the owner.

LIONEL: The owner's already passed a memo to me.

WILLIAM: Thank God for that.

LIONEL: He's sorry you find it so distressing working like this with Ted.

WILLIAM: So you'll take action.

LIONEL: Yes, William, you're sacked.

WILLIAM: I'm sorry? I'm sorry. This can't be easy for you. I'm sorry you've had this unpleasant task. I didn't see what you were driving at. I'm so sorry. You really mustn't blame yourself, here, shake my hand. *(They shake hands.)* I really think the owner might have spared you this, don't you. *(He's clasping LIONEL's hand in both of his.)* I really think it's wrong of him, putting you through something like this. No, don't defend him, he shouldn't have done this to you. It makes me extremely angry when I think of you being used in such a way. How could he? How can you put up with it? How can you allow it? What's happened to your self-respect? Do you get a kick out of doing his dirty work? *(Drops LIONEL's hand.)*

LIONEL: It's natural you're upset.

WILLIAM: Yes. You find it natural. You find the whole thing perfectly natural. That's what's so bizarre, the gross and lunatic distortions which everyone in this company finds perfectly natural. This company is a swarming mess of publications constantly devouring each other, constantly changing their shape, constantly dying and giving birth without ceremony and without reason, like the benighted population of a cursed subcontinent.

LIONEL: I appreciate your straight talking, William.

WILLIAM: People like you swim in the polluted waters of this company all oblivious, opening and shutting your mouths with the idiot complacency of dying fish. *(Opens and shuts his mouth.)*

LIONEL: Yes. We prefer to carry out these things with as little unpleasantness as possible.

WILLIAM: Carry out what things. Dead things. You prefer to carry out the dead with as little unpleasantness as possible.

LIONEL: Yes, we don't like a lot of discussion. Events can speak for themselves.

WILLIAM: Events can speak for themselves, but who hears them? *(Insultingly opens and shuts his mouth like a fish, then leaves. CHRIS returns and tries to retreat unnoticed.)*

LIONEL: Didn't I fire you?

(CHRIS is gone. PEGGY enters.)

PEGGY: As a matter of fact, you didn't. I resigned. I've come here to see William.

LIONEL: William who?

PEGGY: Is he in?

LIONEL: William's about. Everyone's about. Even you.

PEGGY: Is he in another part of the building?

LIONEL: Yes another part completely. William's on the dark side of the building, he isn't very easy to see.

PEGGY: You don't have to protect him, you know.

LIONEL: I'm not.

PEGGY: William's always been accessible, even to people who don't want to talk to him.

LIONEL: But you do want to talk to him.

PEGGY: Yes.

LIONEL: You'll make him feel better I'm sure.

PEGGY: Why. Has he found things difficult without me?

LIONEL: Oh yes.

PEGGY: Thank you.

(PEGGY off.)

SCENE 9

The office.

(ELEANOR and TED. ELEANOR is working..)

TED: And then he just ran from the room. Is he really so jealous? It's true I represent the future.

ELEANOR: Now you're co-editor, you could bring Peggy back.

TED: Peggy?

ELEANOR: William would be glad, I know he would.

TED: Can you really imagine Peggy working for this magazine?

ELEANOR: She worked on it for fifteen years.

TED: I didn't say remember, I said imagine.

ELEANOR: I thought after what you told me, you might want to help her.

TED: Am I being blackmailed here? I shouldn't have told you how guilty I feel. I didn't expect it to lead to anything. I don't think I ought to have her back, I think I'd always feel there was a skeleton.

ELEANOR: Ted, everyone has a skeleton.

TED: I'd rather not feel that I have. I've only just got this job and I'd like to be judged on my achievements, not on what I've done.

ELEANOR: I feel strange. There's something frightening in the room.

TED: Don't worry, I'm here.

ELEANOR: That's it! It's you!

TED: Eleanor, from now on, Footnotes in History is going to be forward-looking. We're not interested in ghosts from the past. *(PEGGY appears at the door.)* Peggy!

PEGGY: Hullo Ted.

TED: Peggy. You look just the same.

PEGGY: It's only been three weeks.

TED: People can change overnight.

PEGGY: Only in horror stories, Ted. Is William in?

ELEANOR: Yes.

TED: No. *(They look at each other.)*

ELEANOR: He's definitely still here.

TED: That sounds a bit vague. *(Laughs.)*

PEGGY: You don't mind if I wait. *(She sits.)* I shouldn't have left as I did. I shouldn't have done that to William. Of course William is tiresome, but he stands for something.

TED: What. What does he stand for.

PEGGY: Informing people. Making people more civilised and less lonely. William has values. You don't know what I'm talking about, do you.

TED: No.

PEGGY: Is he well?

TED: We all are, thank you, thank you for asking. Specially me.

PEGGY: Why, what's wrong with William?

TED: I've been appointed co-editor.

PEGGY: Life goes on, doesn't it. As soon as one's back is turned, life goes on. And is William happy with your appointment?

ELEANOR: He ran out of the room.

TED: We haven't seen him since.

PEGGY: Never mind. I expect it was just the shock.

TED: Were you worried about us, Peggy? Is that why you came in? You needn't have worried. Everything's been fine since you left!

PEGGY: For me as well. The company's better.

TED: Really. I thought you'd miss him terribly. It's really strange. I thought he'd miss you too, but it's as if he's had a new lease of life.

ELEANOR: Ted!

TED: I'm reassuring her. In case she came here thinking we needed her back.

ELEANOR: Ted was the one! He was the one who crashed all the computers! And he didn't tell anyone, he let William think it was you. And you were so upset, you went off and you never got the money!

PEGGY: What money?

TED: She means the money they would have had to pay you, when they made you redundant.

PEGGY: I think you must be mistaken, there was never any question of making me redundant.

TED: The fact is, Peggy, you'd been gravitating towards retirement age and they wanted to, how shall I say, fast-forward you.

PEGGY: William wouldn't have stood for it.

TED: William was about to sack you.

PEGGY: He never said anything of the kind.

TED: He didn't have to. You resigned and saved him the trouble, and he didn't even have to pay you off.

PEGGY: Are you saying he did it on purpose?

TED: Yes. Because of Eleanor.

ELEANOR: Me?

TED: It was Eleanor's presence that made the whole thing possible. I actually did a productivity survey of people in this office. And it emerged that Eleanor was on site and that she was more than capable of doing the same job as yourself but in a more cost-effective way.

ELEANOR: I'm so ashamed. I'm so ashamed.

TED: In fairness to Eleanor, she was unaware.

PEGGY: I'm sure she was. But didn't William like me? He couldn't have done it if he'd liked me. *(Silence.)* Abrupt. Of course he was abrupt. I told myself it was a sign of unspoken affection. *(Silence.)* It was more than unspoken. It was unfelt. *(Silence.)* But perhaps he was right, the magazine must come first, I suppose.

TED: I absolutely agree with you.

PEGGY: Do you? Then I must have said something stupid. Excuse me.

(PEGGY off. LIONEL in.)

LIONEL: Where's she going?

TED: Looking for William.

LIONEL: Haven't you seen him.

(TAMARA in.)

TED: Hopefully he'll come to welcome my appointment.

LIONEL: You think so.

TAMARA: Is that all you can say to poor Ted? After all he's done for you. After he obliged you by speaking against me to the Board.

LIONEL: It's not as if he's done you any harm.

TAMARA: Naturally not.

LIONEL: It was Ted's choice.

TED: Lionel, wait a minute, you advised me strongly.

TAMARA: Hear that, bully, your advice was too strong for him.

LIONEL: I'm sorry if my advice was effective. It's not what I'm used to.

TED: Why is she here? Did she win? *(To TAMARA.)* Darling I'm so glad.

TAMARA: Darling, you're sacked.

LIONEL: *(To TAMARA.)* I've sacked William. There'll be no magazine.

TAMARA: Is that a problem?

LIONEL: *(Indicating ELEANOR.)* She wouldn't have a job.

TAMARA: All right Ted, you can stay.

TED: Did you say you've sacked William? Oh no. Does this mean I'm the editor?

ELEANOR: Poor William.

LIONEL: William won't kill himself.

ELEANOR: But he'll want to. You shouldn't make people want to kill themselves. You should make people want to live.

LIONEL: Well. I'm sorry.

TAMARA: What for?

LIONEL: I'm sorry for not being human.

TAMARA: Oh right.

TED: I think you two have a lot to answer for.

ELEANOR: So does everyone.

TED: Thanks for including me, but why? I'm only an editor.

(ELEANOR picks up the poinsettia in both hands and hits him on the head with it.)

TED: *(Stunned, but unmoved and seemingly oblivious.)* I've had an idea. I've always admired him tremendously. I'll write a tribute to William in my first issue of Footnotes in History. I'll call it Edited Out.

LIONEL: William's an infant! The building's full of them! Infants with gaping mouths and grabbing little hands. They're all babbling away in the infantile certainty that someone's listening. How can anyone listen? They're all babbling at once. They're biting and snatching and pushing and shoving and breaking each other's fat little limbs. One or two on their own would be sweet. Piled up in here they're horrible. How am I supposed to look after them? How am I supposed to care? Has he taken his things?

TAMARA: Lionel, there are two redundant people roaming the corridors. Terminate them properly, can't you! Call security!

LIONEL: Can't we just leave them in peace?

TAMARA: That's not allowed.

LIONEL: Let them just breathe.

TAMARA: No! it's against company policy.

LIONEL: I'm glad you care so much about company policy. You can take over. I need a good night's sleep. I resign. *(He leaves.)*

TAMARA: Don't leave me with these tiny little people! Lionel! I'm coming with you! Lionel!

(LIONEL leaves, pursued by TAMARA.)

TED: *(Timorously.)* Eleanor? (ELEANOR looks at him.) No. Nothing.

(TED leaves. CHRIS enters.)

CHRIS: I'm a person that can talk to anyone. *(Silence.)*

ELEANOR: Are you?

CHRIS: *(Silence.)* Yes. *(Silence.)*

ELEANOR: So I see.

CHRIS: *(Silence.)*

ELEANOR: I'm useless at it myself. You're lucky. Have you worked here long?

CHRIS: I don't work here.

ELEANOR: Have you been sacked?

CHRIS: I've never worked here. I started coming in the summer when the builders were here.

ELEANOR: I've seen you fixing the wiring.

CHRIS: I do what I can.

ELEANOR: I've seen you mending the coffee machine.

CHRIS: I mend it when I need the twenty ps. I'm part of the scenery, that's why people don't see me. Or else they look at me and wonder why I haven't been made redundant like everyone else. That's the advantage of not being on the payroll.

ELEANOR: Do you mean, you work here and you don't get paid?

CHRIS: From what I hear, so do you.

ELEANOR: Why do you do it?

CHRIS: Why do you?

ELEANOR: It's a recent family tradition.

CHRIS: I do it to master my fear. It's the only thing I'm ever likely to be master of.

ELEANOR: I want to make something of myself.

CHRIS: Each different place I go to, like a building site or an office or a hospital, I walk in off the street and make something different of myself. It's nice to belong, isn't it.

ELEANOR: I'm leaving this place.

CHRIS: I wish I'd known.

ELEANOR: Why?

CHRIS: I did something today I've never done before, I went into personnel and got a job.

ELEANOR: Here? Why?

CHRIS: It seems they're anxious about a spate of petty theft, coins going missing out of the coffee machine and such. So seeing they knew my face, what they've done is, they've made me security guard. *(Slowly ELEANOR begins to smile then laugh.)* I knew you could smile *(He kisses her. He looks into her eyes).* Are you crying?

ELEANOR: I hate it here.

CHRIS: We'll go then. I'll give in my notice.

(They leave. WILLIAM comes in, sits at his desk and makes a telephone call. Meanwhile PEGGY enters unnoticed.).)

WILLIAM: I've got the sack... *(Louder.)* I've got the sack... I thought I'd phone and let you know, better than arriving home and telling you I thought... Oh it's your bookbinding class, no no of course you shouldn't miss it, you should bind those books before they bleed to death... all right miss it if you like, I suppose then you'll start saying I'm under your feet, that's how it will be, I'll be a derelict in my own home, if we've still got a home, and you'll complain to your friends about how you have to pick up after me... *(Sighs)...* yes I'm being silly, I'm being silly... Of course there's nothing you can do, how can you increase your earnings at your age, how many vol-au-vents can one woman make... no we can't afford another freezer, get this into your head, from now on we can't afford anything, oh Doodie I'm sorry, I'm so very sorry I've let you down, Doodie, who am I?... Yes I know I'm your husband but who am I?... Yes I'll see you later... Yes goodbye.

(He sees PEGGY, and addresses her..)

You know who's replacing me, don't you. In this building sheep become wolves, frogs become princes, unfortunately I remained the same. So I'm coming to join you in the afterlife.

PEGGY: I'm sorry. It must be hard for you. Especially when you were managing to publish so much more cheaply.

WILLIAM: Much more cheaply.

PEGGY: Thanks to my absence.

WILLIAM: It's true you contributed.

PEGGY: If only by that.

WILLIAM: Anyway, it's all over.

PEGGY: Look on the bright side William. At least they'll pay for your redundancy.

WILLIAM: What did you say.

PEGGY: They'll pay you for making you redundant, as they'd have paid me.

WILLIAM: You're not supposed to know about it, how did you -

PEGGY: I used to think of us as a team. It's odd how one can imagine one is together.

WILLIAM: Well. It's a relief, in a way, that you know. They wanted to make you redundant and I just couldn't face telling you.

PEGGY: But you should have faced telling me. If you'd told me, I'd have got the money.

WILLIAM: Then you walked out and it just seemed easier all round.

PEGGY: And so much cheaper too.

WILLIAM: That wasn't the main thing. I didn't want to hurt you.

PEGGY: So you injured me instead.

WILLIAM: Think if you and I were the last two people on earth and couldn't trust each other.

PEGGY: That won't happen, William. People are everywhere.

WILLIAM: I didn't want to get rid of you! They said they'd axe the magazine.

PEGGY: Yes, and the magazine is so important. Small-minded people might not grasp how a magazine could be more important than they are. We didn't always get on. But there was a harmony. I could hear it. The sound of being useful, that's what I thought it was.

WILLIAM: The magazine is my life.

PEGGY: Such a life.

WILLIAM: A life spent defending civilised values.

PEGGY: William, you cheated me.

WILLIAM: It was a matter of survival.

PEGGY: What's the point of surviving as a civilised person if you've stopped behaving like one!

WILLIAM: You can criticise, but you've never edited anything.

PEGGY: Why should I have to! Can't I trust you to do it? Why should I want to? To be important? And a cheat? Civilised values provided you with a living. Couldn't you have done the same for them? You didn't, did you. You weaseled out, you cardboard cutout, you snob, you fake.

WILLIAM: All you've ever done is help me.

PEGGY: I can see now how pointless that was.

WILLIAM: I wouldn't expect you'd see the point of it, no.

PEGGY: I blame history. History is full of weapons one wouldn't have wished to invent, buildings one wouldn't have wished to build, and magazines one wouldn't have wished to read, and somehow one was always just stupidly wanting to help

WILLIAM: Magazines? My magazine? I think what you're saying proves I was only too right in deciding to let you go.

PEGGY: Perhaps you were, because here's what I think of your stupid magazine! *(Tears it up and scatters it over him. Silence.)* Well. I'd better get back. This place is so many stops further on than Blezzard used to be. More trains arrive here than leave. And they've dug up the ticket office.

WILLIAM: How's your flat?

PEGGY: My flat? Full of rubbish. Just the same. That reminds me. This diskette. *(Reaches for her handbag, rummages.)* I thought you might be needing it. *(She hands the diskette to WILLIAM who drops it on the floor.)*

WILLIAM: Thank you.

PEGGY: Well it's no use to me.

WILLIAM: It's no use to anyone.

PEGGY: So many memories.

WILLIAM: Yes.

PEGGY: My favourite fifteen years.

WILLIAM: Yes.

PEGGY: One does enjoy doing something. If only one had been.

WILLIAM: Yes.

(TED enters.)

TED: William. I'm sorry you're going. If it weren't for you I wouldn't be here after all. What's this on the floor? (Picks up the diskette, reads the label.) "Towards a Life of Fitch". Miles Moore. Isn't that the chap who says he'll write for nothing? *(Nods.)* I think we should use him. *(Nods.)*

THE END

(Revision 2009.)

FAITH

Characters

SERGEANT TOBY SPIERS, 39

LANCE CORPORAL ADAM ZILLER, 28

PRIVATE MICK PIKE, 20

PRIVATE LEE FINCH, 19

SANDRA, 30s

LARRY, American, 30

Setting: A remote island farmhouse at a time of war, 1982

FIRST SECTION

Kitchen of the house lived in by the manager of the farm. Sink full of mugs etc. Bright day, winter.

TOBY, ADAM.

TOBY: If you've something to say to me, say it. (*Silence.*) For better or worse, you're an influence. That's to your credit, corporal. You've become an influence thanks to your achievements. I grant you that. (*Silence.*) Did you speak. Did I hear you speak. (*Silence.*) But influence carries with it responsibility. Doesn't it, corporal. (*Silence.*) I could have you on a charge! Don't think I wouldn't. (*Silence.*) It's not that I like it. You think I like it. What boots are those. (*Silence.*) Where did you get those boots, did you get those boots last night, did you. (*Silence.*) All I'm saying is, what I do, I do for your good. Because I have a perspective. (*Silence.*) I'm looking after you. That's all I'm trying to do, is look after you.

ADAM: Cunt.

ADAM off. TOBY alone.

TOBY: Cunt he says. Quite a definite observation. Cunt he says... The moment she appeared. The moment she appeared I had to press the button to open the doors...

SANDRA enters and sees the mugs in the sink.

SANDRA: I'm not washing those.

TOBY: No love, you leave those.

SANDRA: I'm not washing those.

TOBY: You leave them.

SANDRA: I'm definitely not washing those. (*She runs water in the sink, starts washing mugs.*) The moment I step outside that door. Here comes the skeleton, says one. Like fucking a pair of chopsticks, says another. I'm only going out to empty the slops. I'm not a fucking chorus line. What do they want. A fucking floorshow. The dog runs up and

149

jumps on me. Scratch her tit, says one. Oh yes, we're living life to the full out there. Scratch her tit. Are you going to speak to them.

TOBY: Yes all right love.

SANDRA: You said to me that you were going to speak to them.

TOBY: Yes love.

SANDRA: Anyway. If I'm such a skeleton. How come I've got tits.

ADAM enters.

TOBY: Shut the door corporal.

ADAM: –

TOBY: It's cold with that door open, shut the door.

ADAM: Where am I going to put him.

TOBY: Have you forgotten what a door is, corporal.

ADAM: (*Knocks on the table.*) Hullo.

TOBY: (*Frightened, but determined to continue.*) Forgotten what a door is. You've been out of doors too long, corporal, you've forgotten what a house is.

ADAM: Where am I going to put him.

TOBY: Shut the door.

ADAM: Cunt.

ADAM off, leaving the door open.

SANDRA: That's not very nice. He's not very nice.

TOBY: (*Shutting the door.*) Yes sergeant. I'll shut the door sergeant.

SANDRA: I'm keeping well away from him.

TOBY: You do that, love.

SANDRA: Keep my distance from him.

TOBY: You do that.

SANDRA: Sooner him and his kind are out of here.

TOBY: Soon enough, love. We'll be out of here soon enough.

SANDRA: No-one in my son's room all right.

TOBY: There's people kipping up and down the house.

SANDRA: I'm not having anyone go up in my son's room.
That's my one remaining area of sanity.

TOBY: Yes I can see how special that is, love.

SANDRA: Eh.

TOBY: No-one in your son's room, I promised you didn't I.

SANDRA: Doesn't like you, does he.

TOBY: What makes you say that.

SANDRA: Well he doesn't, does he.

TOBY: I'm not answerable to you, love.

SANDRA: I never said you was.

TOBY: My feet.

SANDRA: Eh.

TOBY: If it hadn't been for my feet. Apart from my feet,
Sandra, I'm fitter now than what I've ever been. I was
carrying my own weight again, Sandra. The night we
set off to come over here, I was carrying my own weight
again. One lad fell in a ditch. He was carrying so much
weight he broke his back. I had no problem with the
weight. I had a problem with the boots. Someone's idea
of a joke our fucking boots. Someone's idea of a bargain.
I took off my boots. In my sock I found the nail of my big
toe. My feet were blue, with a line of red round the edges.
The orderly takes one look, he says to me, You're fortunate
your nail fell off and not your toes, he says. Where do you
think you're off to, he says, you're not going off up the
mountain with those feet. Yes I am, I say. Why don't I cut
them off right now, he says, if I hear any more about you
going off up the mountain, that's what I'm going to do, cut
them off, save myself the trouble later on.

SANDRA: What's his name.

TOBY: Who.

SANDRA: Rude bugger.

TOBY: Angry twenty-four hours a day, the lance corporal.
  (*Laughs.*) Angry with me for being not as angry as he is.

SANDRA: Walks in here as if he owns it.

TOBY: And yet, Sandra. All the time, I'm looking after them.

SANDRA: And what do you do. You do nothing.

TOBY: I don't get emotional see, I don't get angry, there's too
  much at stake to get angry. It weakens me if I get angry,
  Sandra. Some people, it strengthens. The lance corporal
  thrives on getting angry. This makes him useful in certain
  situations. I'm useful in other situations.

SANDRA: I'm keeping well away from him. What's his name.

TOBY: Lance corporal Ziller. The other lads call him God.

SANDRA: Eh?

TOBY: Godzilla.

  *ADAM and MICK bring LARRY in, beaten up. MICK also brings
  some mugs which he leaves by the sink.*

TOBY: Not in here, corporal.

SANDRA: My God what is this.

TOBY: I never said you could bring him in here.

SANDRA: What is this.

TOBY: Christ!

SANDRA: I'm not having that in here.

TOBY: The lady would prefer you not to bring the gentleman
  in here.

SANDRA: Fuck off out of here, put him in the shed with the
  rest of them.

ADAM: Shut your face love.

  ADAM and MICK off, leaving LARRY in the kitchen.

SANDRA: (*To TOBY.*) You hear what he said to me? He'd
  better not say that again. (*Running off after ADAM.*) You
  come here and say that again!

TOBY: ... The moment she appeared I had to press the button to open the doors. Then I had to nip inside the lift and hold the Door Open button pressed down while she and the brass got in... (*To LARRY.*) Come on, you're all right. (*Clicks his fingers.*) Hear that? (*Clicks his fingers.*) Come on. You can hear that. Look, I saw what happened. They hardly touched you. I put a stop to it, didn't I. Soon as they started, I put a stop to it. You try talking about this, you won't get a hearing. You'll do yourself no good by making an issue out of this. Because I stopped it. Straight away. They as good as never touched you. If you want to do yourself some good. I tell you what you should talk about. Minefields you should talk about. Disposition of enemy troops you should talk about. Do us both a bit of good you can. They'd be pleased with me, and I'd be pleased with you. It's not betrayal. Anything you can tell me that helps get this war over quicker and easier is not betrayal. Nobody wants any more fighting and killing than is strictly necessary. Nobody wants that. Do they. You're a rational man. We can do with that. A bit of rationality...

LEE enters, with a tray full of mugs which he leaves by the sink.

LEE: Sarge.

TOBY: This gentleman and I are conversing.

LEE: He's out cold sarge.

TOBY: This gentleman and I are having a chat.

LEE: Yes sarge. When they bring us the stuff sarge. When do you think it will be sarge.

TOBY: I told you Finch I don't know.

LEE: We'll be dead before they bring that stuff, sitting here in the middle of nowhere, one rocket we're history.

TOBY: What do you want Finch.

LEE: Yes well when they bring the stuff it's my turn, that's all I'm saying. Like I said to you, last time, Mick got the last of the Mars Bars and I had a Yorkie. And the time before that, same thing, he got the last of the Mars Bars and I finished up with the Yorkie.

TOBY: My goodness did you Finch.

LEE: Yes I did sarge.

TOBY: I see, Finch. Yes I see. Finch. Why are you telling me this?

LEE: Well can't you see, sarge. Because this time, I want a Mars, is why.

TOBY: What am I going to do about it, Finch.

LEE: What you should do.

TOBY: Yes.

LEE: What you should do. When they drop them. You should take all of them sarge.

TOBY: All of the chocolate bars.

LEE: Yes sarge. And cut them up in pieces all the same, exactly the same, and give them out. That's what you should always do.

TOBY: That seems like the adult solution yes.

LEE: I can't understand why no-one's thought of it.

TOBY: How could they, Finch, they lack your vision.

LEE: How are the feet sarge.

TOBY: You did well last night, I hear.

LEE: Done my duty sarge.

TOBY: You didn't let me down.

LEE: How are the feet.

TOBY: My fucking feet.

LEE: How are they sarge.

TOBY: Getting there, Finch, getting there. I'm looking after them Finch.

LEE: That's good, sarge.

TOBY: It's not as if I could have achieved anything. If I'd have been up there.

LEE: Never say that, sarge.

TOBY: No I couldn't Finch. I'd just have been in the way.

LEE: Never say that. There was a lot of them dead round the rocks up there this morning sarge.

TOBY: Yes I believe so.

LEE: Godzilla, sarge, you should have seen him.

TOBY: Yes I believe he pulled Jennings out of the line of fire.

LEE: Jennings sat up sarge. I thought he was alive. Godzilla pushed him flat again, he just sat up again.

TOBY: How do you mean he sat up again.

LEE: Sat up. Bolt upright. Dead.

TOBY: Must have been something the matter with him, Finch.

LEE: Yes sarge.

TOBY: Did you see that, did you.

LEE: Yes sarge.

TOBY: Yes well you and your prisoners Finch, you haven't half given me a headache, arsing round up there causing people to surrender, we've got more fucking prisoners than we've got men.

LEE: When I saw that fucking white flag, I couldn't have been more surprised if I'd have seen a fucking yeti.

TOBY: No yeti would live here Finch, it's not that hospitable.

LEE: You know what they say, sarge, expect the unexpected. The greatest shock sarge. The greatest shock is when the expected is what actually happens. You've thought of it before. That is what kills you. Things you were only used to having in your mind, like loading your weapon while being shot at for instance, these things are actually happening, this is why it seems like a dream. I hadn't got the foggiest where anybody was half the time, round those rocks, no knowing what I was firing at, no notion of who's firing at me, and I tripped over something, it's a dead man with smoke pouring out of his jacket, like his jacket is hollow, it was fucking mad up there sarge.

TOBY: Was it Finch.

LEE: It was absolute chaos up there.

TOBY: I doubt that, Finch.

LEE: You didn't see what it was like sarge.

TOBY: Chaos was it.

LEE: Yes sarge.

TOBY: That's your opinion, is it.

LEE: Yes sarge.

TOBY: How long have you been with us, Finch?

LEE: Two years, sarge.

TOBY: Long time.

LEE: I wouldn't say that sarge.

TOBY: Long enough for you to have an opinion, would you say.

LEE: No sarge.

TOBY: No sarge. When you've served as many hours as I have days, Finch, then you can have an opinion.

LEE: Yes sarge.

TOBY: If it was chaos, Finch, the victor could have been anyone.

LEE: Yes, sarge.

TOBY: But it wasn't anyone, it was us.

LEE: Yes sarge.

TOBY: Therefore it wasn't chaos. Was it.

LEE: Eh.

TOBY: Superiority is organization, Finch. What is the most superior species on earth. Man. Man is the most highly organized, i.e. the most superior. The British fighting man is the most highly organized of men.

LEE: Yes sarge.

TOBY: That's why we won.

LEE: Yes sarge.

TOBY: (*Indicating LARRY.*) Watch him.

LEE: I'll have a chat with him sarge.

TOBY off. LEE sits listening to music on his cassette player with headphones. LARRY remains seated. ADAM looks in. Withdraws. Sneaks in with a camera, soon joined by MICK. ADAM is secretly photographing LEE from behind.

ADAM: Eh Finch. (*LEE doesn't hear. MICK goes up to him, ADAM too, still taking pictures.*)

MICK: Finch!

LEE: (*Takes headphones off.*) Eh?

MICK: Something crawling on you.

LEE: (*Turns music off.*) Where?

MICK: (*Indicates.*) Look.

LEE discovers a severed hand tucked in the back of his sweater or in one of his sleeve pockets, the fingers placed as if trying to climb out.

LEE: Get it off me.

MICK: (*Pointing at LEE, laughing.*) Your face man! (*To ADAM.*) His face!

ADAM: (*Taking photographs.*) Never mind his face what about his hand.

LEE: You fucking cunts. Get it off me.

ADAM: I'm not touching that, I don't know where it's been.

LEE: (*To MICK.*) Whose is it, is it yours?

MICK: (*Looking at his hands.*) No I got mine here mate.

LEE: (*Trying to bring himself to take the hand off.*) I can't. It's so sad.

The others roar with laughter.

ADAM: It's so sad.

MICK: It is, Lee, it is. So sad.

LEE: You laugh, you laugh! How would you like it if that was you! (*He indicates the hand. The others laugh.*) He's dead isn't he, what more do you want. If you knew what fools you look like, laughing at a dead man. You're laughing in

157

silence. You can't hear it, that's all. I'd rather be mates with wasps. I'd rather be mates with flies.

They're still laughing. LEE gets a tea towel, lifts the hand off and throws it furiously at MICK, who catches it.

MICK: Why am I here. Look at the skin on it. Look at the hairs. Urgh. Thank Christ I'm not a doctor. (*He throws the hand at ADAM, who's photographing him.*) David Bailey. Thinks he's David Bailey.

ADAM: With your disgusting features in my lens. I don't think so.

MICK: What do you want. Marie. (*He mimes her.*)

ADAM: Marie Helvin is the most beautiful woman in the world.

MICK: We know. You told us. The little hands. The beautiful skin like a peach. Old though isn't she. Twenty-what. Face it, Ziller, I'm ten years younger.

LEE: I'd give her one.

MICK: Really. Would you.

LEE: Yes laugh, you laugh. You're not fit to shine her shoes.

MICK: It wouldn't be shining her shoes though, would it, polishing her zimmer frame is what it would be...

ADAM: (*Smashes MICK and then speaks exactly in his former tone.*) Marie Helvin is the most beautiful woman in the world.

MICK: Yes you're right. The most beautiful woman in the world. Yes she is.

ADAM: Where's Tobes.

MICK: Bit old though.

LEE: I come in here, he's talking to that man there.

ADAM: What man where.

LEE: I say to him, sarge, he's out cold. We're having a conversation, he says, we're having a chat.

MICK: Only person that'll talk to him.

ADAM: Cunt.

LEE: I didn't know where to look, I didn't know where to put myself.

MICK: Tobes the feet.

ADAM: If he says one word more about his feet. Just one more word. I'll kill the cunt. Sitting there holding them out to dry. Putting baby powder on them. Know what he says to me. I'm treating my feet as if they were my babies, he says. I say what. Fiddling with them, Tobes.

MICK: The doctor. Going to the doctor with his feet.

ADAM: I never went to the doctor with my feet. Open sores I've got on my feet the size of strawberries. I never went to the doctor.

MICK: The trouble with Tobes, he's been in the military so long, he thought he was safe in the military.

LEE: Job for life yeah.

MICK: Pension to look forward to.

LEE: He joined up for the security.

MICK: His career as a soldier has been ruined by war.

LEE: He keeps going on at me.

MICK: But he's got so much to go on about, hasn't he, cos not everyone has got a wife who's practically completed a –

ALL THREE: Wine tasting course.

MICK: And she's so houseproud –

LEE: You have to leave your shoes by the front door.

MICK: And they've got a lovely –

ALL THREE: Spanish style coffee table.

ADAM: Cunt.

MICK: Who's that woman.

ADAM: A woman of the island.

LEE: What a head case.

MICK: No thanks.

LEE: Eh.

MICK: Head. No thanks.

LEE: Oh... No. Maybe not.

MICK: You're disgusting.

LEE: Maybe not.

MICK: Makes brew for him in a union jack mug.

ADAM: Powerful erotic signal.

LEE: Nothing else for them to do, is there. They've no television.

MICK: They're primitive people. It's like going back in time to 1950.

LEE: They've got no roads. They've got horses.

ADAM: Terrifying animals. Violent. Unpredictable.

MICK: Terrifying.

ADAM: They're throwbacks.

MICK: They're all mentally strange, perverts and weird the lot of them.

LEE: You'll fit right in then Mick.

MICK: Look who's talking. I'm not the one blew a man in half with a rocket.

ADAM: Did he.

MICK: You should have seen it. It was mental. The poor cunt's legs dropped straight down the rocks, the top half goes flying up in the sky like a pop-up toaster.

ADAM: Oh how I wish I'd been there.

MICK: Bonkers though, isn't it.

ADAM: That's a bit evil, Finch.

MICK: That's twenty grand's worth.

LEE: I lost my temper.

ADAM: You're too sensitive.

LEE: (*Indicates LARRY.*) What's up with him then?

ADAM: Who.

LEE: I wondered what happened, that's all.

TOBY enters.

TOBY: You're going to have to get on the radio, corporal, ask what they want us to do with him.

ADAM: Am I sarge.

TOBY: You don't say that. Am I, sarge. You don't say that.

ADAM: Don't I sarge.

ADAM off.

TOBY: You should get some kip, Pike.

MICK: Can't sleep sarge, I'll sleep tonight.

TOBY: Are you looking forward to that are you.

MICK: Certainly am.

TOBY: Like it here, do you.

MICK: Oh sarge this was a master stroke. Wind's like a knife out there.

TOBY: So you're going to kip tonight, are you.

MICK: First night's kip in days.

TOBY: Who says you'll still be here tonight.

MICK: You did sarge.

TOBY: You must be mistaken Pike. They want you back up again tonight.

LEE: We've just come down sarge.

TOBY: Well tonight you're going back up again.

LEE: You might have said before sarge.

TOBY: I couldn't face the look in your eyes Finch.

MICK: Yeah nice one sarge.

TOBY: Don't look at me, I'm coming with you.

LEE: Oh good, sarge.

MICK: What about your feet sarge.

TOBY: Just have to manage, won't I.

MICK: But will you be all right up there sarge.

TOBY: I appreciate your concern, Pike.

LEE: You're going to need your feet up there sarge.

MICK: You need to take care of yourself sarge.

TOBY: Think I'll be a burden Pike. Will I be a burden to you.

LEE: It'll be great sarge. It'll be great to have you there.

SANDRA enters from somewhere inside the house.

SANDRA: Is he still here?

TOBY: Just till we find somewhere else for him, love.

SANDRA: Why don't you put him in the sheepshed with the others.

TOBY: He got in a fight, see.

SANDRA: How do you mean, he got in a fight. I thought that was what you was here for.

MICK: (*To SANDRA.*) It's ridiculous isn't it. See what it is, we have to look at these things as Englishmen. An Englishman should not fear to be ridiculous. Because an Englishman knows that life is ridiculous. An Englishman should expect to be ridiculous and proud of it.

SANDRA: I want to go home.

MICK: Why. Where are you from?

SANDRA: We're from Brixton.

MICK: You're not from here then.

SANDRA: No.

MICK: So did you and your husband have any knowledge of sheep before you came here?

SANDRA: You know Brixton? You know what it's like in Brixton? War, that's what it is. Cars burning in the streets, riot police, people running round covered in blood. Peter and I decided to start again. Somewhere really far away from Brixton. Somewhere really unspoiled. We chose here.

MICK: Yes you need a sense of humour.

SANDRA: We chose here. Ocean, wildflowers, grass, rocks and sheep. No more guns. No more wogs. No more men in uniform running through my back garden. No more helicopters outside my kitchen window.

MICK: Yes you certainly come to the right place.

SANDRA: I keep asking myself, is it us. Is it me. Is it my fault.

ADAM enters, with mugs.

SANDRA: Are you going to wash those.

ADAM: Sarge.

SANDRA: I felt really free coming to live out here. Because nature doesn't press on you the way people do. Now I look round and I've got helicopters breeding out of my suitcases, and soldiers swarming out of my clothes, I feel as if I've brought the plague with me.

ADAM: Can I speak to you sarge.

SANDRA: We'll never be rid of it now. There'll always be soldiers now. Tarmac everywhere, roads, barracks, wire fences and army land, that's what it will be. They'll tread everything flat and piss all over it.

MICK: That's gratitude.

SANDRA: Up till now, these islands used to sparkle.

ADAM: Where's your husband.

SANDRA: Out mending fences you knocked over.

MICK: That's gratitude.

SANDRA: If you don't like what I'm saying, you can piss off.

ADAM: All right Finch? (*He summons FINCH over to him and they prepare to remove LARRY.*)

TOBY: (*To ADAM.*) What you doing.

ADAM: Moving him out sarge.

TOBY: Did you ask my permission to move him out.

ADAM: Oh for fuck's sake.

TOBY: Did you ask my permission.

ADAM: For fuck's sake.

SANDRA: Call yourselves civilized. You filthy animals. Have you ever been to the mainland? They could buy and sell the UK. Think you're so superior. You should spend a day in the capital, it's fantastic, I'm telling you, compared with

London, fantastic, and they've got a Gucci. And a Harrods. Beautiful buildings, big avenues, pavement cafes... (*To ADAM.*) Have you ever been there?

ADAM: No and I'm not fucking going there.

SANDRA: Yes well that's typical that is.

ADAM: Yes I hope so.

LEE: They think we're cannibals, they keep on talking about little black men from the jungle.

MICK: That's the gurkhas.

LEE: No the gurkhas are vegetarians, they eat pickles and that.

MICK: That's gherkins Lee.

LEE: They think we're going to cut their heads off.

MICK: Well I know a guy from Coulsdon that's brought a samurai sword along.

LEE: There's guys that have brought automatics, there's combat knives, there's all sorts.

SANDRA: My son's at school over there.

ADAM: Is he.

SANDRA: I go over twice a year.

ADAM: Yes and what about the poor people.

SANDRA: Eh.

ADAM: All this Gucci and Harrods, but what about the poor people.

SANDRA: You can talk, but you haven't seen them.

ADAM: Treat them like filth.

SANDRA: They live like filth. Little girls of ten having children by their brothers.

ADAM: Shoot anyone that complains.

SANDRA: Best thing to do with them.

ADAM: You're a nice woman.

SANDRA: Well it is. People that won't stand on their own feet, people that won't go out and get a life for themselves.

ADAM: There isn't enough lives to go round though, is there.

SANDRA: Is that my fault? Is that my problem?

ADAM: Why don't you go and live there if you like it so much, you'd save us a fuck of a lot of trouble.

SANDRA: Yes I could live there.

ADAM: Stupid cow.

MICK: I'd live anywhere compared with here.

SANDRA: What's wrong with here then?

MICK: Does this place have a tree?

SANDRA: We don't have the cheap attractions of some places.

ADAM: Sarge.

TOBY: Yes wait, you can wait.

MICK: You mean like vegetation. Habitation. Life.

SANDRA: This place is seen to best advantage when there isn't anybody here.

ADAM: I can understand the logic of that yes.

SANDRA: (*Pointedly ignoring ADAM.*) The spring here is beautiful. It's beautiful with the sun shining, and the wind blowing the grass all up the hillsides and the quiet in the valleys. The little flowers are amazing.

ADAM: Are they. The little flowers.

SANDRA: Sea pinks along the headlands, daisies, there's actually a daisy that smells like chocolate, they call it the vanilla daisy.

ADAM: Well that's intelligent.

TOBY: Who's invaded you, Sandra, us or them?

SANDRA: That's a good question, that is.

TOBY: No say what you think, by all means say what you think, Sandra. That's the point, actually. That's the point of why we're here. What you say disturbs me, Sandra. But I listen politely while you say it. Which is only right and proper I should. Because we're here to protect your freedom of speech. Even if what you say is rubbish. I might think what you say is rubbish but my job is to protect you. Including from myself. That's the difference, Sandra. That is what distinguishes us. The British military undertakes not only to control its enemies but also itself. Now, if we weren't here, and also they weren't here, you could say what you like. But they are here. And you cannot say what you like to them because they will not let you, and they will kill you. So it's a good thing you've got us here as well. Because we can ensure not only that you're safe from them but also that you're safe from us. This is why I'm proud to serve my country. It's a free country. It's a better country...

SANDRA: (*Silently stares at TOBY then returns her attention to MICK and LEE.*) The air in this place is normally so clean, you notice the change when you get within a mile of town, you start smelling the petrol, that's how clean the air is normally. Normally you could go round the beaches and see elephant seals. The animals never learned the fear of man. God they must be thick. I have to get the dinner.

LEE: We've eaten thanks.

SANDRA: Not for you.

MICK: We ate our dinner three hours ago.

SANDRA: You ate your dinner at ten o'clock in the morning.

MICK: Yes, we're still on the time they've got back home. To avoid confusion.

SANDRA: To avoid confusion. What time does the other side think it is?

TOBY: (*To SANDRA.*) They have the same time as you do, Sandra.

SANDRA: You mean they have the actual time which sane people have.

TOBY: Yes, except in the town which we're informed is two hours later conforming to the time on the mainland.

SANDRA: Oh I see.

TOBY: Being three hours ahead may seem strange to you, but it gives us the advantage of surprise.

SANDRA: Surprised! I bet they're surprised! I should think they were fucking amazed.

TOBY: No seriously Sandra, Zulu Time is a tactical weapon.

SANDRA: Zulu Time. Is that what you call it! Zulu Time. And you mean to say, you've got my life in your hands.

TOBY: I'm glad you find it so amusing, Sandra.

LEE: British isn't it.

MICK: British and proud of it.

LEE: Even if it's stupid we're proud if it's British.

MICK: Especially if it's stupid we're proud if it's British.

LEE: Anyone can be proud of things that are clever.

MICK: That's not loyalty, being proud of things that are clever. Loyalty only comes into it when you're proud of things that are utterly utterly stupid.

ADAM: Sarge. Can I speak to you.

LARRY: Fuck you.

SANDRA: He speaks English.

TOBY: (*To LARRY.*) No that won't do, I'm not having that, you behave yourself.

LARRY: Fuck you.

SANDRA: (*To LARRY.*) Excuse me where are you from?

LARRY: (*To SANDRA.*) These fucking assholes.

SANDRA: Excuse me are you American?

LARRY: I told them. I told them.

LEE: Is he American?

LARRY: I was like, glad to know you, I'm American. Then they start beating the crap out of me.

LEE: (*To LARRY.*) You cunt.

LARRY: What's the matter with them?

LEE: Where's your loyalty?

LARRY: Where's yours? We speak the same language here.

LEE: You fucking traitor!

167

LARRY: Neutral. I'm a neutral. (*Yawns.*)

LEE: Don't yawn at me, you cunt.

LARRY: (*Yawns.*)

LEE: You see that. You see him yawn. You want to die, you cunt, is that it. You want to die. You yawn at me once more you'll fucking die.

LARRY: (*Yawns.*)

LEE: (*LEE yawns.*) Fuck. (*Looks around at the others then back at LARRY.*) You'll pay for this.

LARRY: (*Yawns.*)

LEE: (*Yawns.*) Oh fuck! Fucking Yank taking the piss. (*Yawns.*) I'm going to kill you now.

TOBY: Finch. He's frightened, Finch.

MICK: Yes Lee, you frightened him.

LEE: I'll frighten him. I'll frighten him.

TOBY: He's yawning because he's frightened. Sleep is fear.

ADAM: You'd know, you cunt.

TOBY: Sleep is a strategy for putting an end to conflict.

LEE: Put an end to conflict. Him. (*To LARRY.*) We'll put an end to conflict when we're fucking ready. Fucking nerve. Fucking Yank.

SANDRA: What's he doing here, if he's American?

TOBY: (*To SANDRA.*) He's got nothing to complain of, Sandra, there's plenty in worse shape than him.

ADAM: (*To SANDRA.*) We're trying to get this man home. We're trying to get hold of some transport to take him back home. If he'd behave himself, our job would be that much easier.

SANDRA: What's he doing in that uniform?

ADAM: That's it, Sandra, he's nothing but trouble, what does he want. The Hilton.

LARRY: I'm not going anywhere with him.

ADAM: What does he want. Club Class.

LARRY: (*To SANDRA.*) I'm not going anywhere with him.

SANDRA: Is he a mercenary?

ADAM: We're taking him out of here now.

SANDRA: (*To LARRY.*) You scum.

ADAM: He shouldn't have been in here in the first place.

TOBY: No he shouldn't, corporal.

SANDRA: (*To TOBY.*) Why didn't you find somewhere!

TOBY: Now wait a minute Sandra, I never said they could put him in here, it wasn't me said put him in here.

SANDRA: That scum, and you knew this, and you let them bring him in here, into my home, into my kitchen...

TOBY: You're like my wife, Sandra, she's like you.

SANDRA: What the fuck are you talking about?

TOBY: She wants the place just the way she wants it.

SANDRA: Eh.

MICK: He has to take his shoes off before she'll let him through the door. Socks is all she lets him wear.

LEE: She's got beautiful furniture.

MICK: She's got a beautiful Spanish style coffee table.

SANDRA: Get him out.

ADAM: (*He makes to take LARRY out.*) Come on.

LARRY: No.

TOBY: What's so amusing Pike. What's so amusing about a Spanish style coffee table? Can't you take anything seriously?

SANDRA: (*To TOBY.*) What are you talking about, you arsehole!

TOBY: I've gone out of my way to look after you Sandra. Which is part of my job to do, to help you remain innocent and (*He sees the hand on the floor, tries to kick it out of sight.*) safe...

MICK: What's the matter sarge?

LEE: What's the matter sarge are you all right?

TOBY: (*He kicks the hand again.*) What is this.

SANDRA: My God.

Silence.

LEE: Where's that dog.

TOBY: Sandra don't be alarmed.

SANDRA: Oh yes it's funny is it. Waiting for me to set eyes on that. Good joke, is it.

TOBY: Don't be alarmed, Sandra, don't be alarmed...

SANDRA: (*To the others, ignoring TOBY.*) Think it's rubbish here don't you. Think we're rubbish. How you can make out you want to fight for us.. You want to fight because you want to fight and that's all. And if we're rubbish. What are you. You're dossers. If you weren't doing this. You'd all be on the social. If it wasn't for all this. Where would you be. Living in some flat on some estate, and your biggest thrill of the day would be cutting your toenails with the breadknife. Dregs of society, you are. Get yourselves killed, best thing for everyone.

MICK: That's nice, that is. That's nice.

SANDRA: You're fortunate the weather's been so mild.

ADAM: Fifteen days of freezing rain, you call that mild.

SANDRA: We'll be getting the blizzards. You'll be fucked then. There'll be snow blowing by the ton. You'll have no transport. Nothing will fly. Your ships will fuck off home without you and leave you to perish. Mind where you are when it starts, because that's where you'll stay. (*She gets a brush and pan and sweeps up the hand, then throws hand, dustpan and brush into the bin.*)

ADAM: Don't get rid of that, I was intending to dry that out, love, and use it for an ashtray.

SANDRA: It's such a crying shame. That the opposite sex. Had to be men.

TOBY: He'll apologize, love, the corporal will apologize.

SANDRA: I'm not the one leaving this room. You're the ones leaving this room.

TOBY: The corporal will apologize. You're going to have to straighten out your thinking, for your own sake corporal, for your own sake, because you're damaging yourself with this arrogance, it's yourself whom you're damaging, far more than others. You may never even see the damage you've done to yourself, it's going to eat away at your career and hollow you out in ways you never even see. Till you're nothing but a shell. Nothing but bluster and impudence. I give orders to you because that is my right, which I've earned by my own achievements, known, measured, attested and rewarded by those who have the power and responsibility of deciding these matters. A man may dream of giving orders without having been awarded the necessary rank, but if his dreams start taking the place of reality then that man's dream becomes a danger to everyone's real and serious business. That man becomes a liability.

ADAM: A liability. Yes. Yes he does.

TOBY: You're embarked on a dangerous course corporal.

ADAM: I thought it was a fucking picnic sarge.

TOBY: If that's aimed at me, corporal.

ADAM: You fucking disaster! Years you've been trained and held in readiness. Just in order that now, at the crucial moment, you'd be in a position to demonstrate your total incompetence!

TOBY: If that's aimed at me.

ADAM: This is the climax to years of preparation. Where you stand revealed as a complete and utter nothing. A vapour trail swelling into nothingness.

SANDRA: I'm not the one leaving this room.

ADAM: Fuck off love. Go on. Fuck off.

SANDRA leaves.

TOBY: I would have been there last night. I would have been there. This time, when you go, I'm going up there.

ADAM: I don't advise it.

TOBY: Why.

ADAM: It's dangerous.

TOBY: Oh yes.

ADAM: I mean for you. You cunt. If you're up there with me. It's dangerous for you. Finch take this man outside.

LEE: It's freezing.

ADAM: Take him outside.

LARRY: (*To TOBY.*) No.

TOBY: You've made enough trouble, shut your face.

FINCH and LARRY off.

TOBY: You better clean the floor, Pike.

ADAM: Sarge there's something I have to discuss.

TOBY: Don't use the dish cloth Pike.

MICK: Sorry.

TOBY: Did you never learn how to clean things Pike? Don't people clean things in Liverpool? Just cry on them do they, just cry on them cause they're such sorry Liverpool cunts.

ADAM: I've been on the radio sarge.

TOBY: Desert Island Discs was it. Again Pike. Clean it again.

MICK: It's clean sarge.

TOBY: Yes but you've touched it haven't you. Clean it again. After that, you can wash those mugs.

ADAM: Pike, piss off.

TOBY: He's not going anywhere, not till those mugs are washed, Sandra's not doing them, no reason why she should do them is there.

ADAM: Piss off, Pike.

MICK: (*To TOBY.*) Sarge?

TOBY: Glad enough to accept a brew, aren't you Pike, we're all of us glad enough to accept a brew, well sooner or later the time comes along you have to pay for it.

ADAM: Pike.

MICK off.

TOBY: What rank are you lance corporal. What rank do you take yourself for. Seemingly you're not a lance corporal, lance corporal, you're not merely some piss-ignorant cunt of a mere lance corporal, it's almost as if you seem to be under the illusion, lance corporal, that you're my superior officer whereas in fact, lance corporal, the reverse is the case.

ADAM: Sarge.

TOBY: I should make you wash those.

ADAM: I've been on the radio.

TOBY: I should make you wash those. Do the fucking things myself. (*He starts washing mugs.*)

ADAM: Will you listen!

TOBY: Where's the tea towel.

ADAM: He says. We're to shoot the American.

TOBY: (*Drops a mug.*) Eh.

ADAM: Eh.

TOBY: Bollocks.

ADAM: Eh.

TOBY: What does he mean, shoot him.

ADAM: Well sarge, how many ways can you think of to interpret that.

TOBY: What for.

ADAM: (*Patiently.*) It's an order sarge.

TOBY: Whose order. That little twat.

ADAM: Yes sarge.

TOBY: That little tosser.

ADAM: Your superior officer, sarge.

TOBY: I don't have to stand for this.

ADAM: Really sarge. Really.

TOBY: No he can't mean this. You can't have heard him right.

ADAM: I what.

TOBY: You can't have heard him right.

ADAM: Do you think I'm deaf.

TOBY: I never said you're deaf.

ADAM: If you think I'm deaf, why don't you say so.

TOBY: I never said you're deaf, only I thought you said to me the batteries...

ADAM: There's nothing wrong with the batteries.

TOBY: Nevertheless you did say to me the batteries...

ADAM: There's absolutely fuck-all wrong with the batteries. Were you put on earth to drive me mad?

TOBY: I just want to make sure I've got this straight.

ADAM: You were. You were put on this earth to drive me mad. Because if they can't get you with the big stuff, they get you with the little stuff, the little, weak, incredibly irritating stuff...

TOBY: I'm only suggesting the radio might...

ADAM: All right, you talk to him.

TOBY: No no, I wasn't suggesting...

ADAM: You don't trust what I say, you talk to him.

TOBY: I never said I don't trust what you say.

ADAM: Take the fucking radio. Talk to him. Take the fucking radio.

TOBY: I don't need the radio.

ADAM: Take it you cunt!

TOBY: No no I don't want the radio. I don't want the radio.

ADAM: Why can't you trust what I say. What is the matter with you. Why did you have to be my sergeant.

TOBY: Where's the dustpan.

ADAM: Why did they have to bring you here.

TOBY: Where's the dustpan. (*Remembers where it is.*) Oh yes.

ADAM: Why couldn't they have left you quietly somewhere in the barracks to die.

TOBY: Just like that. Shoot him, just like that.

ADAM: Can you think of some other way of shooting him, sarge.

TOBY: He gave himself up. He's a prisoner.

ADAM: So he is.

TOBY: Why.

ADAM: Who knows.

TOBY: Trouble with the Americans. They'll be panicking over the thought of trouble with the Americans. I'm being asked to murder a man in case of trouble with the Americans. And he's an American. Oh yes, it makes absolute sense.

ADAM: Yes sarge. As soon as possible sarge.

TOBY: I'm trying to think.

ADAM: Stop thinking, sarge, and concentrate.

TOBY: I can't.

ADAM: No sarge.

TOBY: I can't think, because I can't find where anything is, corporal. Everything is in a different place. The air. I used to think it was safe. Now it's got bullets in it. A clear sky. I used to think a clear sky was empty. Now I see a plane come out of it with a bomb. Grass. I used to think it's for walking on. Now each time anyone puts their foot down I think he's treading on a mine.

ADAM: I don't need this. I'm so fucking tired. I don't need this.

TOBY: I haven't debriefed him. He may have information.

ADAM: I'm tired of information.

TOBY: Well it's all very well to talk about these things but to actually pick up a gun and do it, to pick up a gun and do it now, well I'd like to see anyone that would enjoy the idea.

ADAM: Least of all you sarge.

TOBY: All right. If that's the way you see it. If that's the way you want it. You want the responsibility, you take it. That's what you're saying to me. You're saying to me, you think I'm not fit. So what you come running to me for. You do whatever seems best to you. Do what you think best.

ADAM: I'll shoot him then, shall I sarge.

TOBY: Nothing to do with me.

ADAM: I'll shoot him.

TOBY: Don't know what I'm worrying about. More trouble than he's worth. We've lads of our own to worry about.

ADAM: That's right.

TOBY: He doesn't deserve it.

ADAM: That's right sarge.

TOBY: World's upside down in any case, what difference does it make.

ADAM: That's right sarge, you forget about it sarge.

TOBY: You think I wouldn't do it.

ADAM: No sarge, no, I don't think anything sarge.

TOBY: Do it if I have to.

ADAM: I'm not saying you wouldn't sarge.

TOBY: I could, you know.

ADAM: Do you want to do it, sarge?

TOBY: Oh no not me, too much of a fucking coward, aren't I, no no, you're the one that wants to do it, you fucking do it.

ADAM: Suit yourself.

TOBY: No point my doing it, is there, it wouldn't change anything.

ADAM: No sarge.

TOBY: I'd still be a fucking coward, wouldn't I.

ADAM: Yes sarge.

TOBY: You'd still be wanting to put a bullet in me. I don't know. It might come as a relief.

ADAM: To all of us, sarge.

TOBY: Yes I do see that. I do see that.

ADAM: Not your fault sarge. Made that way. Some people are
made that way.

TOBY: They shouldn't be. Should they.

ADAM: We can't choose how we're made.

TOBY: I expect you mean well by that. Thank you.

ADAM: Better get on, sarge. Things to do.

TOBY: I'm going to come out of this.

ADAM: Better get on.

TOBY: No listen to me. I'm going to come out of this now.
I've hit the bottom of this, and now I'm coming up out of
it. I'm not going to let you do this thing.

ADAM: Eh.

TOBY: You don't understand. We shouldn't be doing this
thing.

ADAM: Oh fucking hell.

TOBY: It's not right, corporal.

ADAM: Oh fuck me.

TOBY: You think I'm a coward. I'm not such a coward that
I'm going to let you do this. The task of the military.

ADAM: Eh.

TOBY: The task of the military is to make things reliable,
even things which are not reliable.

ADAM: Eh.

TOBY: That order's against the law.

ADAM: An order is the law, sarge.

TOBY: No, orders change but the law remains reliable.

ADAM: Don't start please sarge.

TOBY: He's not a traitor.

ADAM: Don't fucking start.

TOBY: He's not a traitor. He's a neutral we thought was on our side.

ADAM: Well put, sarge.

TOBY: Supposing it gets out that we shot him.

ADAM: It's not as if I like it sarge.

TOBY: We'll be the ones take the blame.

ADAM: But that's what we've come here for, to do things we don't like. I say to myself, if I don't like it, that proves it must be right, because that's what we've come here for.

TOBY: There are people up there looking down on all of this.

ADAM: No there aren't, sarge.

TOBY: Just because we're tiny it doesn't mean we're invisible. People up there can see anything they want, they're not stupid the people up there.

ADAM: Up where, sarge. Up in the sky are they sarge.

TOBY: They can see you, and me, and all the other thousands that are here. And if once they focus on you, you won't be tiny, you'll be magnified thousands of times in those eyes of theirs, and everything you've done will be seen. How will you feel about that. When that speck of dirt is caught and magnified thousands of times in those great big eyes, and nothing in your life is ever the same again.

ADAM: I don't really think anyone up there is bothered sarge.

TOBY: Yes they are.

ADAM: You know that, do you sarge.

TOBY: Well at the very least they're people, the people up there. I've met them, some of them. They talk like people, behave like people, I'm a person, it bothers me, are they immune? no, how could they be, if I'm a person, they must be more so, otherwise why would they be up there. They wouldn't be up there if they was less, they have to be more, don't they. Mrs Thatcher herself is a mother.

ADAM: I tell you who will be bothered sarge. He'll be bothered.

TOBY: That little twat.

ADAM: If we don't carry out this order, he'll be bothered. Our lives won't be worth living. Will they sarge.

TOBY: What are we, murderers. I'm not a lackey. I'm a free man who's freely chosen to fight in defence of the laws of my country. I'm not the hired help. That little twat. Thinks that's all we're fit for. Get back to him corporal. Ask him for confirmation.

ADAM: Confirmation?

TOBY: Yes.

ADAM: Confirmation.

TOBY: Yes.

ADAM: (*His patience is absolutely exhausted.*) Oh yes of course. Confirmation.

TOBY: Tell him I want it confirmed from higher up.

ADAM: Yes but sarge, he will get it confirmed from higher up.

TOBY: He won't.

ADAM: They're mounting an attack. They're busy, sarge.

TOBY: That doesn't mean they'll confirm whatever he says.

ADAM: It's hardly the time to question an order sarge.

TOBY: They have to be better than that. Otherwise, what am I doing here.

ADAM: I don't know sarge, I really don't know.

TOBY: They operate in the full light of day up there. Not like us in the dark. It's part of their job to ensure that we are in the right. That's their part of the bargain. It's for them to ensure that we are in the right, so that we can go into action feeling confident. Their job is to make it right, then we can feel confident and secure about making it happen.

ADAM: Oh good, sarge.

TOBY: You'll get back to him, corporal.

ADAM: If I get back to him, and they confirm it, will you be happy.

TOBY: Yes but they won't. They won't. They wouldn't. (*ADAM off.*) Because I don't see the point of us fighting the other side if we're no better than they are. Unless we're simply fighting to win, and for no other reason. I wouldn't mind fighting to win, as such. But dying to win. Me dying. Simply in order for them up there to win. And them up there being no better than the other lot. I'd have to think about that.

...Once I was sure that she and the brass were all safely inside, I had to step out the lift, turn round and salute while the doors were closing. Then, as she began to ascend, I had to run like buggery up three flights of stairs so as to be standing there outside the lift at attention, not out of breath, ready to salute her as the doors opened up again...

SECOND SECTION

Later the same day. SANDRA and ADAM in her son's bedroom.

SANDRA: We should never have sent him to that school. How can he hold his head up in that school with all of this going on? What must they be doing to him. I never wanted to send him to that school. It was Peter who said we're sending him to that school. There's never any discussion, you know what I mean.

ADAM: No discussion. How does he manage that, then.

SANDRA: Peter always goes to bed at eight o'clock. Every night. He's up again at five o'clock. Hot breakfast every morning. He chews everything thirty times. He read it in a book.

ADAM: So where's this school then.

SANDRA: And here's my son's room just waiting here. For all the good this room's doing him, it might as well not exist. And by the time he comes home, perhaps it won't exist. Perhaps this house won't even be left standing. So I hope Peter's satisfied.

ADAM: He speaks Spanish, your son, does he.

SANDRA: More than you do.

ADAM: I speak English. I prefer it.

SANDRA: Then you can just wallow in your ignorance, can't you.

ADAM: They're the ignorant ones. What's he going to learn from them, except their ignorance.

SANDRA: This is the best room to see from. Peter and I were in here last night watching, it was better than Guy Fawkes.

ADAM: That's where I was, up there.

SANDRA: What's all the white bits on the grass up there.

ADAM: Field dressings.

SANDRA: Eh.

ADAM: They press them on wounds to control the bleeding.

SANDRA: Dreadful.

ADAM: Carrying men around with drips in their arms, don't know if you're in a battle or a hospital.

SANDRA: It turns my stomach. (*They kiss.*)

ADAM: You're a strange one. (*He turns to go.*)

SANDRA: Don't go, I'm frightened, you make me feel safe.

ADAM: I what.

ADAM off. After a moment, TOBY comes in.

TOBY: The corporal's not in here.

SANDRA: No.

TOBY: Your one area of sanity.

SANDRA: Oh definitely.

TOBY: I'd like to apologise, Sandra, for the events in your kitchen.

SANDRA: Nothing you could do, was there.

TOBY: I'm still responsible Sandra. I'm still responsible. I'm sorry you had to see such a thing. See it once, it's with you forever.

SANDRA: Yes thanks for reminding me, thank you very much.

TOBY: And you've got to cook in there.

SANDRA: Yes, fish fingers will take on a whole new meaning.

TOBY: My wife's allergic, you know.

SANDRA: Oh. What's she allergic to. Personally, I'm allergic to bits of dead people in my kitchen.

TOBY: Sensitive yes. She's almost completed a wine tasting course. Seventeen kinds of champagne. And her palate was able to differentiate between them all. She tasted the lot. Seventeen glasses. She spits it out of course. Fastidious you see. A sergeant's wife has to set an example. Her garden has to be weeded. Her doorstep has to be scrubbed. My wife's doorstep is as clean as most women's pillows. Look Sandra. I've apologized.

SANDRA: Yes.

TOBY: You could try to be a bit more understanding, Sandra.

SANDRA: What's that mean.

TOBY: Not everyone's in your bad books.

SANDRA: What are you talking about?

TOBY: I saw the two of you chatting on the stairs. That savage. If you can stomach that, Sandra, well then.

SANDRA: What.

TOBY: Well then.

SANDRA: What.

TOBY: So what would be the prospects for me.

SANDRA: You're all the same, you're all the fucking same.

TOBY: The question is bound to arise, Sandra, if him, then why not...

SANDRA: You poor broken-down watery-eyed little sod.

TOBY: I don't think that's quite fair Sandra, but be that as it may, Sandra, I need a little bit of light, that's all, a bit of light shining on me from your face, that's all, a bit of warmth to save me... No, I'm sorry. I'm sorry. I know it hasn't been easy for you... I'm sorry about your toilet Sandra. I advised it should be placed out of bounds. Others disagreed with me. I'm sorry about your goose. It may come back. It may just have gone for a walk. I'm sorry about the trenches in your lawn. Anyway you might be glad of one yourself if our presence draws an air raid to this place.

SANDRA: Oh thanks very much. Yes thank you.

TOBY: I'm sorry Sandra.

SANDRA: How much do they pay you.

TOBY: That mercenary probably makes ten times what I do. But what are they, they're just cowboys, ghouls, they're mad, they've got to be fighting, blow their legs off they'd try and sign up in a wheelchair. They're doing it for kicks you see, selfish, running wild, you can't tell them anything, mercenaries is all they're fit for. They're not good men Sandra. They hold nothing sacred. Not even violence. But no. I'm lucky enough to be serving in a volunteer force which is both moral and necessary, defending democracy, freedom and the law.

SANDRA: Don't you love your country then.

TOBY: Eh.

SANDRA: Do you only love your country because it's a democracy? What if it wasn't a democracy? Wouldn't you love it then?

TOBY: I'd have to think about that, Sandra.

SANDRA: You don't love it then, do you. If you have to stop and think, it means you don't love it.

TOBY: No no wait a minute Sandra, there has to be an element of reason.

SANDRA: That's what I say. You don't love it.

TOBY: No that's not patriotism. That's hysteria.

SANDRA: I love my son. Whatever he does. I love him now and always. Whatever he does. Are you calling me hysterical?

TOBY: No Sandra, of course not, no, all things considered, but put it this way Sandra I might love my country whatever it does, but that's not to say I'd fight for my country whatever it does.

SANDRA: Oh.

TOBY: What does that mean. Oh. What does that mean.

LEE and ADAM enter, with LARRY.

TOBY: What's this. (*No response.*) What you bring him up here for.

ADAM: It's all right sarge, don't worry yourself.

TOBY: I never said you could bring him up here.

ADAM: No sarge.

TOBY: Did I say you could bring him up here.

ADAM: It's all right sarge.

TOBY: Take him downstairs.

ADAM: He's better off up here sarge.

TOBY: Take him down.

ADAM: He's out of the way up here.

TOBY: I promised Sandra, nobody in this room.

ADAM: You promised Sandra.

TOBY: Yes.

ADAM: Keeping on the right side of Sandra, were you.

TOBY: Have you got anything against that, corporal?

ADAM: Looking after Sandra's interests.

TOBY: Eh.

ADAM: She can see through you. She doesn't want any favours from you sarge. Do you Sandra.

SANDRA: I said to Adam he can put him in this room.

TOBY: You said to Adam .

SANDRA: I said he can put him in this room. Is that all right with you?

TOBY: This is the thanks I get.

ADAM: What thanks were you expecting sarge.

TOBY: Eh. What do you mean. How dare you.

ADAM: I said to Sandra, just till we know what his transport's going to be. Just till we know when he's able to go back home.

TOBY: Have you –

ADAM: No sarge.

TOBY: Why not, corporal. Why haven't you –

ADAM: I can't get through to him sarge.

TOBY: Try again.

ADAM: Yes sarge.

> *TOBY off. LARRY goes and lies on the floor in a corner, falls asleep.*

SANDRA: (*Referring to TOBY.*) What you give him such a hard time for.

LEE: He's a sergeant, isn't he.

SANDRA: The state of him though. I think it's all too much for him.

ADAM: Yes he's exhausted by his efforts to stay out of combat.

SANDRA: What you so mean to him for.

LEE: Sergeants are so boring, everyone hates them. Everyone hates them cause everyone wants to be mad. And sergeants want to be sane. They want to be sane so badly. They wind up being madder than all the rest of us put together.

SANDRA: (*To ADAM.*) Are you coming out of here?

LEE: No, this is it, they have an impossible task, because they have to train us.

ADAM: He's got a point there.

LEE: They have to train us to be hard, see, which means they have to be hard on us. There was one used to get me up five o'clock every morning my first three weeks. Out running before the sun came up, all round the barracks with ice all over the roads and they'd be shouting at us how we were the worst they'd ever had, so weak, no puff, they were all day telling me how thick I was and I'd never make it, it's just, I like to stop and think but you're never supposed to, so they're all the time making out I'm a halfwit because I have thoughts.

ADAM: Yes but Finch, they're halfwitted thoughts.

LEE: I don't see how you make that out.

186

ADAM: (*To SANDRA.*) Recruiting officers give you a little intelligence test, nothing very taxing you understand, nothing very difficult. They score them, one two three four five. Fours and fives they can't be doing with. They're too stupid even for the military. But they chuck out the ones as well. They don't want the ones, cause the ones might ask questions. Twos and threes are their favourites, twos and threes. Smart enough to fight. Dumb enough not to ask why.

LEE: (*Continuing his talk to SANDRA.*) They break you right down, they make sure you know exactly how bad life can be when they don't respect you, nothing you do seems to please them and they make you feel like a boil on the face of the earth. Then one day you do something right and someone gives you a good word suggesting they don't hate you quite as much as before. So then the joy of living starts up again, it's like you're born again and they've become your parents, a few weeks down the line and by then you're well in. You're not allowed home the first six weeks. They know what they're doing see. By that time they've become your family, you've won the acceptance and you're really happy they let you belong. Only that's why it comes as a bit of a shock when they let you go off and get killed, because families aren't supposed to be like that.

ADAM: You're just a number, Finch, to be crunched in that big black mouth.

LEE: But this is the sergeant's problem. Because the reason he takes the trouble to be hard on you is that he cares. The more he cares, the more he treats you like a bastard. The more he treats you like a bastard, the more he cares. I don't think it's good for them. They get really strange, some of them. They get really nice to you. It's horrible.

SANDRA: (*To ADAM.*) Are you going to stay in here?

ADAM: No.

SANDRA: I'm down the hall.

SANDRA off.

LEE: She's down the hall.

ADAM: She is.

LEE: Are you going down the hall?

ADAM: Might do. I don't want her coming back in.

LEE: No, that's right, no.

ADAM: Shut your face Lee.

LEE: Amazing though.

ADAM: What.

LEE: It's everywhere.

ADAM: Are you clear in your mind about what you're going to do?

LEE: Tell you the truth, I'm not really in the mood you know. It's our day off, you know.

MICK enters.

You have to keep on, don't you, it's like the dog in the cartoon, he runs over a cliff and just keeps on running, he can run along in thin air just as long as he doesn't look down. Once he looks down, he falls.

ADAM off.

MICK: The way I look at it. An order which is so obviously questionable has to be, by definition, an order that was made with very good reason. It's not as if they like making questionable orders. So obviously if he finds he has to make an order like that, such an obviously questionable order, the last thing he wants is for anyone to question it.

LEE: Sooner we get this over with.

MICK: The problem with something like this. A questionable order like this. We assume it results out of careful deliberation. We assume there are special circumstances.

LEE: I'm so tired.

MICK: We assume that all the careful deliberation which people have been doing for years has finally resulted in someone having the right to make this questionable order in special circumstances.

LEE: So tired.

MICK: Of course all the time it might just have come from some twat.

LEE starts spreading a poncho on the floor.

I don't like this in the house.

LEE: No.

MICK: Why am I here. (*Pause.*) Do you want a drink?

LEE: Yeah.

MICK leaves. LARRY lies still for a while, then, half asleep, gets up and starts climbing into the bed.

LEE: Get off that.

LARRY: No.

LEE: Here's where you should lie, get over here.

LARRY: Clean cotton. So smooth. I can't feel it.

LEE: You can't get in there. You have to kip here.

LARRY: It's so little.

LEE: You won't fit in there.

LARRY: Yes I will.

LEE: I'm warning you.

LARRY: I'm getting in here and I'm staying in here.

LEE: You're disgusting. You're filthy.

LARRY: This your room?

LEE: Doesn't have to be mine for me to know what's right.

LARRY: Yes it does.

LEE: Yes but you should know what's right as well. You should know what's right as well.

LARRY: I don't.

LEE: (*Threatening LARRY with a gun.*) Get off.

LARRY: Like you said. You know what's right. I have to sleep.

LEE: Get off.

LARRY: I'm ready to die so long as I die right here. (*Closes his eyes.*)

LEE: (*Goes over and shakes him.*) Come on wake up.

LARRY: (*Half asleep.*) Haven't slept in thirty-six hours.

LEE: (*Yelling in his ear.*) Neither have I! (*Slaps LARRY's face.*) Right. Keep them open. Selfish cunt. I can't sleep. Can I! I can't sleep and it's on account of you! I'm supposed to be resting! I'm going to die because of you! I won't see the danger when it's coming. My eyes will be too tired to move. I'll be dead, and it will be your fault!

LARRY: Quiet.

LEE: (*He grabs a toy drum and bashes it.*) Sleepy? (*Bashes the drum again.*) Night night! (*Bashes the drum again.*)

TOBY enters and watches him for a moment.

TOBY: What are you doing, Finch?

LEE: Nothing sarge.

TOBY: I could have sworn I heard a noise.

LEE: It's only pretend sarge.

TOBY: The face on you. Struck dumb. What would I find if I went in through your face. A thousand paths through the forest. Which one brings me to the centre.

LEE: I don't know sarge.

TOBY: Is there a centre, Finch?

LEE: I don't know sarge.

TOBY: Put the drum down Finch.

LEE: Yes sarge.

TOBY: Asleep is he.

LEE: Yes sarge.

TOBY: We have to treat him properly, Finch. There's no end to what he might be able to tell us, there's no end to what we might be able to learn, if only we treat him properly.

LEE: Yes sarge.

TOBY: Hardly going the right way about it, are you Finch.

LEE: No sarge.

TOBY: Who knows what's inside that head of his. There's only one way to get that information out. By the delicate mechanism of speech. By carefully encouraging those mysterious little puffs of breath. We're going to have to coax the words out of him like little kittens.

LEE: Yes sarge.

TOBY: We have to be patient.

LEE: Yes sarge.

TOBY: And not smash his brains in.

LEE: Yes sarge.

TOBY: Otherwise what will become of all the little kittens.

LEE: Yes sarge.

TOBY: He shouldn't be on that bed though.

LEE: Mick and I can get him on to the floor sarge.

TOBY: Yes but nicely Finch. Be nice. With what he could tell us, fighting could well be avoided.

LEE: Yes sarge.

TOBY: Anything wrong with that, Finch?

LEE: No sarge.

TOBY: I never heard there was anything wrong with fighting being avoided, Finch.

LEE: No of course not sarge.

TOBY: It troubles me what you might be thinking.

LEE: Don't trouble yourself sarge.

TOBY: I do trouble myself. Finch. I'm walking around thinking nothing is solid. As if the ground was going to melt away from under my feet and I'd look down and see daylight through the hole. Whatever I touch, it starts to melt, as soon as my fingers touch there are hollows forming. Everything I pass through is falling into wreckage, and I can only manage to escape by moving forward. My mum and dad.

LEE: Eh.

TOBY: I never used to know what was the matter, all the time at home it was like there was a cold wind blowing on me so hard, so hard, I couldn't stand upright. And then I joined up and I wasn't living at home any more and all at once I found the wind had dropped, it had simply stopped blowing and everything was quiet, what a relief. And I slowly straightened up, and I stretched. Because what I'd learned was, there are things which work. There are things which can be controlled.

LEE: Yes sarge, thank God for that sarge, you taught us that, didn't you sarge.

TOBY: I hope you won't forget what I've taught you, Finch.

LEE: No it's really useful sarge.

TOBY: Has the corporal said anything to you.

LEE: What about, sarge.

TOBY: Good, good.

> *MICK enters.*

If you see the corporal, Finch, tell him I'm looking for him.

> *TOBY off.*

MICK: Wake him up, we'll have to get him off there.

LEE: Just you try, that's double sleep he's got there, that's my sleep as well he's got there.

MICK: (*Speaks in LARRY's ear.*) Larry. Wake up. We have to move you. (*No response. They shrug. To LEE.*) Here. (*He produces a bottle of whisky.*)

LEE: Where'd you get it.

MICK: Swapped some loot for it. Pistol. I've still got two more.

LEE: We'll have to move him though.

MICK: Yeah. (*They go and sit on the poncho, and drink out of the bottle.*)

LEE: See this.

MICK: That's your piece of shrapnel.

LEE: This was in my chinstrap.

MICK: Yeah, Lee, you told me.

LEE: Here. It was here.

MICK: You told me.

LEE: That would have been my eye.

MICK: Yeah, you need to be careful, Lee.

LEE: I think of it in my brain.

MICK: Yes well that's where people normally think of things.

LEE: It's almost like it's been in there and come out again knowing everything about me. I feel as if it could tell me all about myself.

MICK: Well. Good luck.

LEE: Yeah.

MICK: Why am I here.

LEE: (*Unpacking things from pockets.*) You got these? The night vision glasses? Magic these. See and not be seen. When you get married Mick I'll be standing in your bedroom with these.

MICK: Do you think we ought to move him.

LEE: Ammunition. Pack of enemy fags I'm going to take home for my mum.

MICK: Done your holiday shopping then.

LEE: All right we'll move him shall we.

MICK: I haven't thought about anything back home since we got here. How many people back home have ever been tested. How many of them would be ready die for their faith. What's your faith Lee.

LEE: Being ready to die.

MICK: Is that it.

LEE: Yeah.

MICK: I'm not really ready to die.

LEE: Aren't you?

MICK: No, Lee, I'm not.

LEE: So then. What brings you here.

MICK: Why should I die for them. All they want is a chance to get on with their selfish little imaginary little lives. I'd die for my mates. Because we've earned it. As for the rest of them. Living on in their kingdom of light with their cities and their glorious pavements and their freedom parades, walking on the dust that used to be us, well they're laughing aren't they. Fuck them. I hate them. Maybe it's not even worth hanging round if I just have to be with them. Come on, we have to move him.

LEE: See these.

MICK: (*Looks at LEE's photos.*) Ooh! pig.

LEE: Pig??

MICK: (*Grunts.*)

LEE: I don't think she's a pig, I think she's nice.

MICK: What's she written on it. Hullo soldier whoever you are, friends tell me I look like Olivia Newton John so let's get physical. No I don't think so. Where'd you get these, off the pigs' notice board. I put one or two on there, I threw the rest of mine off the ship to frighten the sharks.

LEE: These didn't come off the pigs' notice board.

MICK: Yes they did, there's dart holes in them.

LEE: Let's see.

MICK: Only joking.

LEE: I thought that was out of order, throwing darts at them.

MICK: Oh disgusting yes, having to aim at them, having to look at them, oh God that took courage, oh my God.

LEE: You're no oil painting yourself Mick.

MICK: Am I not.

LEE: No you're not.

MICK: I know that.

LEE: How would you like it if someone talked that way about you.

MICK: So what you're saying is, if I don't want to be talked about like that, I shouldn't talk like that.

LEE: Yeah. That's it, yeah.

MICK: (*Indicating picture.*) So you don't think that she would talk about anyone like that.

LEE: No. I don't think she would.

MICK: It hasn't stopped me from talking about her though. It hasn't saved her from having me talk about her. Has it. Has it.

LEE: No, but.

MICK: Well there you are then. What good has she done herself. None.

LEE: That's not what I was trying to say.

MICK: None. What were you trying to say.

LEE: I don't know. Something different.

MICK: Don't try to be different, Lee. You've got enough problems trying to be the same.

LEE: See this one though. This is a nice one, this one is really nice, this one is not a slag. She sent a picture of herself with her mum and dad in their garden see, and she writes, To a brave soldier, thank you for what you are doing for our country, we are all praying for you, love, Lorraine. She has sympathy, I know she has sympathy, she's got a really gentle face, don't you think she has, and she's got true eyes, she's sending her thoughts and I can feel them reach me.

MICK: Her thoughts eh.

LEE: Yeah.

MICK: She should send her tits. Look at them.

LEE: Yeah. What I'm going to do, if I get home, I thought I'd go and introduce myself you know, say I am the soldier who received your card and I cherished it, I kept it on me in times of danger and as you can see it must have protected me.

MICK: Nice one.

LEE: If they don't let me fuck them, what does that tell us about their patriotism.

MICK: They.

LEE: I've got nineteen.

LARRY wakes up screaming.

MICK: Here. Cut that out. (*LARRY stops screaming, stares at MICK.*) Stop that. What's your game. You stop that all right. Frightened the life out of me. Are you awake? You should be ashamed of yourself. Misbehaving yourself like that. Give you a spanking I will if you do that. Don't try to make me sorry for you, carrying on like that. The only thing you make me feel is disgust. You should have guards on yourself to stop you from doing that. Not doing their job are they. Naughty guards. You're going to have to watch them guards. You'd better not sleep any more, because if you do, they'll see their chance and slip away again like the sly little rascals they are. Are you ready to stop misbehaving. Are you going to be good, yes. If you're good you can come to our party. We're having a party, aren't we, Lee. What sort of party are we having.

LEE: Poncho party.

MICK: We're having a poncho party. (*He shows LARRY the bottle.*) The rules of a poncho party are, it has to take place on a poncho. Doesn't it Lee. Because that's our magic carpet. Isn't it Lee.

LEE: Yes flying carpet.

MICK: Where shall we fly to, Lee.

LEE: Fly and never land. Wherever you land, all you're going to find is just the force of gravity.

MICK: So are you going to come and have a drink.

LARRY: No.

MICK: Why not.

LARRY: No.

MICK: What's the matter, don't you trust us.

LARRY: No.

MICK: Why don't you trust us.

LARRY: Bureaucrats.

MICK: Are we bureaucrats, are we. I don't think you're all there.

LEE: No it's just. Waking up in a strange bed.

MICK: Is that what it is.

LEE: It's frightening, waking up in a strange bed.

MICK: Well you'd know.

LEE: He just needs to remember where he is.

MICK: Oh yes Lee, that will make him feel so much better.

LEE: Anyway I hope he's ashamed.

MICK: I think he is ashamed, Lee, I think he's got a guilty conscience.

LEE: I hope he has.

MICK: (*To LARRY.*) Some would say death's no more than you deserve.

LEE: Some would say death's too good for him.

MICK: We've always thought America was so great.

LEE: I've always thought America is. Bugs Bunny.

MICK: You'd have shot us down last night as if we'd been just anyone.

LEE: As if we'd been just foreign.

MICK: Pretending not to know us.

LEE: Pretending not to know your own kind.

MICK: There's blokes out there, they'd hang you if they knew what you are.

LEE: You should be glad it's us mate.

MICK: But we're not vengeful, are we Lee.

LEE: No.

MICK: Because that would be childish.

LEE: Childish.

MICK: Because who knows what your reasoning is.

LEE: No-one.

MICK: So fuck it, have a drink.

LARRY: I'm dead.

MICK: We're not going to hurt you.

LARRY: I can see it now, I can see the hand of the bureaucrats in this.

MICK: What do you mean, bureaucrats.

LARRY: The bureaucrats are in favour of England. They govern America, but they are not American. I'm an American, and I say I'll fight who I want, where I want. The bureaucrats are not in favour of that.

MICK: They're after you, are they.

LARRY: Because England is the birthplace of bureaucracy.

MICK: Are they after you then.

LARRY: Top people.

MICK: Top people, are they.

LARRY: In America. In England. They'll be working on this together.

MICK: Thatcher's after you, is she.

LARRY: She's a bureaucrat.

MICK: They all want to kill you do they.

LARRY: I think so. Because the American people would take a dislike to this situation. They would take a dislike to English soldiers fighting against an American boy. They would criticize the bureaucratic obsession with England,

and this is what the bureaucrats will be working to prevent. Sure, I'm crazy. Sure.

MICK: I never said that.

LARRY: Do you even know why you're here.

MICK: To safeguard the sovereignty of British people.

LARRY: Antarctica is the reason you're here. This is the point from which England intends to claim a piece of Antarctica. Antarctica. The icebox of the world, full of fish, full of phosphates, and the ground there is all composed of jewels and precious metals and oil, everything man needs is there under the snow just waiting to be uncovered. One of these days they're going to thaw it out with mirrors, and people there will make their homes in bubbles.

MICK: Bubbles eh. Beautiful bubbles.

LARRY: See people say they're doing one thing, but the big thing is happening beyond their conscious mind, you look down one day, you find a new continent has risen up under your feet.

LEE: There's this pool there you can swim in.

LARRY: What pool? Where?

LEE: There's this warm pool. In Antarctica.

MICK: This jacuzzi is there Lee.

LARRY: You mean there's a geyser.

LEE: No, there's no people, no. Oh. A geyser. Yeah. There's a geyser. In a pool.

LARRY: That would be neat. Swimming in that pool with ice all around. That would be neat.

LEE: Yeah. I'm not sure what part it's in.

MICK: Come on, come and have a drink.

LARRY: You guys are only doing what you have to. I'm sorry to meet like this. But guys, if there was some way you could see my way out of this, I sure would appreciate it.

MICK: What's he talking about.

LARRY: Please.

MICK: Come and have a drink.

LARRY: Bring me a drink over here.

MICK: No, you come over to us mate.

LARRY: Why can't I have it here.

MICK: Don't you trust us.

LARRY: Bring it to me here and I'll trust you.

MICK: No you insulted us now. I'm not giving you no drink if you don't trust me.

LARRY: Fuck your drink then.

LEE: Fuck you and all. You can fucking stay there and rot.

MICK: Wait a minute Lee.

LEE: I wouldn't take a drink with him if he asked me.

MICK: Lee.

LEE: Won't take a fucking drink with us, well fuck him.

MICK: Lee. He's frightened Lee. He had a frightening dream. We don't want him feeling frightened Lee.

LEE: Frightened of his own fucking shadow.

MICK: (*To LARRY.*) Are you coming over here then?

LARRY: No.

MICK: We're going to have to get you out of this. Come on. (*Starts pulling LARRY out of the bed.*)

LEE: Come on.

LARRY: No, fuck you, no!

LEE: He's bringing the whole fucking bed with him.

LARRY: No!

LEE: Get his fingers loose.

MICK: (*Trying to undo LARRY's fingers.*) Be reasonable, you're being hysterical, be reasonable.

ADAM enters and stands watching.

LEE: (*To ADAM.*) He won't take a drink with us.

MICK: He's refusing to take a drink.

ADAM: (*To LARRY.*) Don't you want a drink?

LARRY: Give it to me here.

ADAM: Why won't you give it him there.

LEE: Eh.

ADAM: Give him a drink. Give it him there.

LEE: But you said –

ADAM: Give it him there. (*They give LARRY the bottle. LARRY doesn't drink.*) You might as well. Pity to waste it.

LARRY: Sure. (*LARRY drinks.*)

ADAM: Bring him over.

> *LARRY screams. MICK and LEE drag LARRY over on to the poncho and ADAM kills him with his bayonet.*

Cover him. (*They cover him.*)

LEE: (*To ADAM.*) Only you said. He has to be on the poncho. That's what you said. We were doing every fucking thing to get him on the poncho. Then you walk in. Give it him there. We might just as well have saved ourselves the trouble. Give it him there.

ADAM: Shut up Finch.

LEE: But you said –

> *TOBY enters.*

TOBY: I thought I heard a noise.

ADAM: What noise.

TOBY: I thought I heard a noise. (*Silence.*) Have you tried getting through to him.

ADAM: Yes I have sarge.

TOBY: You haven't got through to him then.

ADAM: Yes I have sarge.

TOBY: When did you get through to him.

ADAM: Just now.

TOBY: You didn't tell me.

ADAM: The order's been confirmed sarge.

TOBY: You didn't tell me.

ADAM: He said to get on with it sarge.

TOBY: I don't understand why you couldn't come and tell me.

ADAM: He said to get on with it.

TOBY: All the more reason. All the more reason, corporal. They want us to get on with it, why aren't we getting on with it. It's these problems of communication, corporal.

ADAM: Yes sarge.

TOBY: Once again, these problems of communication.

ADAM: Yes sarge.

TOBY: Who'd have believed it, eh.

ADAM: I believe it, sarge.

TOBY: I never could have believed it. Is it possible.

ADAM: Yes sarge.

TOBY: Is it possible.

ADAM: Would you like to check with him sarge.

TOBY: No, that's all right corporal. Is it possible. Yes it is. Well. Anything's possible. Only in practice, you rely on certain things not happening, don't you, even if they're possible, you rely on certain things not happening. How wrong can you be.

ADAM: This isn't one of those things though, is it sarge.

TOBY: I bet that little twat never even asked anyone.

ADAM: Your senior officer, sarge.

TOBY: Or if he did. He asked someone who thought the same as him.

ADAM: Most people would think the same as him, sarge.

TOBY: No, most people are not like you lot.

ADAM: Yes. They are. And the proof of it is, they recruited us.

TOBY: But it's wrong. You know it's wrong. Everyone knows it's wrong.

ADAM: They know it's wrong sarge, but they want it done. There are times when wrong things have to be done.

TOBY: So they don't care.

ADAM: No sarge.

TOBY: Well then. If they don't care. Why should I.

ADAM: That's right sarge.

TOBY: If the law, for which you and I are fighting, corporal, means nothing to them that have the power, then what is this golden banner I've been carrying around. This banner above my head, this pride. What's this banner I've got left on my hands, perishing in my hands, it's just an old thin piece of cloth which I'm carrying for God knows what reason any more.

They have their daylight voice, they have their golden voice. But they also have their night voice, and in the daylight hours they pretend it isn't theirs, even to themselves.

Get him up, take him outside.

ADAM: Eh.

TOBY: Wake him up.

LEE: But sarge.

TOBY: Wake him up, take him outside.

LEE: But sarge, he's –

ADAM: We can do it in his sleep sarge.

TOBY: Now. You mean now.

ADAM: I'll do it. I'll do it sarge.

TOBY: Where's your bayonet.

ADAM: I'll do it.

TOBY: Give it here.

ADAM: Sarge. Are you sure you want to do this.

TOBY: Show me up would you. Give it here.

ADAM: (*Giving him the bayonet.*) In his eye sarge.

TOBY: Don't fucking tell me what to do. I know what to do.

ADAM: Straight in his eye, then you know it's done.

TOBY: What I happen to think of it doesn't matter.

ADAM: You can do it sarge.

TOBY: Do it. Course I can do it.

ADAM: What we all joined up for, isn't it sarge.

TOBY: Course I can do it.

ADAM: Come on sarge, give him a good one.

TOBY: Frankly I don't think much of it. I don't think it's any great achievement frankly.

ADAM: Are you all right, sarge.

TOBY: I don't think it amounts to very much at all. Perfect myself. That's what I wanted. Mentally and physically. Perfect myself. What must they think of us. That twat won't even want to know me after I've done this job. In giving me this job, he reveals how little they think of me. Whenever he sets eyes on me, he'll remember. And he'll say to himself yes, he really is the garbage I thought he was, he proved himself fit for the job.

ADAM: Give it here.

TOBY: Fuck off.

ADAM: Give it here.

TOBY: No wait. No listen. Wait.

ADAM: Give it here.

TOBY: If this is how low they are. They're not worth it.

ADAM: Oh you cunt.

TOBY: No listen. If we can't be proud of what we do, then where's our motivation.

ADAM: I'm proud, you cunt.

TOBY: Why.

ADAM: Because I exist. I'm proud because I exist, and I exist because I'm proud.

TOBY: But you can't be proud if you do things that make you ashamed.

ADAM: That's why I'm never ashamed of what I do.

TOBY: But you should be. They're asking you to do a shameful thing. Therefore they're not worth it. There's nobody to do it for. We're free. We can enjoy our time on earth. We don't have to harm anyone. Everyone can live.

ADAM: (*In total exasperation.*) I don't think so. I really don't think so.

TOBY: I don't want to harm this man. Even this man is infinitely more valuable to me than nothingness. Even this man, lying there asleep, has the depth and life of a forest.

ADAM: A forest, sarge.

TOBY: Yes, even this man is a forest.

ADAM: Listen sarge I understand the principle, but the principle is there for human beings and this man's not what I would call a human being. This man has no conscience, he doesn't know what it's like to be us. He's a setback to the human race.

TOBY: What gives you the right to say that, corporal.

ADAM: You've got a conscience sarge. You're better than him. So it's all right for you to kill him.

TOBY: What's my conscience worth if I don't follow what it says. See, in this engagement, corporal. Already in this engagement the decency is slipping away. Just for the sake of getting on with it. But it slips away so fast, and then it's gone, and everyone's left crawling in the mud not knowing why. Look at him sleeping. (*He looks at LARRY more closely, pulls back the poncho covering him.*) What have you done.

ADAM: Who's asking me.

TOBY: What have you done.

ADAM: Who's asking me. You cunt.

SANDRA enters. TOBY hastily covers LARRY.

SANDRA: (*To ADAM.*) Remember me?

ADAM: Eh.

SANDRA: I'm still down the hall.

ADAM: I know.

SANDRA: Just down there.

ADAM: I know you are.

SANDRA: Are you coming.

ADAM: In a minute.

SANDRA: You do what you want. What's it to me what you do.

TOBY: Go out of here will you love.

SANDRA: I beg your pardon. I beg your pardon.

TOBY: Go on, bugger off out of it.

SANDRA: What's the matter with you? (*To ADAM.*) What's the matter with him?

ADAM: I wish I knew.

TOBY: (*To SANDRA.*) I'm warning you.

SANDRA: (*To TOBY.*) What's your game?

TOBY: For your own sake I'm warning you.

SANDRA: What's happened? (*Registers LARRY.*) He's dead.

ADAM: Well done sarge.

TOBY: She can see for herself.

ADAM: Well done.

TOBY: Can't you love.

SANDRA: Oh my God.

ADAM: (*To SANDRA.*) He shouldn't have told you.

SANDRA: How do you mean, he shouldn't. How do you mean.

Pause.

ADAM: Don't be upset.

SANDRA: Stay away from me.

ADAM: Don't be upset. I'm not going to hurt you. What you take us for.

SANDRA screams.

SANDRA: Stay away from me.

Pause.

ADAM: He's got no business upsetting you like this.

SANDRA: What are you going to do.

ADAM: All that happened, Sandra...

MICK: He tried to escape.

TOBY: Eh.

ADAM: He tried to escape.

Pause.

TOBY: This is it, Sandra, he tried to escape.

ADAM: He was dangerous.

SANDRA: Yes.

TOBY: A dangerous man.

SANDRA: Why did you bring him into my house. Why did you bring him into my house.

TOBY: I never brought him into your house. I'm not the one.

ADAM: No he's not the one, he's never the one, he's never ever been the fucking one! He calls himself my sergeant, and not one fucking thing has he ever done, oh no, he leaves it all up to me, he leaves it all up to anyone who actually cares what actually happens! I can't look to him! Can I! I might as well be looking at a black room through a broken window! What am I supposed to be? I'm only human! I never wanted this! He says to me, special treatment. This man's to have special fucking treatment...

SANDRA: (*To TOBY.*) Now see what you've done! Are you satisfied? You –

TOBY: A hypothetical question Sandra. Just a hypothetical question. Just so I know your opinion. A British platoon captures an American mercenary. What are we supposed to do with him.

ADAM: Oh yes give him special treatment.

TOBY: He's an embarrassment. What are we supposed to do with him?

ADAM: (*To SANDRA.*) Come out of here.

SANDRA: Yes.

TOBY: They want it kept quiet. They don't want it known.

ADAM: Come on.

SANDRA: Yes.

TOBY: How far should they go?

SANDRA: This is a hypothetical question you're asking me.

TOBY: What's it worth to them to keep it quiet? Is it worth his life?

SANDRA: Yes but this is not happening.

TOBY: What's his life worth?

SANDRA: (*To ADAM.*) It's a hypothetical question he's asking me.

TOBY: They'd be making us murderers, wouldn't they. We're not murderers, we're citizens. What are they putting us on the level of. Creatures of the dark. We hate the dark. We're afraid of the dark. We want to live in the light with everyone else.

SANDRA: This isn't a true question he's asking me.

ADAM: No it's not a true question. How could he ask you that question unless it wasn't true. Because if it were true, that would have to be a decision made by very senior people. Very senior people would have decided to keep this man's existence quiet. They would be wanting to keep his existence quiet, so as not to jeopardize the special relationship between England and America, a relationship which is very important to us in this conflict, which is a

208

very difficult and dangerous one. Now Sandra. If this man's existence was having to be kept quiet, then his death would also have to be kept quiet, wouldn't it. Anyone who knew about his death would have to keep it quiet. Wouldn't they.

SANDRA: But none of this is true.

ADAM: No.

SANDRA: What he said isn't true.

ADAM: Some people here, Sandra, have trouble facing up to the reality. There are some people wandering away from the reality, physically and also in their minds, they wander in their minds. Don't they sarge.

TOBY: This is it, Sandra, I think I must be wandering in my mind. Because I'm sane. And all of you are mad. So what does that make me.

ADAM: (*To SANDRA.*) Come on.

SANDRA: Yes.

TOBY: Don't listen to me. Whatever you do. Don't listen to me.

SANDRA: (*To ADAM.*) He frightens me. I'm frightened of him.

ADAM: (*To SANDRA.*) Come on down the hall. (*ADAM and SANDRA off.*)

MICK: (*To TOBY.*) What the fuck's got into you.

TOBY: Who are you speaking to, Pike.

MICK: You'll get us all destroyed. Will you be happy then. Will you finally be happy.

TOBY: Who are you speaking to.

MICK: What's the point of trying to tell her anyway, she doesn't want to know. Nor should she! It's a specialized matter. For specialists.

TOBY: Am I mad?

MICK: Who cares if you're mad, do the job, that's all, do the fucking job.

LEE: Yes but Mick.

TOBY: Am I mad.

LEE: What is the job.

MICK: Do the job.

LEE: What is the job.

MICK: (*To LEE.*) Don't you start.

LEE: (*To MICK.*) I always want to be proud of what I've done.

MICK: Who's stopping you.

LEE: Yes but I'm not.

MICK: Have a drink sarge, put your thoughts in order. (*He retrieves his bottle of whisky from the floor.*)

LEE: I'm not.

MICK: Cheer up sarge. (*Offering the bottle to TOBY, who takes no notice.*) Have a drink.

TOBY: The moment she appeared.

MICK: Who sarge.

MICK and LEE start wrapping LARRY's body.

TOBY: Press the button just as she came round the corner then stand to attention.

LEE: Are you all right sarge.

TOBY: Soon as the doors were open I had to slip inside the lift and hold down the Door Open button.

MICK: Did you sarge did you really.

TOBY: Once she was safely in, I had to stand outside saluting while the doors closed. Then I had to run like buggery up three flights of stairs, and be stood there at attention and not out of breath ready to salute her when the lift arrived...

LEE: Brilliant eh sarge.

TOBY: I trained three weeks for that.

MICK: Nobody does it like we do sarge.

LEE: Brilliant eh.

THE END

HER MOTHER AND BARTOK

Characters

MAN

WOMAN

A man and a woman of a certain age, the man older than the woman.

WOMAN: He opens the door.

MAN: Yes.

WOMAN: The shabby door.

MAN: The shabby shabby door.

WOMAN: He opens his shabby door, which is not the same as the doors at home. The doors at home are new, flat, clean doors, because her parents like new, clean, flat things. Her parents don't like history. Her parents have rejected history as being the history of oppression, but she's oppressed by her parents' new, clean, flat things, and she likes old things. She's young and the world is calling her with its oldness, and that's what she's going to dedicate her young life to discovering.

MAN: He asks her in.

WOMAN: She and her parents live at home eating salad straight from the fridge, and they cut the tomatoes in flower shapes. But she's recently been discovering other people, with other salad, and these people –

MAN: These people tear salad roughly –

WOMAN: They tear it roughly and mix it all together, and they serve their salad at room temperature, in a warm room, and the oil and vinegar and garlic, which these people have used copiously, eat into the lettuce leaves, until the salad swoons and melts under the corrupting influence of the foreign ingredients.

MAN: He studied in Hungary.

WOMAN: She can't move her neck. Her neck has suddenly been gripped by the force of her own nature, or is it the force of nature itself. She's standing at his shabby door, paralysed

by the force of nature, working inside her,
although the force of nature working inside
her is working because of him, and he's
outside her, and it's as if the nature inside her
were trying to join up with the nature outside
her, and she's being gripped and taken apart,
because she's in the way, and he giggles...

MAN: In fright. He's giggling in fright. He's the
older one. He studied in Hungary. He knows
just how much she'll be expecting. And she's
moody, she's one of those moody girls who
make him feel as if he's done something
wrong, before he's even...

WOMAN: She likes his giggle, she wants him with his
odd giggle, yes, because he's not one of those
regular men who put on deep voices, trying
to be men. She prefers him to all those men
competing to be men with their deep voices
and their urgency and their money and their
dread of being effeminate, she prefers him
to all those men driven by the dread of not
winning the competition to be men, they
all dread not winning the competition, but
she's the judge of the competition, and it isn't
going to be them, with their dread and their
manliness, no the winner of the competition
is going to be the one who laughs at the
competition, the one who giggles at the
competition, the winner of the competition is
going to be the one who doesn't care about
the competition, and who makes all the
others look like children, it's going to be the
unreliable giggling one, the hyena, the thief,
the trickster, the wolf, the jackal, the rat...

MAN: She likes him.

         (Pause.)

WOMAN: She walks down the hall.

MAN: She lunges down the hall.

WOMAN: He finds her unfeminine, because when
he thinks of femininity, he thinks of tiny
footsteps, tiny footsteps like tiny obedient
children, and the competition to be women is
even fiercer than the competition to be men,
except that it's rigged as well, because men
think women are supposed to be, not women,
but tiny obedient children with tiny footsteps.
Women who walk like women –

MAN: She's fond of saying –

WOMAN: Women who walk like women are thought of
as walking aggressively, they're thought of as
walking like men, so in order to avoid walking
like men, women avoid walking like women,
they carefully avoid lunging, and trot around
with their elbows tucked into their sides, they
trot around like tiny high-heeled dinosaurs.

MAN: She lunges. She's a university girl, and she's
talked about these things with her university
friends, and she's decided, after careful
deliberation, that she's going to be natural,
and spontaneous, and lunge. She lunges along
the hall, and into the room, where she opens
her violin case.

WOMAN: And he opens his violin case, and fetches his
editions of Kodaly. His Hungarian editions of
Kodaly. They're printed on yellow thin paper,
he bought them in Hungary, he studied in
Hungary.

MAN: She unwraps her instrument, releasing puffs of
rosin.

WOMAN: At the first lesson, he said he's going to have to
change everything she does, everything she's
been taught is wrong, and he's surprised she's
managed to get this far, with such a cramped,

unnatural way of playing the instrument,
she'll certainly injure herself, if she carries on
playing in this cramped, unnatural way, and
she's always known it, she can feel how the
joy that should be flowing through her has
been blocked by everything she's been taught,
and she's very happy that he's going to free
her of this unnatural cramping and release
her natural joy... and that's when they start on
his editions of Kodaly, he brought them back
from Hungary, all the way from Hungary in
his suitcases with his things, she looks at them
and thinks about his things, his shirts and
things, and the yellowish paper of his editions
of Kodaly makes her think of his things and
his shirts and his sheets and his bed.

MAN: And they play folk tunes, which Kodaly
collected from Hungary's fertile plains. She
plays the melodies, while he plays the descants
which are more complex and difficult...

WOMAN: But despite these complex and difficult
descants, the music is music of the open air,
music you might hear on the river banks or
in the fields under that vast pale open sky she
can imagine stretching above, and the song
they're playing is frail and melancholy. The
tune is like sighing, but with sighs that go
up instead of down, and then softer echoes
of the same upward sighs, and then a long
downward sigh, and the harmonies he plays
are like the wind blowing on an empty plain,
in the sun, and it's so beautiful, so beautiful...

MAN: And it stops.

WOMAN: It stops in the middle.

MAN: He says to her –

WOMAN: "What are you doing?"

MAN: And she says, "Why have we stopped?"

WOMAN: "I stopped because you stopped," he says. "Why did you stop?"

MAN: "Did I stop?" she says.

WOMAN: And he says, she did.

MAN: She stopped because it was so beautiful. She thought she was playing. She'd gone so far into the music, she forgot to play.

(Pause.)

MAN: He says to her, it's no use being so far into the music you forget to play. You should never be inside the music, he's never inside the music when he plays, he's ice cold, ice cold, and she says but that's the reason she plays music, to be in it. She says it's like a golden castle, it's like being in a castle in the air and walking through the rooms which are all golden, and that's where she wants to live, it's the only place she's ever wanted to live, in that –

WOMAN: Gold.

MAN: Is she planning a career in music, he asks.

WOMAN: Yes. She is. She wants to use her ability, use it to the full. She says she isn't going to wind up like her mother and Bartok. Yes, she says, there's this thing my mother always says about Bartok. She always says this thing, whenever Bartok's name is mentioned, especially if it's mentioned by a man, and as far as my mother is concerned, mentioning Bartok is the kind of thing that's best done by a man. If I mention Bartok she immediately starts treating me as if I were a man, she immediately starts being girlish and coquettish and wayward with me, because in mentioning Bartok, as far as she's concerned, I've assumed the role of a man. And by the way, in treating me as if I were a man, she scores a point, because just as when

two men are together, both of them are usually
wanting to be masculine, and so the more
masculine one of the two becomes the winner,
when two women are together it's the more
feminine one who wins, it's the more feminine
one who actually dominates, and I refuse to
be girlish and coquettish and wayward just in
order to compete with her, so she always gets
possession of the girlish wayward feminine
high ground and I'm left being a lump, a
churlish masculine lump, and I don't think it's
very nice of her, seeing she's my mother and
says she cares for me, I don't think it's very
nice, the way she drives home her advantage
in a situation like that. Anyway, someone
mentions Bartok and she'll say, with a
childlike eagerness which wouldn't be spiteful,
if it weren't for its obvious glee at wrecking
something, she'll eagerly say, "But Bartok is
so cold and mechanical, don't you think?" and
there it is, she's pushed forward her Bartok
opinion as if she were pushing forward her
counter in some board game, she's established
her credentials as a woman with a Bartok
opinion, and a wayward opinion at that, and
then she'll look from under her lashes at the
man who's mentioned Bartok, or at me if I'm
the one who mentioned Bartok and there
isn't a man available, she'll look in a slightly
flirtatious way, as if to say, "You see, there's
more fire than you think in this irreproachable
housewife and mother", and also as if to say,
"I'm not cold and mechanical, like the cold
mechanical Bartok", so the very name of
Bartok is like a sort of starter's pistol for my
mother, her starter's pistol in the race to sexual
victory, it's her cue to flirt, and to hint that
she's capable of putting up a fight as well, and

what's more it will be an intellectual combat,
not some merely physical thing – with her,
the word physical is always accompanied by
the word merely – yes it will be an intellectual
combat, and of course the man is going
to win it in the end because of his greater
brainpower, which Nature gave him so he'd
be able to bludgeon her into submission with
it, like a caveman with his club, my mother
wants to be bludgeoned into submission as
Nature intended, but not by a club, she wants
to be bludgeoned into submission by a brain;
her opinion isn't designed to win against
his in the end, and because of that, any old
opinion will do as far as she's concerned: it
doesn't have to be her own fully thought out
committed opinion, it might just as well be
an opinion she's picked up from somewhere
like a magpie with a blue bead, because its
main function is simply to be attractively
coloured, its main function is simply to draw
attention to itself so that she can be dealt with
and tamed, it doesn't want to be well founded,
it doesn't want to be too powerful, because
then it might win. My mother has this vision
of herself being wrestled to the ground by an
intellectual giant, she's moved the battle of the
sexes into the arena of aesthetics, and that's
all she thinks art is for, and I don't want to be
like that, I've promised myself, I'm not going
to be like that, it's difficult, when you feel your
attractiveness might depend on your being
like that, but anyway, I love Bartok. And I
keep thinking, why won't she just sit down
and listen to Bartok and then she'd know, cold
and mechanical is the last thing he is, why
won't she listen, why won't she do herself that
favour, but she won't, even though she knows

Bartok's important to me, her daughter, she won't, even for me she isn't prepared to let go of this ridiculous little counter she has that she keeps pushing in her own private game of being attractive...

MAN: She doesn't want to be like her mother. It's political, they don't want to be like their mother, whereas he, on the other hand, wants to be like his father, and why not, it works. Because his father was away, and was loved, while his mother was there, and was looked down on.

WOMAN: She wants to play as she does in her dreams.

MAN: She says to him that, when she plays, it's as if her fingers are groping in the dark, trying to find their way up to the golden notes in the sky...

WOMAN: She says that even if her fingers never find their way out of the dark to that sky of golden notes, it will have been a life well spent.

MAN: It's all sex, he says.

WOMAN: He says to her that music is all sex, he says he knows it is because he's a musician, he plays the music so he ought to know where it comes from, it comes from here, he says, that's where it comes from.

MAN: He knew, ever since he was eight, that he was going to be a musician, that's when it started, when that woman in the soft dress looked at him specially while he played, that's when he started sawing his way out of the prison of his childhood with his constantly practising bow, yes he sawed his way out of his childhood, playing The Flight of the Bumble Bee, his puberty took wing on the vibrating nuptial Flight of the Bumble Bee and he rose into the

air up out of his childhood home, and never
went back...

WOMAN: And she wants to do the same.

MAN: The same.

WOMAN: She wants to do exactly the same.

(Pause.)

WOMAN: He opens the door.

MAN: She's an exceptional young person.

WOMAN: A person, what does he mean, a person.

A person like all the rest.

MAN: What's wrong with that?

Although, if he really thought it was so nice
being a person like all the rest, why would he
have gone to so much trouble and worked so
terribly hard in order not to be a person like
all the rest, why would he have gone to so
much trouble to rise up out of that calm flat
sea of persons... natural ability, he was blessed
at the outset with natural ability, but natural
ability is only the beginning, natural ability is
meaningless unless you work, and work, and
apply the highest, the very highest standards,
constantly criticising yourself and others and
ensuring you can do everything others do
and more, yes, this is his unique destiny, he's
repelled by the thought of others doing the
same, it has been his unique destiny to rise up
out of the calm flat sea of persons, he's spun
himself up in the air like a twister, and he
maintains himself up in the air by spinning
and spinning, and if he really thought persons
were so nice, he'd be one, but instead he turns
himself inside out, and around and around,
in order to be something more, and that's

why he's never inside the music, because he's turned himself inside out...

WOMAN: And she's impressed by him, he wants her to be impressed by him, and she is, but being so impressed by him, it's doubly important for her to be impressed by herself as well, he must see that. It's doubly important for her to be able to whirl herself up in the air and spin alongside him, it's true, she wants him because he impresses her, so she can't see how he could want her unless she impresses him as well.

MAN: She does impress him.

WOMAN: As a person.

MAN: As a person.

WOMAN: She's afraid of making the attempt to be more than a person, but she's even more afraid of not making the attempt, so she will make the attempt...

MAN: But a young person who loves music, in the wonderful way that she loves music, shouldn't really be a musician. If she turns into a musician, she'll find she's unable to love music in the wonderful way she did before. He wishes he were brave enough to love music as she does, without controlling it, he's not brave enough, he has to control it, and in controlling it, he loses his peace of mind, he wishes he were brave and humble enough to love music fully and forget himself, as she does...

WOMAN: And doesn't she realise, he says, that having her there, listening, is what makes him play so well. Why does she think he was playing so well just now, he says, it was because she was there, listening. He says listening is all she has to do, and she doesn't have to take all those terrible risks, she doesn't have to play.

MAN: Because listening is part of music too. Having her there, listening, is part of his music.

WOMAN: So he'll do the playing.

MAN: He'll do the playing, and she'll do the listening.

WOMAN: She doesn't have to make music, he says, because –

MAN: She is music.

WOMAN: She's music.

MAN: She is music.

(Pause.)

WOMAN: She opens the door.

And she's music, she is music –

MAN: She doesn't have to play music –

WOMAN: And take all those terrible risks, no it's a job for life, being music, and she's almost sorry for him, because all he can do is play it.

MAN: Whereas she'll be a goddess, and he'll burn incense to her –

WOMAN: But not a contemptuous goddess. She'll be a kind one, because it's such a pleasure, listening and not having to play, so much pleasure, it's almost more than she's able to enjoy all at once, which is why she keeps thinking about it later, so that every bit of it can be properly enjoyed, if only memory didn't have a way of fixing things and holding them still which changes them... He's made the fireplace into a strange sort of altar, that's where he burns the incense. He's got parrot feathers there and bits of silver paper and a picture of Bach, and actually it's all a bit pretentious, he has long curly hair and he wears labourer's boots, and he drives an army surplus jeep, it's rather pretentious and strange, that fervent way he

talks to her and looks at her, like a caricature,
it's almost as if he's laughing at her, and if
she's really being honest with herself, she
doesn't entirely like his giggle, any more than
she's entirely sure about liking strange food,
but if she doesn't eat strange food, she'll be
back to eating home food, and she definitely
doesn't want to go back to doing that, now
she's on her way.

MAN: He brings her treasures, rare and curious
things.

WOMAN: He encourages her to eat strange food, even
forces her to eat it.

MAN: And if a particular person encourages you
to eat strange food, or even forces you to eat
it, you begin to like the fact that he takes the
trouble. And the repulsion you feel at having
to take the strange food into your mouth and
swallow it becomes inseparable from the
strange charm of that particular person.

WOMAN: And eating it changes her, and the man
who can change her, owns her, and she's
bound to adore him, and she'll ride in his
jeep, she'll ride around the city like a queen
in his pretentious broken-down jeep! with
the canvas flapping off it, and he'll clash the
gears and jar the handbrake and slam his
boots on the pedals, and oh, him changing
a wheel at night on some forecourt out of
town, he drops the jack bang on the ground
and then starts jumping up and down on
it, his hair flying, and the next minute the
car is lifted up and he's spinning a spanner
like a mad cook stirring a pot, he makes the
wheel fall off in his hands and runs around
the forecourt wheeling it like a hoop, then
he comes running back with the spare wheel
and flings it into place, the spanner starts

whirring again then the jack is thrown clunk
into the boot and he jumps into the driver's
seat and they're off... And she'll sit beside him
at night, sitting beside him while he sleeps,
with the moonlight and the night air falling
in on them through the broken window,
and his ribs like ivory in the moonlight, and
black shadow in the hollow beneath his ribs,
lying like a pieta in the bedclothes, and the
way she feels about him, it's like gold. It's
like having a hoard of gold. She sits beside
him while he sleeps, and it's like one of those
tales where the hero finds his way through
the underground caverns, and outwits the
guard dog with its eyes as big as clocks, and
finally arrives in a cave all full of gold, and
sits there bathed in the glow of all the heaps
of gold which stretch into the distance all
around. Sitting beside him as he sleeps, she
feels like a miser sitting secretly with the gold
which even at night is brighter to the miser
than the sun, because this is the brightness
she comes and communes with in secret, this
is the brightness she can lend himself to and
fully abandon herself to, unseen. She feels as
if she'll never need to sleep again, because
where could sleep take her that she'd rather
be, than here? Where could she go in her
dreams that could be better than here? She's
rolling in gold like a miser, she shouldn't
think of him as though he were gold, it isn't
right, secretly enjoying someone like that,
secretly deriving this enjoyment without his
knowledge, because he isn't able to know,
he wouldn't be able to reach to where her
enjoyment is, it's her innermost hunger for
being owned which is feasting on him. Her
infinite appreciation cuts her off from him, her

appreciation separates itself from him by the
very fact that it's appreciating, appreciating
and secretly feasting on him, this little beast,
her appreciation, is feasting and gnawing on
him, privately taking advantage of all the
opportunities it's being offered to gratify itself,
it's watching him when she watches him, even
if she watches him adoringly, especially if she
watches him adoringly, because that adoration
she feels for him separates him the adored
from her the adoring, that appetite she feels
for him can only exist precisely because he is
the object of it, she is the appetite and he is the
object, and they're separate, and what could
be more solitary and despicable than a miser,
besotted with gold which exiles her from
human company, or perhaps her love of gold
reflects her inability to be in human company,
but anyway her love of her gold defines her
as being sad and unnatural, suffering from
a social deformity, and she glimpses that
about herself, she senses a sort of deformity
in herself which she hastily conceals from her
own eyes and from everyone's eyes, she senses
the miser in herself, besotted with a glittering
treasure, cut off from other people, stunted,
because nothing is shared, nothing is being
shared...

(Pause.)

MAN: He opens the door.

WOMAN: Nothing is being shared.

MAN: He opens the door, and she's there in
a summer dress, and the quality of the
workmanship that went into her takes his
breath away, the richness of the jewels
that were selected to be her eyes, and the
smoothness of the stuff her lips are made of,

and the incredible expressive range built into the delicate muscles around those perfectly incised lips, and the unified fineness of the weave of her white skin, and the wonderful extravagant blue twists of vein and sinew in her white swan-curving hands, and the clean shape of her nose, because some people are assembled out of rough clay, but she's the work of a master, using the finest and most sumptuous materials...and there in the house, over and over, he'll take off her dress and she'll become solemn, she'll become reverential, he'll take off her dress and she'll become reverential, like someone offering a plate of sacred wafers –

WOMAN: And he'll marvel, he lifts up his hands, marvelling –

MAN: He lifts up his hands, marvelling, and he says a few holy words, and he's very moved by her frantic young warmth and her tentative young hands, and her frank young gaze and her noble young body, he's very moved and full of gratitude and ardour until eventually there comes a time when he hears himself saying, "Couldn't you resist me a bit?".

WOMAN: Resist him?

(Pause.)

MAN: He opens the door.

WOMAN: Resist him?

(Pause.)

MAN: He opens the door.

WOMAN: The shabby door.

MAN: And she's there in a summer dress, looking sulky.

WOMAN: Sulky.

MAN: Unsmiling.

WOMAN: Do girls in summer dresses always have to smile?

MAN: There's something fierce about her.

WOMAN: Because she's disturbed, violently disturbed, even if she does happen to be dressed in Laura Ashley.

MAN: Something almost masculine.

WOMAN: He means desire.

MAN: Is desire masculine?

WOMAN: She didn't make the rules.

MAN: Something frightening.

WOMAN: Is that what he wants?

MAN: She thinks she isn't frightening, standing there in her dress and her dumb turbulence, as if untouched by civilisation, reminding him how little there is to separate cultivated human beings from their heritage of unreformed savagery.

WOMAN: If that's how he sees her.

MAN: She doesn't know herself. A tigress.

WOMAN: A cliche.

MAN: Yes, the closer he comes to the centre of his emotions, the more he resembles everyone else, the closer he comes to the centre of his emotions, the old emotions, the overpowering emotions, the flash of red emotions, the old, the deceptive, the fetish emotions, the closer he comes to the centre of those pure, natural, corrupt, misleading emotions, the more cliches he discovers, and he's not alone in that. Well. He wouldn't be.

WOMAN: He wants to be frightened.

MAN: Yes, because being frightened gives him courage. He gets his courage up by being frightened.

WOMAN: So he invents a fright for himself by looking at her, violently disturbed in her summer dress, and thinking she's a frightening tigress. Whereas the frightening thing about her, the only really frightening thing about her, is that she isn't a frightening tigress, she's just her, so she isn't very frightening, so he might not get his courage up.

MAN: He has no trouble getting his courage up. At the beginning.

WOMAN: But he said all he wants is to do what she wants, that's what he told her, and he called her a goddess, and burned incense to her, etcetera. And of course she wants to do what he wants, of course she does. But she thought she was doing what he wanted, exactly what he wanted, by letting him do what she wanted.

MAN: Yes but now he's tired of doing all the work.

WOMAN: The work.

MAN: He's been working to make it wonderful for her. But she might like to do some work as well. To make it wonderful for him.

WOMAN: But it is wonderful for him. He told her.

MAN: Telling her is part of the work.

WOMAN: Isn't it wonderful for him?

MAN: Is it wonderful for her?

WOMAN: Yes.

MAN: But she doesn't tell him.

WOMAN: It's too wonderful to tell.

If it were less wonderful, maybe then she could tell. Only then it wouldn't be sincere.

MAN: Couldn't she just for once do something that isn't sincere?

WOMAN: Isn't he sincere?

MAN: He's been telling her how wonderful it is.

And now he's tired.

He wants her to help him play the game.

WOMAN: Play the game?

MAN: Well for instance, by resisting him.

WOMAN: The very thing she's in it for is that wonderful feeling of being totally unable to resist him, that wonderful feeling of being totally without resistance. But in order to be with him so she can have that wonderful feeling of being totally unable to resist him, she has to resist him. Is that what he's telling her?

MAN: Yes.

WOMAN: But that's pretending, she says.

MAN: Pretend, he says.

WOMAN: Is pretending what he means by work.

MAN: Yes pretending is what he means by work, pretending is making the effort to surpass herself.

WOMAN: No. Pretending is making the effort to stifle herself. All her short life she's been pretending to want to get up when the alarm rings in the morning, pretending to pay attention in class, pretending she never noticed the boy in the garage, and now at last, for the first time in her short life, she's finally stopped pretending, and now he's asking her to start again.

MAN: It's wonderful for her, not pretending.

WOMAN: Now he's asking her to start again, she's only just escaped into these golden fields and already he's saying she's got to go home again, and what if this is the only time she's ever going to have been in these golden fields, what if this is going to have been the only time in her life?

MAN: It's always wonderful for the person not pretending.

WOMAN: He's been pretending!

MAN: By pretending, he means presenting. It's when he chooses to do something. It's how he chooses to do something.

WOMAN: She doesn't want to do chosen things. She doesn't want to choose.

MAN: She doesn't want to work.

WOMAN: Goddesses don't work.

MAN: It's obvious that she shouldn't have believed an overenthusiastic figure of speech like that, people who use overenthusiastic figures of speech like that are people who may have temporarily lost their reason, they've lost their reason and forgotten that over-enthusiasm like that is unsustainable and they imagine, at the time, they can sustain it, when any reasonable person would see at once that it can't be sustained. But unfortunately, reasonable people are all just waiting for someone unreasonable to come along and tell them that they don't have to be reasonable after all, reasonable people are all just waiting for someone to come along and relieve them of the burden of being reasonable, so reasonable people are always believing the overenthusiastic figures of speech used by people who've temporarily lost their reason... And she is a goddess, in the sense that she's worth his pretending she's a goddess.

WOMAN: And when he said, she didn't have to play, she just had to listen –

MAN: He was being over-enthusiastic.

He was strong at the beginning. He liked being strong at the beginning, strong and alone. It's how he likes to see himself. But it's hard enough being alone when you're alone, without being alone with someone else, stuck all alone at the centre of their swoon like a rock stuck in a swamp, the only thing for miles around that possesses any resistance...

WOMAN: Girls have always been told to resist what they want, they've always been told they're being strong if they resist what they want, but she decided a long time ago it isn't strong, it's weak, she decided it's weak to let people talk her into resisting what she wants just for the sake of appearing to them to be strong. Girls shouldn't resist wanting what they want, they should be strong and want it, that's what she calls being strong.

If she resists him, he knows she'll be pretending. What's the point of pretending, if he knows?

MAN: He'll pretend not to know.

WOMAN: Is he saying, he likes pretending more than he likes the real thing?

MAN: Pretending is the real thing.

(Pause.)

MAN: He opens the door.

WOMAN: Listening and not playing, she should have known he didn't really...

MAN: Pretending is the real thing.

WOMAN: He's complicated.

MAN: She's easy. Is she always this easy?

WOMAN: She doesn't make low calculations of the sort he seems to be making.

MAN: She's accusing him of making low calculations. But she's the one making herself cheap.

WOMAN: She's surprised he thinks like that, because he's a musician, and music isn't like that, she knows, because she is music, but he isn't music, he's just a musician, after all, and if he wants to know what she thinks is cheap, she thinks it's cheap when people calculate whether people are cheap. And she's fought hard in this respect, she's fought hard to overcome the belief she was brought up with, the belief that desire in women was low and disgusting, worse, it was ridiculous, because women were supposed to know their place, like the old and the deformed, they were supposed to know they weren't of the proper rank to be allowed to feel desire. They were supposed to know that if they did feel desire, it was inappropriate and ridiculous. Desire was an animal manifestation. In the snakes and ladders game of society, desire was a slip down the snake, and if men were alarmed by a slip down the snake in themselves they positively condemned it in women, they were indulgent towards it in themselves but merciless towards it in women, because women were of a lower rank and not entitled to the same indulgence. She was brought up believing desire and defeat were the same thing.

MAN: Which they are, because if you desire a person who considers himself superior to you, you are, by the force of your desire, endorsing his impression of his superiority.

WOMAN: And that's what she's had to overcome, because if, in your fear of endorsing his impression of his superiority, you bury your own desire, if you become afraid to feel desire,

237

you wind up being afraid to feel anything,
you wind up being afraid to know what you
feel, she was afraid even to know what kind
of salad she liked, she was afraid to know
anything she felt or believed because if she
knew what she felt and believed, then she'd
also know she felt desire, and if she felt desire,
that would have meant she'd been defeated
by men, and men would ridicule her defeat.
That's what she's had to overcome, in order
to be anything, in order to be, she's had to
overcome her fear of feeling desire. And it
follows that her acquiescence to him is not
the acquiescence of a slut, her acquiescence to
him is her stand against the force of history,
and he should be happy that she's standing up
against the force of history by desiring him.

MAN: But he can't help asking what sort of girl
        allows herself to be fucked in a place like this?

WOMAN: It's a beautiful place. And anyway he's going
        to clean it up, he said so, he said he'll cut
        down the weeds in the yard, because that's
        why he wears those boots, to protect him from
        spiders when he goes to the toilet –

MAN: And he'll buy some toilet paper, he'll buy it
        for her and it will be pink, to go with the part
        it's intended for.

WOMAN: And he says to her, the place needs knocking
        down, and he's only saying it because
        she's made a point of liking it, and finding
        poetry where others might see immature
        pretentiousness and squalor, no, she likes it,
        she thinks it's poetic, and he must like it too,
        because it's his, but he can't endure having
        her agree with what he thinks, he interprets
        her agreeing with what he thinks as being an
        attempt by her to appropriate what he thinks,
        and in his determination to prevent her from

appropriating what he thinks, he abandons what he thinks, like the Russians abandoning Moscow to Napoleon. And she doesn't like being thought of by him as Napoleon. But she likes being able to understand these things, and of course he's intriguing and complicated, anyone so valuable is bound to be intriguing and complicated, like a valuable watch with a complicated action, and she doesn't mind his complications, even if they might have an unfortunate effect on her sometimes, she doesn't mind how complicated he is, she likes it, because there's more and more for her to understand and she's finding it more and more absorbing, and she wants to be absorbed in him, totally absorbed.

(Pause.)

WOMAN: He opens the door.

MAN: She wants to be totally absorbed in him.

WOMAN: Being the younger one.

MAN: But he thought she was a different sort of younger one, wilder and more difficult to approach, more like the great untamed outdoors, without which human life seems so barren, he had in mind a younger one who wouldn't be all that impressed with his artful courtship, that's why it was so artful, because he didn't think she'd be all that impressed, he expected a bit more youthful scorn and derision, a bit more judgment, he wanted a stronger sense of somebody there judging him, somebody stronger. He wanted some hate, he wanted something physically hotter. For her it was all about the angels in heaven. But the angels in heaven aren't hot... And he tries to provoke her into standing off away from him, he tries shocking her with his peculiar words and actions, like the day on the beach, when he found a lump of driftwood, huge and waterlogged and full of barnacles and he said he wanted to take it back, but could she carry it, because he couldn't carry it because of his precious hands. He couldn't have cared less about his precious hands, but this is the effect she has on him, he made a fuss about his precious hands because he wanted to see whether she'd carry this huge lump of driftwood up the beach for him, or whether she'd be shocked and reluctant.

WOMAN: And of course she dragged it up the beach for him, to protect his precious hands, knowing he couldn't have cared less about his precious hands, but glad to be asked and particularly glad to be understanding everything, and also quite glad to be showing him he couldn't shock her.

MAN: Yes she dragged the log full of barnacles laboriously up the beach, under the incurious eyes of a few people loitering there, she dragged this huge cumbersome penis up the beach for him, and she was happy, happy and proud as if she'd been his dog, and he walked beside her in the deep shame of having got what he asked for, barely suppressing the urge to kick her.

WOMAN: And he saw an acquaintance of his in the restaurant up above the beach –

MAN: And in the embarrassment of his triumph he introduced her by her Christian name only, like his dog –

WOMAN: Like his dog that belonged to him –

MAN: Like his despised familiar dog –

WOMAN: And she liked it.

(Pause.)

WOMAN: He opens the door –

MAN: She liked it.

(Pause.)

WOMAN: He opens the door –

MAN: She liked it, and she seems to regard being despised by him as some sort of saintly vocation. She seems to regard his anger as a gift. But he doesn't want to learn to like giving it. He's lonely enough without that.

WOMAN: He doesn't understand the dreadful fear she has, of finding that he and she might not be living in heaven but somewhere ordinary! He doesn't understand the fear she has, of not being the chosen one, the one with special properties, the only possible counterpart, the fellow, the accomplice, the soulmate –

MAN: The soulmate of the thief, the jackal, the rat –

WOMAN: The soulmate, the one whose mind he gazes into, he doesn't understand the fear she has of being interchangeable –

MAN: And he doesn't understand the impossible, contradictory, mythical properties she's intent on endowing him with, who is this **him** she's communing with? he thinks, she sees **him** when she looks at me, but I can't, and he sees her communing with **him** and it makes him almost afraid to speak to her, as if her mind were in a state of sanctuary, thinking about **him**, yes he's almost afraid to speak, he's afraid of blundering in and spoiling the radiance of dawn in which she appears to be sitting, the radiance of dawn on her mountain top, yes he knows that sitting in the rarefied air of the dawn on her mountain top, she's being

disturbed and annoyed by the clatter of his
packhorses and his cooking pots further down
the slope, but he has to disturb and annoy her,
because he's the rescue expedition, he has
to rescue her, he knows he's disturbing her
worship, which is an old and hated crime, he
knows when he speaks, he'll make her hate
him, she'll hate the infidel, but it's cold on her
mountain top, she'll freeze, she'll starve, the
clatter of his pots and pans is the sound of her
rescue, and he's going to have to cook warm
food and wrap her in blankets and massage
her frozen extremities and so on...and the
truth is, she annoys him, contemplating this
mythical presence at his expense, she has
to be interrupted, she has to be disturbed, it
has to be done and he's glad to do it...And
he's taken to thinking about dirty legs, white,
bow-legged, dirty legs in scuffed black boots,
and she'd be coarse and aggressive, with
knuckledusters and fake rubies on her dirty
fingers, and she wouldn't be the work of a
master using the finest and most sumptuous
materials, she'd be rough, she'd be bored,
she'd be sly, she'd be practical with her hands!
and she'd know absolutely nothing about
Bartok... And she'd call him a dirty little
swine...

WOMAN: She couldn't.

MAN: No.

(Pause.)

MAN: He opens the door.

WOMAN: She just couldn't.

MAN: She's shy.

WOMAN: She's a shy tigress.

MAN: Shyness can also be attractive.

WOMAN: In a tigress.

MAN: Shyness can be attractive, if she'd just, for instance, act shy.

WOMAN: She can't act shy.

MAN: She's too shy to act shy. She's too shy to exploit her feelings of shyness.

WOMAN: He wants her to be an exploiter.

MAN: If only she could exploit her natural shyness and reluctance, so he could see them. She has these feelings of shyness and reluctance, but she's been hiding them, perhaps she's ashamed of them in this modern university climate, but she should let him see them.

WOMAN: She couldn't.

MAN: At last he's found something she won't let him see. Despite the fact that she's so free, freely bestowing herself, as she thinks, freely acknowledging the strength of her desire, which is what he does, he freely acknowledges the strength of his desire, but the reason why he does it, is that by freely acknowledging the strength of his desire he tricks himself into thinking he's not afraid of the strength of his desire... and what she doesn't freely acknowledge is that every animal in the world fears the strength of its desire, every animal in the world, except university girls apparently, fears the humiliation of being driven towards another, driven towards a potential enemy, by the strength of its desire. Every animal has the sense, and the self-respect, to fear its desire, except university girls like her, who seem to have decided their desires are something to be welcomed with inane beatitude, like visiting sitar players from the subcontinent.

WOMAN: She's supposed to want it, but resist. But she just wants it.

MAN: Is there never a time when she's not in the mood.

WOMAN: It's not a mood, it's a –

MAN: Vocation.

Is there never a time when his one-track mind starts to annoy her.

WOMAN: His one-track mind, his one-track train and what she'd really like to do is lie down on the track in front of his one-track train as it thunders towards her...

MAN: Deferred gratification isn't something she's learned much about with her university boys.

WOMAN: Although her mother knew a woman who educated her sons in the following way. When they were out in the car and the boys were small and they wanted to pee, she'd say no, we can't stop yet, we can't stop yet, wait a bit longer, you'll just have to wait, she did this every time they were out in the car and wanted to pee, and she boasted in later years they both became excellent lovers. Divorced, but excellent lovers.

MAN: Can't she see the point of making the effort to contain herself in favour of a longer-term objective?

WOMAN: No.

MAN: If she can't see the point of making the effort for herself, he says, could she make the effort for him.

(Pause.)

MAN: He opens the door.

WOMAN: What does he want her to do?

MAN: No not like that, he's not supposed to tell her what to do.

WOMAN: But he is telling her what to do.

MAN: He's telling her to do something herself.

WOMAN: But she won't be doing it herself, because he's told her!

(Pause.)

WOMAN: He opens the door, and she listens not plays, except now she has to play, and she's accepted the strange food, except now there's more strange food, and after all she's on a voyage of discovery –

MAN: "A voyage of discovery" –

WOMAN: A voyage of discovery which is increasingly producing the crudest kind of stereotypes and cliches –

MAN: She doesn't like his cliches, but the only reason she doesn't like his cliches is, they're not her cliches, her cliches are just as much cliches as his, the difference is, she doesn't know it –

WOMAN: She's embarked on this voyage –

MAN: "Of discovery" –

WOMAN: And she doesn't want it to stop. So she'll have to go on with it.

MAN: He caught his first fish on a greasy blue boat smelling of engine oil and fish guts. His father stuck a knife in the fish to stop it flapping, and the other men praised him and patted him. And when they got back to the hotel that night, they gave him the fish to take round to the kitchens. A victory procession. Only somehow the fish was bigger, and the scales were coarser, and he knew without wanting to know that his father and the men must have swapped his fish for a bigger one he could be proud of, which meant his own fish wasn't one he could be proud of, but his own fish was the one he could be proud of, the real one, the only one, with the small silver scales, and he wanted it back. But then the chef caught sight of the fish, and his eyebrows went up and he whistled, and he said, "What a monster," and the boy held it up to him proudly, and even the wriggle of shame at the deception felt somehow delicious inside him, and they took a photograph.

(Pause.)

MAN: He opens the door.

WOMAN: And he wants to know what she used to be like when she was a schoolgirl, and she thinks it's quite nice that he's interested.

MAN: And she tells him about her voracious reading.

WOMAN: Which doesn't seem to interest him particularly.

MAN: She tells him about her voracious reading, and her cat, Timmy.

WOMAN: And he says, was she naughty.

MAN: And she wasn't.

WOMAN: He says, was she bossy.

MAN: And she wasn't.

WOMAN: And did she do anything with boys.

MAN: And she didn't.

WOMAN: And what about fantasies.

MAN: Her fantasies –

WOMAN: What about –

MAN: The boy in the garage –

WOMAN: He'd be standing in the garage on her way to school, on the forecourt of the garage, and she used to wait for that, morning and afternoon, it was the most important thing in the day, she used to look forward to walking past his garage the way she looked forward to eating a sweet, the flavour on your tongue that goes right through you, because it's eating you, the flavour from that one little sweet is eating you...

MAN: And what did she do with the boy in the garage?

WOMAN: Nothing.

MAN: And what was her fantasy about the boy in the garage?

WOMAN: Saving him from a shark.

MAN: What?

WOMAN: She used to fantasise about him in the jaws of the shark and she'd punch the shark on the nose and set him free. You can punch a shark on the nose, she said. Their nose is sensitive.

MAN: Right.

WOMAN: And sometimes she talked to the shark and asked it to let him go, and it did, because she was queen of the animals.

MAN: You be the queen of the animals and I'll be your shark, he says. You're making fun of me, she says. No, he says.

WOMAN: He laughs when he catches sight of people's privacy.

MAN: In recognition, purely in recognition.

WOMAN: Oh in recognition, of course in recognition. Recognition without mercy. Like an owl recognising the stirring of a mouse. And does he really want to know about her childhood things?

MAN: Of course he does, because she's so wonderfully –

WOMAN: Young.

MAN: Young.

WOMAN: Yes, because the things she says to him have the fresh naive colours of a primitive painting.

MAN: And he feels she's very dear to him, with her dear, fresh –

WOMAN: Youngness. And he laughingly tells her not to be embarrassed, but she is embarrassed, and what if he's just thieving among her childhood things, peering and prying among her childhood things, and watching her through her childhood bedroom window –

MAN: And laughing at her through her childhood bedroom window, and gaining pleasure from the little girl things on her dressing table, the grubby empty perfume bottle, the child's plastic lipstick –

WOMAN: And betraying her behind her back with her childhood things?

MAN: It's not that he means to be furtive or insincere, but it's something that happens once you get outside the music, no matter how much you might want to get back inside the music, you can't, you're condemned to be always outside it, furtively watching even as you take part in it with the greatest sincerity, and the furtive watching is an appetite in itself...

WOMAN: And he asks her to pretend he's some disgusting man on a bus, and as it happens, there was a disgusting man on the bus.

MAN: Pretend I'm him, he says.

WOMAN: Yes there was, a disgusting bloated old drunk, with a big underlip, and he was sitting next to her on the bus.

MAN: Pretend I'm him.

WOMAN: Pretending to be asleep.

MAN: What did he do?

WOMAN: But he wasn't asleep, he was leaning all his weight on her and –

MAN: Groping her.

WOMAN: She was shifting in her seat trying to get away from him, but as she was shifting she heard him muttering under his breath, "Do it again, I almost come". He thought she was doing it for his benefit!

MAN: Was she?

WOMAN: He was horrible.

MAN: And did she tell him off? Pretend I'm him.

WOMAN: He was horrible, that's why she couldn't stop him, because she was ashamed at finding him so horrible. She was ashamed, she thought her judgment on him was too terrible for anyone to be able to bear, because she was young, and she thought her judgment on him was as terrible as a judgment from God, because it was the truth, she was too young to be able to imagine that her judgment on him was just

the judgment of one absurd, dying creature inflicted on another absurd, dying creature, she was young and afraid that even the smallest gesture on her part would show him how horrible she found him, and that the revelation of how horrible she found him would be as terrible to him as a judgment from God, which indeed it might have been, because beautiful people and young people are often seen, by those confused in their minds by drink or desire, as heavenly messengers. So she sat and did nothing, she sat fearing that if she did anything, she'd wind up inflicting some dreadful blow on the old man pressing against her, and as she sat without doing anything, her mind began creeping into

his, her young foolish mind began creeping
into the still young and foolish mind of the old
man pressing so closely against her, the still
young and foolish mind tragically entombed
in his derelict body, her mind began creeping
into his young, foolish, saucy mind where the
young music kept playing even as his body
slumped unable to move to it. Yes her young
mind crept in and watched the performance
playing on that secret stage, the performance
unfolding in the red behind his eyes, behind
the red velvet of his eye sockets, yes there in
the dark in the red soft seats, her young mind
hid and watched him striding around on that
red velvet erotic stage that we maintain for
ourselves inside our own heads, unable to
bear the thought that our life may not offer
the erotic swaggering piratical personage
striding around on that stage any role to play...
You can go through a door, you can stumble
through a door into that inner world – it can
happen with anyone, that you see them too
close and you're through the door and into
that inner world, and you could love anyone...
and besides, when you see people do certain
things, anyone, you can't help but love them,
it's fortunate we don't often see people doing
these things, she saw a young man in the
park lying beside his girlfriend and he raised
himself on one elbow, and gently shifted
his hips closer while his eyes were locked in
hers, it's fortunate we hardly ever see these
things, because if we did, we'd all be in love
with everyone, ugly or beautiful, young or
old, we'd all be in love with the ceremony of
certain gestures, we'd all be in love with the
love-worthiness shining out of certain gestures,
we'd all be saints knowing nothing but love,

free of that sense of self, that painful sense of self, the grazed knees, the trudging feet... and the world would come to an end...

MAN: Pretend I'm him!

WOMAN: Is that all he can say?

MAN: It's all he wants to say.

WOMAN: He doesn't want to know her. He's contemptible.

MAN: She thinks he doesn't understand the hope of being known, and the despair of not being known. The despair of ever being known is one that some people arrive at early in life, but he hasn't arrived at it, he still has enough hope of being known to be able to experience acute pains, the same as her, when once again he fails to be known...But these pains, far from being banished by intimacy, as she appears to believe, often strike most ferociously within the privileged walls of intimacy, where people have come to know each other well enough to reveal to each other the full force of their mutual incomprehension, and knowing this, he refuses to subscribe to her ignorant theories of how well and how fully and how intimately he and she are supposed to know each other. Not only can he not subscribe to these ignorant optimistic theories, but their very ignorant optimism goads him on to flout these theories of hers in the most decisive way, opposing some stubborn whim of his own when she's trying her hardest to put these ignorant theories of hers into practice, and besides, these stubborn whims of his should surely be part of their mutual knowledge, which she so much wants to promote, yes she ought to take account of these stubborn whims of his in all their brutishness, and perhaps it's

the accumulated pain of failing to be known
that makes him insist so brutishly on these
whims, these deliberate crude simplifications,
and perhaps he finds some paradoxical
comfort in being so deliberately and crudely
contemptible, yes contemptible...

MAN: He should be punished!

WOMAN: No.

MAN: He must be punished!

WOMAN: No.

MAN: She's punishing him by saying no.

WOMAN: No.

MAN: And he's a dirty little swine!

WOMAN: No!

MAN: Again!

WOMAN: No!

MAN: Again!

WOMAN: No!

MAN: Again!

WOMAN: And she's tired. And she's outside the music.
And she was right after all about that giggle of
his, it's the giggle of a madman trapped on the
outside of everything

he does, only able to do it at one remove,
because he's lost the vital spark, he can't find
the vital spark –

MAN: And little by little he looks at her and sees that
she's becoming ugly.

WOMAN: And why is she becoming ugly, because
thanks to him she's no longer inside the music,
thanks to him she's beginning to play the
music, more and more she's playing the music,
she used to be inside the music, and now she's
outside it, and she finds herself noting how
effective it is if she plays this way, or that way,

she gets into the habit of remembering how effective it was the last time, so she can do it again the next time, just as effectively, and again the next time, just as effectively, and each time she does it, she finds herself moving further and further away from the music, and still she's following him, further and further away from the music, growing more and more certain she's never going to find her way back inside the music, ever again –

MAN: Sometimes he looks at her stern face and he's really afraid of her.

WOMAN: He dares to be afraid of her stern face!

MAN: Yes sometimes he looks at her stern despairing face and wants to snivel like a guilty schoolboy...She could easily have him snivelling and sniggering like a guilty schoolboy. She hates it when he snivels like a schoolboy, but somehow the more she hates it, the more he snivels, and the more he snivels, the more she hates it...

WOMAN: And the more she hates it, the more she comes to resemble him, and it's making her so tired, and still she finds another sharp answer to throw at him, and she feels as if her brain her mouth her eyes were full of sand and she can hardly bear to rouse herself to say even another word to him, but she does rouse herself and out of her sand-filled mouth she does say another word...And she wishes she were leaning on her father's coat, or leaning on the wall of the house when the sun's been on it all day, she wishes she were leaning on that warm rough man-smelling coat, her father's coat, but the wall, and her father's coat, and her father, all turned to sand long ago...And she herself is turning to sand, under the corrupting influence of tired old routines, tired old rituals enacted in order to summon the vital spark which becomes ever more elusive as the ritual becomes ever more absurd –

MAN: She used to talk about the truth in physical things, she and her university friends always used to be talking about the truth in physical things, and saying how the truth in physical things is spontaneous, not some tired old routine, some sorrowful ritual. But he said to her, that physical things are rituals, physical things are sorrowful rituals, and that she ought to admit there might be more to discovering physical things than discovering what she used to refer to as freedom.

Discovering physical things is discovering limitations, habits and cliches, but a sorrowful ritual, as she calls it, is better than nothing...

WOMAN: So he and she are supposed to engage in these sorrowful rituals...

MAN: Better than nothing, and the more accustomed you become to these sorrowful rituals, the less sorrowful and the more normal they become, and the more pleasure you're able to find in them, the more pleasure and mastery you're able to enjoy within these rituals which you've come to know so well and which you can manage and drive so well...

WOMAN: And more and more she does find pleasure in them, because they're all she knows, these rituals where they meet every day and jockey for advantage, and the advantage they're jockeying for is the advantage of being the weaker one, dominated and enveloped by the other's powerful presence, and he gradually emerges victorious from this jockeying to be the weaker one, because he's the stronger

one, and every day he incites her to despise
him, until she does despise him, every day he
incites her to abuse him, until she does abuse
him, and she might just as well dress herself
up as a witch with a broomstick to beat him
with, or as his old schoolteacher who used
to scold him and hit him with a book, or as
death dressed in black, the colour of rotting
flesh, and carrying a scythe, yes she might
just as well, she might just as well dress up in
black, tie her flesh up in black so it bulges in a
parody of youthful abundance, and she might
just as well take a whip in her hands, and
there's never any mercy!

MAN: There's never any mercy, isn't that what he's
been telling her all along, and he's glad she's
finally able to admit it, and why did she ever
imagine anything else, because was it merciful
of her, making him out to be her firebird
and her hoard of gold, was it merciful of her,
foisting that travesty on him, in the service
of her boundless appetite, is that any better
than the travesties he tried to foist on her,
in the service of his boundless appetite, and
they've foisted their travesties in each other's
direction, and missed, and there's never any
mercy, on either side!

        (Pause.)

MAN: He opens the door.

WOMAN: And they're old...

MAN: She's run her course, he's comfortable
with her, it's a long time since he felt
uncomfortable in her presence, those days
of feeling uncomfortable in her presence,
uncomfortable because of the sense of peril
brought about by the possibility of fulfilment,

those days of anguished discomfort in each other's presence are gone, he's comfortable in her presence now, because he no longer feels the dangerous possibility of fulfilment. He's so comfortable in her presence now, she might as well not be there.

WOMAN: They've been progressively inoculated against each other's presence, and the longer they've been together, the more perfect their immunity to each other's presence has become.

MAN: He sometimes thinks about starting again with a younger one, he sometimes thinks he'd like to start again, in the hot frantic embrace of a younger one still capable of ignorance, yes he needs ignorance that he can slowly consume, the slow consumption of ignorance is a source of light and energy for him. Yes a younger one, a new one, one who hasn't been here before, because this one is ashamed that he used to thrill her, and her boredom and dismissiveness are her revenge, and they've done up the house, and they've gloss-painted the door –

WOMAN: And she plays music.

MAN: And she always used to be behind the rhythm, but now –

WOMAN: Now she's learned how to lift herself up into the condition of the rhythm, she's learned how to call up the core of her being through the rhythm and it rises, the core of her being becomes the voice of her instrument, and her instrument is muscular, it's so muscular she can aim it, and she throbs and chugs with the energy of the music, she's become an engine, throbbing and chugging... And she wishes she didn't throb and chug, because she wanted to be sustained by the music, not play it, even though she does play it, but he wants to be sustained by the music too, and not play it, even though he does play it, and she should have known, as soon as it started, she should have known how it would end –

MAN: And she's never understood the risk she runs, being so bored and dismissive, he accepts it of course as her right, he accepts it as a consequence of the long and complicated contractual arrangements that exist between them, but just the same she's amazingly careless about wounding him, she's amazingly careless about wounding someone who could break her arm, or smash her face in, he could very easily strangle her with his bare hands, and cut her up, and post her limbs to different parts of the country... Though of course, the price of any co-existence with her is a polite abstention from even the merest suggestion of physical force, even the slightest reminder of his physical superiority... But he wishes she'd think of it sometimes, and give him some small credit for his forbearance... He himself can't help but be aware of the constant forbearance he exercises towards her, and he's amazed at the thoughtless vanity with which she walks up to the cannon's mouth and pipes her dissatisfaction into it. She seems quite unconscious of his forbearance and not in the least grateful...

WOMAN: She deceives him in her mind with a younger violinist.

MAN: And they're always fleeing from what they are into what they used to be, which in turn brings them back to what they are, and then they have to flee again...

(Pause.)

MAN: They could go to the place around the corner.

WOMAN: If that's what he wants.

MAN: They've often enjoyed themselves there.

WOMAN: Just because they've sometimes enjoyed themselves there, the tragedy of their lives is of no importance.

MAN: He's offering her some relief from the tragedy of their lives.

WOMAN: She doesn't want relief from the tragedy of their lives. Tragedy that can be relieved is tragedy that can be discounted, tragedy that can be relieved is as good as no tragedy at all. He can feed her all he likes at the little place around the corner and she'll eat it, she'll eat it all and more, but all the time she's eating it, she'll be tragic. She can eat and be tragic at the same time, she can weep even as she's cramming her mouth full of food, she'll be eating, and the flavour of the food will actually be enhanced by the flavour of her tears and that in itself is tragic, it's tragic because it's ridiculous, living in this ridiculous non-tragic situation is their tragedy, and the more they eat, the more tragic it becomes, the more they eat, the more tragic the triviality of their tragedy becomes.

MAN: So she doesn't want to go to the little place around the corner.

         (Pause.)

WOMAN: The first day at school.

MAN: Watching children being propelled around the playground by incomprehensible forces.

WOMAN: Running and grabbing at each other and shouting incomprehensible things.

MAN: You're in the midst of this frenzy, thinking you must be there by accident, and you don't see how you're ever going to fathom the madness of their comings and goings, or the energy that propels them.

WOMAN: Then as you're watching, you see someone else watching too, and you and she exchange glances, and in that glance is transmitted the entirety of what she's seeing and what you're seeing, and the fact of both seeing at once.

MAN: And suddenly it's as if the others are rushing about underwater.

WOMAN: Rushing about in an element that you and she have lifted your heads out of just in time to catch each other's glance, and another layer has been added to the world, a layer where you and she can look at each other and know you're both seeing the same things around you, surprised and delighted at both seeing the same things at the same time.

MAN: Then you and he start to rush about like the other children, you and he can rush about like the other children now because you have each other's eyes to steer by, and between you, you're able to map out a whole comprehensible universe, with the link between your eyes as the centre of it.

WOMAN: And you know you won't deny each other, or pretend to forget the acknowledgment you've made of each other, because it was so hard to find each other in the first place, and so lucky to find each other, and to deny each other would be to sink back into chaos and pain, the shared intelligence is a lovely haven, so why would either of you ever want to be without it...

MAN: Everyone dreams of encountering a figure on the path, armed exactly the same as you are yourself, weapon for weapon, and you dream of the day when you and that other figure will stand exactly facing each other and carefully lay your weapons down, one at a time, never taking your eyes off each other, carefully take off your armour piece by piece and lay it down, watching each other, until at last you slip into the river together, naked and happy to drown...

WOMAN: And touching each other with a touch that has eyes, touching each other with a touch that sees everything...

THE END

SHADOWMOUTH

Characters

MAN

MOTHER

BOY

PAUL

DAISY

shadowmouth

MAN   The ward was full of old men

Babbling, wandering about

Counting up to ten, not reaching it

He was fifteen, fresh as a rose, apart from the bandage

His mother was saying

MOTHER   I've brought his pyjamas from home

MAN   He never wore pyjamas

MOTHER   He won't wear them

MAN   No

MOTHER   He resents me

I try

He resents me because I try

I put on lipstick

He says I'm putting on an expression

I make myself presentable

And it feels like a betrayal

Sweetheart!

BOY   Mum

MOTHER   Look at you

BOY   I'm

MOTHER   Slippers, where are your slippers

You must have your slippers

BOY   Mum

MOTHER   They don't sweep under the beds

> They actually sweep things under the beds,
> I've seen them
>
> All sorts of things
>
> Dressings, tubes, fruit, flowers

BOY   I'm sorry

MAN   I didn't know what to say, any more
than she did

She'd made sandwiches

MOTHER   It's nobody's fault

Is it

MAN   She put the sandwiches on the bed cover

As if he were going on a train journey, leaving
her small on the platform

I live alone

I'm fine with that

In summer, I make a bed on the balcony

And when the neighbours' music has
throbbed itself to a standstill

And the silence is beginning to be louder than
the traffic

And the city breathes out

That's when I can almost bear to…

I first met him in a cinema

They had a knife

A collector's item, I'm sure

Anyway, they'd collected it

Still, I was honoured they showed it me

It bespeaks a level of trust

Also on my side

He was homeless, he said

Well

I have the space

I don't believe a place of safety is a place you lock

It's a place you decide not to lock

He was new to my method of tea making

I've discovered after years of experiment, if you keep the tea in the pot all day you can simply put this much into a mug and top it up with hot water, you can hardly tell the difference

It's an efficient method

BOY   Thanks

(*Sips tea.*) Interesting

MAN   I found his presence extraordinary

His bag his shoes his jacket

His hand around the mug of tea

BOY   It's very kind of you

MAN   Not at all

MOTHER   He let the cat on the good white couch

That I bought after his father left

He deliberately

And then of course it descended into a row about the drugs and

I didn't mean it

Perhaps I did

As revenge

Because I couldn't help him

I told him it was for his own good

I ripped up his posters

MAN   He liked hamburgers, Radiohead, Frida Kahlo

Footballers' Wives

None of his socks matched

He made a hammock for his stuffed owl

MOTHER   His father was an animal

Why did I marry him?

Because he was an animal

End of story

For me, inside

It doesn't show

I wouldn't give him the satisfaction

MAN   He told me, even as a kid he used to sneak out at night

He used to climb out of the window

He didn't want any pane of glass or piece of wood between him and the moon

He was in love with her

He loved her bleak little face shining coldly so far away

He felt a chill that was a thrill looking up at her

He loved her even more at midnight than in the evening when she swung down close

In the evening she loomed large like a mother

But at midnight she rode high in the sky like the skull of a little princess, and when he looked up at her, he could feel the vertigo of immense times and distances, seen from her vantage point

He didn't want anything as much as he wanted
that cold thrill

At times when he missed her, he'd steal a few
mouthfuls of his mother's scotch, and then a
few more

BOY   School's, you know

       Not where I am in my head

MAN   School

       School people

       Sniggering with embarrassment in the face of
anything true

       They know they're faking it but you'll never
get them to admit it, never

       And they practise cruelties large and small on
you, if you show them up

BOY   Sports day

       Cheering and yelling and acting as if it
mattered

       If you didn't, teachers noted your attitude
problem and kids threw your lunch over the
fence

       It was the one thing they definitely agreed
about, you had to act as if it mattered

       Sports day was when I discovered I could be
there and go somewhere else in my mind

       Really go

       I went into a wood with huge leaves

       And leopards

MAN   Daylight people scare me

       The ignorant certainty they profess

       The confident ring of their footsteps

Their desire for everyone to be up and in
harness

Day is always fresh and new

Exhausting

Night is what you return to

Where everything that used to be still lingers

And Juliet still talks to the moon

He used to walk by the rail yards in the
moonlight

BOY   One night, I reached the centre of town

It was like discovering a whole unknown tribe

People awake at night

Like me

Going about their business in the middle of
the night as if it were the most ordinary thing
in the world

While everyone I knew was asleep in bed

All the rules were turned upside-down

Drink, drugs, visions and sex were everyone's
serious business

While the business buildings, the government
offices, the gallery, the museum, slept like dark
forgotten giants

There were lit up places floating like boats on
the city darkness, and in them were pirates
and ruffians, girls with smudged eyes and
bare flesh, drinkers staring down into wells of
alcohol, fat hairy men in black leather, women
in bowler hats, people with cigarette holders
and rings on their fingers

It was like seeing through the skin of the city
down into where it had always been like this,
century upon century

It was like seeing the hidden life now visible
and glowing, everyone decked out as the self
of their dreams

I didn't know who I might see lining up to the
bar

Christopher Marlowe

The Queen of Sheba

I'd never seen a floor with so much dirt on it,
the dirt of centuries

Fag-ends in drifts

Grit piling up against the skirting boards

And people slopping drinks as they passed,
calling to each other across the noise

The air was at saturation point with alcohol,
smoke and sweat

The place felt ready to burst into flame

It was here

Whatever would make me real

I was in the room with the animal

I could see its rolling eye, its velvet mouth, its
foam-flecked shoulder, its huge flank

I could feel the heavy stumbling of its hooves
in the straw

I loved it

MAN   You see, I couldn't see anything wrong
with

On the contrary

In his love of what he saw and experienced,
he seemed to me to be magically beautiful

And through him, if I had him near me

I could see the whole world as magically
beautiful

He adorned my life

271

He probably brought the drugs to school to
hold on to like good magic

As much as to sell them

He was expelled of course

He found himself a job at a filling-station,
casual employment

MAN   What about your age

BOY   Identity card

MAN   What

BOY   It says I'm eighteen

Look

I made it

MAN   Yes

I see

BOY   No-one asks

This is the city

PAUL   How much

BOY   Cocktail shaker twelve twenty

PAUL   It's got a mark

BOY   I can't take money off, you tosser

PAUL   See the mark

It's damaged

BOY   I know it's damaged, you damaged it

PAUL   I've done bar work

The manager had it in for me

I said, life's not worth living, if I can't give my
friends a drink

Twat said I couldn't control my temper

So I nutted him

MAN   He met a girl there

She was older

A cradle-snatcher

She took him out, bought him things

Glamorous

DAISY I want pizza

BOY But it's

DAISY Shut up. I want pizza. Where's the fridge

This is what you've got in your fridge

A lemon

A lemon

How do you people exist

Let's go shopping

BOY It's the middle of the night

DAISY I'm going shopping

BOY Sit down before you fall down

Sit down. I'll go shopping

DAISY Come here. You're not going anywhere

He can go shopping

Hullo!

BOY Quiet you'll wake him up

DAISY Hullo!

BOY Shut up he's asleep

DAISY He won't mind

Your landlord

Landlord!

BOY Shut up. No-one's going shopping

DAISY All right darling

You darling

Are you angry with me darling?

Come here

I love you

        God

MAN I was glad he was straight
      No, really
      The worst thing is hope

      I've always watched boys
      Ever since I was a boy
      Vaulting over railings
      Kicking cigarette packets
      Eyeing girls

      I was always watching
      Learning how to be one

      I never did learn

BOY Morning
MAN Good morning
BOY Sorry about the noise last night
      We didn't disturb you
MAN Hardly at all
BOY You don't mind
MAN No
BOY You're not upset with me
MAN Why would I be upset
BOY So everything's all right then
MAN How are you this morning?
BOY She's nuts
      I think I'm in love

MAN Well, of course he knew I
      He was indispensable to my peace of mind
      His beauty was my redemption

That room, when he was in it, was satisfied

It was filled

I didn't even have to think about it

That's how absolutely solved the problem of
that room was

Before when it was empty it was on my mind
obscurely

A sense of something lacking, barely conscious

A worry about lopsided bookshelves or bad
chairs or the room somehow eating itself

Suddenly everything in the room was perfect,
glowing and secure

And I could get on with making toast or
writing my history of monasteries

Knowing he was there

While he

I don't know

Entertained, why not?

Or smoked

Sharpened pencils

Listened to the music of the spheres

He said he found himself dragging the knife
across his wrist

And suddenly awoke to a knowledge of what
he was doing

And that's when he came and showed me

What had he done

What had he suffered

It was the last thing I ever thought he'd

It was the opposite of everything I thought he

He was life, generous life

He wasn't even distorted in the minor,
unhappy way most people are
There was nothing twisted, mean, narrow or
obsessive about him
No mark of pressure, no deathly misery
Just a profusion of loveliness, dreams
Yet he

How could I not have seen?

What had I been looking at?

I half expected the shine on the hospital floor
To throw up earth and boulders

And how could he have had to go through this
alone, when I

Loved him

I shuddered with terror thinking he might
have died
And I'd been happy, useless, criminally
contented

And what was I going to say to his mother?
The shock would be

MOTHER   Of course, it's not the first time
         He did tell you
   MAN   No
MOTHER   Are you all right?
   MAN   He'd told me nothing
         I felt
         Like an orphan

MOTHER I want you to know

It's nothing to do with you

MAN Like an orphan

Selfish

In his darkest hour

But I did, I felt cheated, bereft, insignificant, criticised

While hating myself for feeling like that

But is it possible to love someone without needing them?

How would you know it was love, if your very existence and comfort didn't hang on theirs?

DAISY I thought he and I were together

I was

He wasn't

MAN I know

DAISY The little sod

I've been outsmarted by a fifteen year-old

It's all secret with him

Secretive

I feel like tearing him apart

MAN I know

Then she went out and bought him a watch, to cover up the scar

One isn't consistent

Perhaps it was really as he said, a thing secret from him as well as from us

A lake of tears, rising unnoticed, until the banks broke

And after that

Emptiness

MOTHER What happens
When you come out of hospital
You might like to come back home

BOY I

MAN He said he wouldn't
His mother didn't try to dissuade him
She wasn't very confident
Especially after that

Whereas I revived
I meant something
I could do something
He'd be saved

I got rid of the bathmat
Bought some new towels
New records
Daisy cooked for his homecoming

DAISY Are you hungry?
Do you want to sleep
What do you want

MAN I'll make some tea

DAISY Do you want tea?

BOY It's strange

DAISY What

BOY Everything

DAISY Us, are we strange

BOY Everything

DAISY Where are you going

BOY The toilet

DAISY   Do you want us to go with you?

MAN   Strange
        Yes, we were

        I found I was always wanting the world to put
        on its best face
        The one that would woo him and keep him
        The perpetual question was
        What face was that?
        Should I empty the ashtray (or would that
        prompt thoughts of mortality)?
        Should I not (or would that prompt them even
        more)?
        Should I switch on the light (or would that be
        too bleak)?
        Should I let the darkness grow (or would that
        be too symbolic)?
        What did he see?
        What lifted him? What threw him down?
        What reassured him? What made him afraid?
        What if that which reassured him actually
        made him afraid because it seemed to be
        trying to reassure him?

        I bought fruit to nourish him
        A pot of daffodils to cheer and strengthen him
        I'm not claiming any of this was rational
        I felt like some sort of kaleidoscope, with all
        surfaces splintered, shaken up, disturbed and
        disturbing
        We drank tea, played chess
        Normal as could be
        Nothing was normal
        I kept imagining how things might look to him

What might set him off

I began to hate the daffodils

Their sturdy cheerful brutish flowers

I hesitated too long over the chessboard and
started seeing dead horses

I dreaded his mother's visits

MOTHER   I wanted him home but he chose this

Do you know what I've decided?

I'm not the problem

He's the problem

If I think of it any other way, I'll go quite mad

It's good of you to let him stay

I hope he's grateful

I think he finds me far too boring, don't you
sweetheart

I was bohemian when I was young

Cockroaches in the saucepans, that sort of
thing

You're lucky to have kept your cool

Whereas I have an almost irresistible urge to
get the hoover out

Perhaps you'll be the saving of him

I hope something will

He's keeping his appointments, isn't he

With the psychiatrist

I'm sure if anyone can make him do what he
should, it's you

He pays no attention to me

MAN   She was always trying to make me into her
representative

MOTHER   I have absolute faith in you

My friends say I'm crazy

But I know you're a truly good person

A selfless person

If I thought for one minute there was anything wrong about his being here I'd be doing everything in my power to put a stop to it

MAN   I saw each sentence as an arrow threatening his fragile peace of mind

Or mine

But he

Gave her his washing

PAUL in.

As for Paul, he was so young, but he never smiled

He was a graven image

He seldom looked at me

Sometimes a scrap of a glance

Moving his face would have been giving too much away in the poker game of life

His nerves were always on edge and that was why he was so still

Once he brought me some opera glasses, once, a bag full of shoe-trees

Thank you

So many

Are you sure you don't have a use for them?

It dawned on me

Paul and he were

Oh God

Well of course I kept thinking about times he'd

I don't know

Helped with the rubbish

Borrowed my aftershave

DAISY He's not gay

He's just

Too young to know the difference

I'm not jealous

It's him I'm worried about

Laugh at me, go on

Fucking gays

MAN But anyway, I couldn't have invited him under my roof and just

Above all, in the circumstances

Even forgetting his age

And mine

If he'd wanted

If he'd ever shown the slightest

The fact is, nothing took place

And that was as it should be

PAUL (*To DAISY.*) I'm going now

DAISY Good riddance

BOY (*To DAISY.*) Paul and I are going

Do you want to come?

DAISY Where?

I'll come

MAN   My pot plants had drugs hidden in
them, I'm sure of it

PAUL   What are you doing?

MAN   These plants need a good soaking

PAUL   Yeah

MAN   What's the matter?

Jealousy

Not just the fear of loss, but the fear of being
dried away to nothing

A prophetic fear, of course

If a choice had existed between him being
happy with Paul

And him being dead

If that had been the choice

What would I have

Paul made him well

That's the paradox

The three of us went to the shop one night and
stole cloth, for Paul's mother's curtains

It's never been missed

I'm the only one who knows the stock

The owners are idle and unpleasant

I still work there

The greatest love, they say, is the love that lets
another person be

I didn't want to want anything from him,
nothing at all, just his freedom

That's how I felt, in moments of clarity

        You're home early

BOY   I went in the door and Paul was at the other end of the bar

        Talking to the Civil Servant

        Bicycle Man

        He waved

        By the time I got through the crowd I couldn't see him

        I kept looking

        Then I waited

        Got drunk

        Got thrown out

        Smashed a window

MAN   What do you want to do

        With your life

BOY   Maybe art school

MAN   Art school

        It wasn't impossible

        He needed the O levels but he could be signed up somewhere, I began making enquiries

        He started on a portfolio

BOY   Bollocks, it's bollocks

MAN   But these are

        Not bad

BOY   They're bollocks

MAN   What's this

BOY   I can see it in front of my eyes when I close my eyes

It's a tree with its roots in a rock and the light
shines through it and it flies

This isn't anything like

MAN   You've only just begun

BOY   It will never be anything like

MAN   That was the end of the art school idea

PAUL in.

BOY   Where were you Saturday

PAUL   Where were you

What have you been up to

BOY   What have you

PAUL   (*To MAN.*) Hullo

(*To BOY.*) What's he looking at

BOY   You

MAN   He's busy

BOY   It's fine

PAUL   He's fine

What's your game?

MAN   I beg your pardon

PAUL   What do you want?

MAN   I

PAUL   I know what you want

I know what you want

Nonce

PAUL leaves with BOY.

MAN   I bore it for his sake

DAISY in.

DAISY   Is he here?

Where is he

The little shit

Have you got a drink?

What's that you're writing?

I'm not disturbing you

How could you let him run around with Paul?

Don't you care?

It's irresponsible

It's not good for him, all this

He should be in an institution

He should be locked up

Crazy little shit

And as for you

No, go on with your work

I'll just sit here

MOTHER   Is he here?

The thing is

I'm dead inside

Since his father left

Do you understand what I'm saying?

So when he started having all these problems I
think what I felt, deep down, was

He was acting out everything that was wrong
with me

I felt so ashamed of myself

I could hardly stand the sight of him

Isn't that terrible

I think he and I have more in common than
you think

I'm a survivor, that's all

Oh God, I don't mean he

But if life's trying to kill you, you fight it

Does that make sense?

Have you ever been married?

BOY in.

Sweetheart

MAN   One could easily spend all of one's
time just living

Steering a course, that's what I felt I

Sometimes they all visited at once

MOTHER   Is he in?

DAISY   Is he in?

PAUL   Is he in?

MAN   I generally retreated to the balcony

PAUL   (*To MOTHER.*) Do you want a cigarette

DAISY   She doesn't smoke

MOTHER   I'll have one

I've brought your washing

PAUL   Lucky boy

BOY   Yes, aren't I

MOTHER   What do you do, Paul?

PAUL   Oh

DAISY   What doesn't he do?

MOTHER   Are you two together?

MAN   I constantly felt like someone trying to
guide a sleep-walker

Talking sensibly, doing everything sensibly

My mind in a panic constantly seeing him fall

PAUL   Catch

BOY   What is it

Thanks

PAUL   How much will you give me

BOY   For this?

PAUL   Twenty

BOY   Keep it

PAUL   Don't you want it? It's a present

Give me fifteen

BOY   I thought you said it was a present

PAUL   I got that for you

BOY   Where are you going?

Stay

PAUL   Get off

BOY   Stay

PAUL   I'm going now

BOY   Tramp

PAUL   (*Hits him.*) Don't you ever

BOY   You're just a little tramp

PAUL   (*Hits him repeatedly.*) Don't you ever call me
that again

What did I say

(*Hits him.*) I said what did I say

MAN   I went for him

MAN winds up on the floor, badly beaten.

Of course, he took Paul back again

PAUL   He said he loves me

It's patronising

He wants me to stop him thinking

So he won't top himself

Wanker

He thinks he can get emotional

If he thinks I'd cry over him

Fuck him

BOY   I don't know what's the matter with me

I'll always be alone

Have you always been alone?

BOY kisses MAN.

MAN   I have

BOY   Sorry, I'm sorry

MAN   Forget it

It didn't happen

BOY   I'm sorry

MAN   He called Daisy then

He made her coffee with honey

On his sixteenth, his mother took us out

The restaurant was Italian

It smelt of vegetables being kept warm

MOTHER   What's everyone having?

What's Paul having

PAUL   Nothing thanks

MOTHER   Nothing

PAUL   No thanks

MOTHER   Is there nothing here you like?

Minestrone?

Cannelloni?

There's chips

BOY   Don't you like this place?

PAUL   It's OK

MOTHER   Does Paul not like this place?

BOY   He's OK

MOTHER Are you all right, sweetheart?

BOY Yeah

MOTHER They'll bring us a tiramisu at the end, with a sparkler

MAN It's a cake

Do you like cake, Paul?

DAISY You can have some of my spaghetti

MOTHER And mine

PAUL whispers to BOY.

BOY He'd like some bread

MOTHER Of course

Waiter!

MAN I took him walking out of town near the reservoir

Sitting on the ground with grass waving all around us in the sun, lit to vanishing point, substantial and insubstantial, with the glittering water beyond

I hoped he found it as beautiful as I did

I was looking at the scene, hoping it would be enough for him

When I found myself not hoping but questioning whether it was indeed enough for him

And to my alarm as I tried to hold to the vision

It started to seem faded

Or like a thin painted scarf drawn over a void

And I seemed to be seeing it with the light gone out of it, fading to ashes

As I thought oh no, oh no

Because if it wasn't enough for him, he might die

And suddenly it wasn't enough for me,
because I'd questioned it

And I couldn't even tell any more why I'd
ever thought it was enough

He was eating an apple quite happily

And I certainly couldn't ask him if he saw
what I saw, in case he did

BOY I'm glad we came here

I feel all right with you

At home, I can't explain it

The loneliness, looking at the sofa, linen
texture, round fat feet

It's so plump

Sitting on its fat feet alone in the universe, all
dressed up and nowhere to go

And the haircord on the floor

So empty and busy, with a square of sunlight
on it

MAN Just then

We could have –

The moment was so –

It was so –

It was too –

To use it for anything would have been
vandalism

He would have said no in any case

I hope he would

Because otherwise, that could have been the
moment that changed everything
One ordinary evening he got ready to go out
In a cloud of Paco Rabanne (mine)

They found his body two days later

I didn't see it, but I keep seeing it

You can be right next to someone and still
they

I still don't know what he suffered
I'm still trying to, I follow all the pathways,
sitting here at night

It's a strange thing
I never saw him weep

And he never said hullo or goodbye, he was
always just there or gone again

Of course it could have been his childhood,
his love-life, something coherent
Any or all of the difficulties
But if a difficult life made people kill
themselves
Millions would do it every day

Depression, that's a thing people talk about
In affluent societies
Maybe at the top of the tree, you see more,
you see all the way to the boundary
And everything between
All this shackled complicated half-life

I stand accused by his death of finding the
world good enough

I don't find it good enough but I can't find the
place

The extreme place where

So many times I've tried to follow him there

To be company for him

Not leave him going through it alone

But

His wound isn't mine

Perhaps I'm unworthy

I'm left here wishing the world into some kind
of state where he could thrive

The funeral was

His mother had him cremated

Empty grey room, rows of empty seating

Piped music

She cut me

Didn't even look at me

Wherever he was, he wasn't there

His presence was always radiant

You can bring forth all sorts of reasons why it
might have happened

Maybe even read the circumstances in such a
way that it was bound to have happened

But that's not how it seemed, not at all

I don't understand any of it, not even the first
thing, that one moment he was there, warm
and breathing, the next, vanished

I look for him all the time

In drinking places, or under the street trees at night

I look for him

Waking or sleeping

In some way, I always knew it would happen

But not because of any particular circumstances I could see

It wasn't the circumstances that made me know he'd do it

It was him, something about him

Nothing tragic, just something

Unearthly beautiful, that you know you're not good enough for

He climbed into the park to do it

Had a drink

He died leaning up against a big park tree mottled in the lamplight

Ranks of worshipping flowers erect in the night air

The small moon visible through the leaves

A tryst, that's what I really believe

He died going towards beauty as I

Go towards him

He died going towards the life he was born to know

THE END

GLIDE

Characters

Tentatively two voices, as different as possible, both women. M a 'concerned' sort of motherly voice with a big expressive range that includes light, deprecating, ironic and sentimental aspects, m some kind of fierce younger voice

SECTION A

M   Glide

m   (Fierce) Yes

M   Not dwelling on it

m   No

M   Glide

m   Yes

M   She shouldn't dwell on it
     Just because people note it

m   (Distress) Ah

M   They could hardly fail to note it

m   Ah

M   The survival instinct
     Forces us to note
     Only in passing
     But it does still
     Force us to note
     Any defect
     Not dwelling on it
     But we do just instinctively note

m   Ah

M   Even if only in passing
     Any defect
     Any discrepancy
     Any imbalance

        Just as we instinctively desire to note
        Whether the house we live in
        Has a rotten floorboard

m   He caught sight of me
        There was a flash of expectancy on his face
        Dispelled at once by a blankness

M   Glide

m   Ah

M   Glide

m   Yes

M   Glide

m   Foot forward
        Roughly treated in return for its pains
        The stronger one
        I also punish the weaker one
        I stand on it hard when it hurts
        I punish the weaker one for being weak
        And I punish the stronger one
        For not sharing the misfortune of the weaker
        one

M   Glide

m   Yes
        When I desire someone
        I cease to be attractive
        Because desire is self-forgetfulness
        And in forgetting myself
        I forget to disguise my unattractiveness

M   Glide

m   Yes

M   The hardest thing to change, the saying goes
    Is the way you hold your spoon
    So it's surprising
    How many people do change the way they
    hold their spoon
    And much else
    Glide

m   Yes

M   They do change deeply rooted things that
    betray their origins
    And they do even betray their origins
    In changing these things
    A person who changes the way he holds his
    spoon

m   Wrenches himself into a shape unknown to his
    family

M   Breaking the stubbornest fibres of loyalty
    And becoming strange to those people
    To whom he was formerly
    Known down to the very elbows at the kitchen
    table
    Down to the very scrape of his chair
    Throwing up a screen of calculation and
    practice
    Between himself and them
    Rendering himself homeless

m   A lost spirit

M   Glide

m   Yes

M   So it is surprising

How many people do actually change the way
they hold their spoon
No matter how much tedious repetitive self-
instruction is required
No matter what harsh and severe reminders
they have to ply themselves with
Glide

m   Yes

M   They do change the way they hold their spoon

m   And much else

M   Impelled by the most terrible fear
The fear of sexual relegation
Because when for instance they see

m   A sexually convincing acquaintance

M   Holding the spoon in a different way
So the spoon in that hand
Is mesmeric
So the spoon in that hand
Has authority

m   Then they are afraid that the way they hold
their spoon
Will mark them out as a sexual loser

M   Condemned by their unthinking childhood
way of holding their spoon
And then with fear in their throat
They come to look on their own vulnerable
childhood way of holding their spoon
With wild alienation and hatred

m   And they never hold it that way again

M   It is a mistake

To believe there is no connection
Between fear and learning
Glide

m   Glide

M   A lovely walk is a regular walk
Regularity confirms expectations
And protects against bumps and surprises
A lovely regular walk is a lullaby
As a result of which there are dreams
As a result of which there is love

m   Glide

M   A swaying regular walk
Strokes
It shapes the air and strokes it
As a result of which there is pleasure

m   Glide

M   Some people are attracted to a walk that has a
spice of irritation
The banging of high heels
Brings them to attention like a call to arms
Jostling thighs
Make them want to wrestle
Others prefer the slow sleepwalking walk
Of one just woken from a sleep
That plumbed the depths
And visited the oracle
The walk of the satisfied deep dreamer

m   Glide

M   But the one essential thing in any walk
Is regularity

Freeing the mind from the jolts and shocks of
mundane existence
Expressing the symmetry and safety
Of two powerful hips!

m   Glide

M   A failure of symmetry
Is a failure of momentum
A failure of momentum
Is a failure of aim
A failure of aim

m   Is a failure of love

M   Jerky movements
Suggesting alarm, timidity, incompetence
Will always be the inferiors of smooth
movements
A lovely woman
Should glide forward smoothly
Like a mental process
On and on through the bright water
The prow of the little boat
Barely skimming the lake
On and on
To the enchanted isle!

m   *(Despairing)* Glide

M   The beautiful butterfly stretches out his wings
Stretch your wings, children

m   Stretching
I'm stretching my wings

M   Stretch them right out, as far as they'll go
Are you stretching your wings?

m   Yes

M   Take a deep breath

m   Yes

M   And out

m   Yes

M   And another deep deep breath

m   Yes

M   Are you ready, children? And - fly!

m   But I -

M   Flying around, up to the ceiling

m   I -, I -

M   Swooping down, floating up, flying

m   I -, I -, I -

M   She thought the other children could actually
    fly

SECTION B

m   One of the boys stooped absentmindedly,
straightened up and threw something
There was a puff of dust near my shoe
Another stone tapped my arm, and slowly
bounced off
I, struck dumb, calmly dumbly acknowledged
The animal correctness of what they were
doing
Even though I would have preferred kindness,
and being saved
But shame which does not bring death
Becomes a particularly stubborn form of life

He took me walking to all his favourite places
Along the ruts of the old timber trail
The old timber trail
Which made me think of men like him
Congregated there on the mountain
Joking and cutting timber
Quiet now
Trees in the grass high on the mountain
And we walked into a big patch of wild mint
Right up to our shoulders
Another time I remember setting off with him
in the dawn
Black shadows across the dew
And smoke coming off the cows where the sun
hit them
He took me through the paperbark swamp
And down to the huge yellow headland that
ran down to the sea like a roller coaster

In the city he liked the old parts near the
harbour
Low crooked stone streets linked by stone
stairs
And I was always trailing behind
Walking was his way of talking to me
And as we walked through all these treasures
of his
I kept asking if we could sit down
My head full of beauty
My body full of pain

Shame catches everyone
Turning this one's golden hair to white fluff
Piping knotty veins into that one's muscular
calves
Stiffening this one's sinews to a tightness
That pulls her askew
And draws her up to strut on her toes like an
ostrich
It finally catches everyone
Even as a child I was always able to see who
else had been caught
Old Mr Maher with his geese and his falling-
down trousers
Down the road by the broken swimming pool
Old Mrs Job and her potty chair with the table
mat on it
The simpleton with the rolling walk passing
our house each day
Any one of us at any time might have to run
the gauntlet
Of boys on street corners
And there is no way to be sure the eye of god
is compassionate
The eye of god might just as well be

The jeering eye of a street corner boy

At first you only know yourself
By what you see around you
And what you see around you is beautiful
So you imagine yourself to be beautiful
But when at last
The voices of others reach you
And following their direction, you turn your
eyes upon yourself
Then you see the chaos
Then you see the difference
Between what they see and what you thought
you were
And the blade of fear is in you
There were children at our school
Who had a game of going round asking
everyone
"Do you love yourself? Do you love yourself?"
And it seemed the most dangerous thing that
could happen
Would be if you did

I wanted to take shape
I wanted to become myself, like everyone else
And in trying to resemble myself

I tried to resemble everyone else

I shunned my own taste

Shame loses track of its intentions

Its thoughts make it ashamed

So it does not pursue them

I saw myself as a halt in the music of the spheres

Lopsided, an irritating check, a halt

A check, a halt

Is the time I spend in front of the mirror

Spent in trying to assimilate an unacceptable truth

Or in trying to make that truth acceptable after all?

Shocks repeated

Are shocks mastered

But a relaxation in vigilance

Leaves the way open for more shocks of course

Some things are quite inexorable

And thoughts can flail against them all they like

And falling exhausted

Forget them for a while

Then flail again

Then fall exhausted again

And flail again

And so on

SECTION C

M   He sat down beside her
And rubbed his upper arm against hers
And then upstairs with the sun coming
through the curtains
He praised her and said she was beautiful
There are times when everyone is beautiful
When you can feel the vigour and fluency
Of nature's rich paint
Even in a mottled weighty forearm
Or a pendulous cheek
The deficiencies of those we love
Are as beautiful as their beauties
So for instance his grim thin mouth
Seemed to her to bring an irresistible whisper
of death
A smudge of charcoal or grave dust
To his honeyed face
And perhaps he found
In her
Something wild and formless
The darkness before creation
Seeking light

Or perhaps he saw her
As a lame wolf gnawing at herself
Elemental
And perhaps it was for that reason
He called her beautiful
Beasts are beautiful
There is a religion of the senses
Where everything seen is meaningful
Ink in sunlight on paper
Trickles dries and leaves its fossil
On a blazing desert
Stripes over a parrot's eye
Frown spick and span
The bent frown of the war god
And the bird's quiet stare
Is the field where the war dead sleep
Everything seen
Is seen as a message
Things not originating in our mind
Seem sent to us
Shadow branches
Nodding at the window
Are saying yes to some love of ours
She felt sure of her place with him
As withered leaves, rots and diseases
Have their place in the life of the tree
Still all the time she was with him
There was a lump in her throat
The fact that she was happy
Encouraged her sorrow to think it might be
allowed out
And it dared to make itself felt
But waited in her throat
Unsure of its welcome
Crouched there

And who would want to coax a thing like that
Out of its hiding place

SECTION D

m   Hospitals are buffed shining disinfected
horizons
Silently crossed by rubber-wheeled trolleys
Moving easily unlike people

M   In hospitals
You see in every direction
Flesh that has lost its meaning
Cut measured like fatty cloth
Instead of having sprung into shape of its own
volition

m   And when you look at all this botched flesh
These botched afterthoughts of flesh
These clumsy ruptures and repairs
At these wobbling skewed walkers
At these flesh ghosts that have lost
The light and logic from within
Then you curse all second thoughts
All remedies
All determined attempts to mend
You only want to run from that place
And not stop running till you reach the
primary fountain
That throws up instantly complete beautiful
forms
Where everything you see is a promise
A message sent by the great intelligence
That expresses itself in bursts of symmetry
Enchanting facet after enchanting facet
Each enticing you with the promise
Of enchanting depths you can dive into
And no droplet with a broken skin

313

M People's vulnerability can attract others
If people have the confidence of their
vulnerability
But they wouldn't be vulnerable if they did
And heaven knows
There is nothing fixed or permanent
About the turn of a foot

m The angle of a limb to the body

M The shape of a torso
The curve of a cheek
It can all be pulled out of shape

m Puffed up twisted and changed

M And the thing which is fixed and permanent
Is not physical reality
But the idea of physical reality

m The thing which is fixed and permanent
Is not the realization
But the intention behind it

M A beautiful person
Is an oracle
A messenger of a higher mathematical order
Symmetrically unfolding

m A distorted person
Is a messenger of a lapse in that order

M But the orderly doubling of cells
Has a clear goal
Easy to recognize
Even if there is a mistake

m They knew me
They greeted me as their child

Hurt on my way to meet them
They could have pretended not to know me
Instead they claimed me

M   What she should have been
Was more important than what she was

m   They knew me

M   Our child

m   They cherished me

M   We knew her

m   As if

M   It was just as if

m   As if I was what I should have been

M   We knew her for what she should have been

m   In spite of what I was

M   So perhaps she came to believe
She was what she should have been

m   They said I was not my imperfection

M   Love, for instance
She thinks of the love she feels as having the
power to save others
She thinks of the love she feels
In just the way people always think of the love
they feel
She thinks of her love as a remedy that could
heal broken limbs
She

m   They gave me
A sense of inner rightness

And outer wrongness

M   You are not what happened to you

m   Even the wildest contradictions
    Don't cancel each other out in me

M   You are what happened to you

m   But simply move on different paths
    Where they don't meet

M   I blame no-one. No-one is to blame
    No-one is to blame
    Because no-one is in control
    Nothing is in control
    But something should be in control
    Something should be in control
    Otherwise the idea of trying to order one's life
    Or choose one's behaviour
    Or permit oneself to become accustomed to
    anything
    Or fond of anyone
    Is terrifying, sickening
    The idea of it all changing at any moment
    Or disappearing altogether
    Makes me feel sick

m   But she doesn't blame me

M   No-one is to blame
    Although it would be easier
    If someone were to blame
    And she is not
    So I do blame her for that
    Nevertheless
    We tried with all our skill
    To make her resemble what she should be

So she could lead a normal life

m   The demon sister
Used to lead her nurses through the ward at
night
Throwing fantastic shadows with their torches
They had on their trolley
Little bottles of cascara
That gleamed like black essence of eye pupils
This poisonous mixture of pitch and aniseed
'Cleaned you out', as they said
It was the source of their power over the
children's bowels
With it they turned your shit to a fearful hot
liquid inside you
And sent it running out through your helpless
arsehole
Filling your nostrils with the smell of your own
defeat
And if any child refused to take it
They held your nose as they pushed the spoon
into your mouth
And if you struggled
The demon sister had them wheel you out
On to the verandah
Where you were left all night
At the mercy of the bogey man

M   Oh. You catch sight of yourself
And know the whole amoebic absurdity
The two-legged improbability
Not just of all mankind -
Of yourself specifically
The fault
Through which frailty and unease enter the
whole pattern

m   Glide

M   Yes

m   Glide

M   Yes

m   Down the corridor

M   Yes

m   To the three young men in pyjamas
Who every tea time form themselves into an imaginary three-piece band
The double bass taking great pinches of air between thumb and fingers
And going zum zum zum furiously with his lips
The amputee playing a comb and tissue paper
While the percussionist
Bashes his tray on wheels with such irresistible rhythm
It flies to the end of the bed
And has to be caught and bashed again

M   Meanwhile the old man puts on his dressing gown
And shuffles by inches to the room of his old friend
Where they greet one another with great containment
In the manner of farming men
Then fall to discussing their imaginary farm
Whether the crops need spraying
Whether fruit trees would be a good investment
Or whether the cattle should be moved to a pasture further from the river

On account of the heavy rain running down
the hospital windows
Glide

m   Yes

M   Glide

m   Yes

THE END

THE MIND OF THE MEETING

Characters

The characters are: CHAIR (man),
ESTELLE, CAROLINE, BOB, RAY, JENNY,
all middle-aged-ish, some younger

CHAIR: Their inaction yes? Their general

ESTELLE: Chair?

CHAIR: Yes, Estelle

ESTELLE: Chair, I don't actually think they are inactive,
            I think in many ways they are active, I don't
            mean to say we always see it, but I think the
            signs are there, if we know how to look for
            them, it's just we don't always know how to

CHAIR: Yes, thank you Estelle

ESTELLE: Well, for instance, the prostitutes seem to
            have gone from the trees and I heard a green
            woodpecker has been sighted

CHAIR: Oh good, yes

            (Internal.)

CHAIR: She's mad

            (To the room at large.)
            Yes thank you Estelle

ESTELLE: It's not that I want to try and impose what I
            think

BOB: No worries there, Estelle

ESTELLE: That's nice of you Bob, but I do think people
            have to find their own

CHAIR: Yes thank you Estelle, that's considerate, thank
            you

ESTELLE: People have to find their own way, I can't
            always [find it for them]

CHAIR: No, of course you can't

ESTELLE: I mean to say, chair, if the meeting feels
             strongly, then I agree we should write to them

CHAIR: Yes, good, does everyone feel we should write
             to them

SEVERAL: Yes/No

CHAIR: What does everyone feel

SEVERAL: Yes/No

CHAIR: So, shall I take that as a

             (Internal.)

             I don't honestly know what to take it as, one of
             them's drawing purple blobs on the minutes,
             another one's waving her espadrille about,
             another one's eating a doughnut

             (To the room at large.)
             Shall I take that as a

ESTELLE: Chair, I don't think we should write just to
             question and find fault

CHAIR: I'm sure that's correct, Estelle, I'm sure we
             should be ready to

ESTELLE: I think we should also give praise where praise
             is due, we've been promised new bins

CHAIR: Yes I'm sure we should celebrate some of the
             aspects...Thank you Estelle

             (Internal.)

             Mad

             (To the room at large.)

ESTELLE: I think we should always try and give them
             some thanks and give them some praise

CHAIR: Thank you

             (Internal.)

CHAIR: Mad and she's got a hair ribbon

(To the room at large.)

ESTELLE: Some thanks and some praise, for everything they

(Internal.)

CHAIR: A labyrinthine mauve-coloured chiffon hair ribbon

(To the room at large.)

ESTELLE: For everything they've been trying to [do for us]

CHAIR: Does everyone feel we should write to them and give them thanks and

BOB: Chair, I personally don't know what in the world Estelle thinks she's talking about, I personally think they're a bunch of absolute/

RAY: Definitely write and get some action/

JENNY: If only they weren't so stupid, they're just so incredibly/

CAROLINE: By all means write, but what exactly do we think they're going to/

CHAIR: Does everyone feel we should write

(Silence.)

Some form of letter

(Silence.)

CHAIR: Everyone?

(Internal.)
Sometimes everyone just looks down.
Just looks down. A mysterious glimpse of consensus, a mysterious

(To the room at large.)

BOB: They're a bunch of absolute/

RAY: We definitely should write, definitely definitely/

JENNY: So incredibly stupid/

CAROLINE: Oh by all means, by all means/

ESTELLE: If the meeting feels we should write

(Internal.)

CHAIR: Unfortunately short-lived, a glimpse of some higher consensus

(To the room at large.)

CHAIR: So I'll take that as a

(Internal.)

CHAIR: Some higher consensus briefly ennobling the meeting, I have to confess that in general, consensus only happens when the group is faced by some extreme of peril, like the threat of having to pay for residents' parking, equally the possibility of a giant meteor striking the earth would be generally unwelcome, I think, though there might be one or two dissenting voices

(To the room at large.)

CAROLINE: By all means, why not, it will make no difference at all

(Internal.)

CHAIR: But I've always grasped the importance of a unified attitude, it's as if I can't rest until I've crystallised the mind of the meeting into some sort of

(To the room at large.)

May I suggest we write to them and say we're puzzled by their inaction yes? their general

(Internal.)

Crystallised the mind of the meeting into
some sort of more composed and transparent
form, it would give me pleasure not to say
relief, it would bring to me a welcome sense
of light and of repose, but it isn't always
easy, and especially when Bob starts leaning
forward on the more collapsible end of the
more collapsible sofa

(To the room at large.)

BOB:	Chair
CHAIR:	Yes Bob?
BOB:	The word puzzled
CHAIR:	Yes Bob, I'm with you
BOB:	Chair, I'm rather puzzled what you mean, when you use the word puzzled, to be perfectly honest, chair, I doubt if anyone here is puzzled in the least, I think everyone here is very well aware what's wrong with them
CHAIR:	Yes and what's that, Bob
BOB:	They're evil
ESTELLE:	Bob, I don't think we should be negative
CHAIR:	Are you sure? I don't think I know what you mean
BOB:	That's how evil they are, you don't know

(Internal.)

CHAIR:	I always like to imagine we're going to find some common ground, it isn't always immediately apparent, but my function as I see it is finding some sort of common ground and clearing away the various troublesome differences that

(To the room at large.)

BOB:	They're evil sods, that's all

ESTELLE: I think that is quite negative, Bob

(Internal.)

CHAIR: The various troublesome differences that

(To the room at large.)

ESTELLE: Totally negative, Bob

BOB: All right, I'm negative

ESTELLE: I'm not negative, I'm never, ever negative

(Internal.)

CHAIR: That cloud the mind of the meeting, yes, I'm always setting out to find some common ground and somehow crystallise the mind of the meeting into some sort of letter we can send them, a clear sort of crystallised letter we can send them, a reasoned letter, I always feel they're open to reason, I don't know why, I feel as if they're open to reason more than almost anyone I actually ever

(To the room at large.)

BOB: Evil, evil sods

ESTELLE: If they're so evil, who made the nature strip, for instance

(Internal.)

CHAIR: More than almost anyone I ever actually have anything to do with, I've always thought they're open to a clear and reasoned letter, and that dialogue is possible and that the right sort of reasoned letter will produce the right sort of dialogue, of course the failure to reply can itself be construed as simply another form of dialogue ... my wife thinks I'm an idiot

BOB: What nature strip

(Internal.)

CHAIR: My wife thinks I'm an idiot, writing letters to
them, my wife says it takes all my time, but
I reply that reason does take time, it takes
all the time in the world, trying to consider
everything, this generally seems to make my
wife impatient, but I believe everything should
and must be considered, because only then
can a reasoned letter emerge, the pitfalls are
numerous, such as signing myself for instance
with the name of the man I was writing to,
yes I've done that, talking to myself, my wife
would say, she says I might as well talk to
myself as write them these

(To the room at large.)

BOB: What nature strip, what do you mean, nature
strip

(Internal.)

CHAIR: Write them these carefully reasoned letters...
Bob doesn't reason, Bob knows, Bob knows
and laughs, he's got an aftershave face and a
salesman's manicure

(To the room at large.)
If we could try to focus on the letter

ESTELLE: The nature strip on the island

BOB: What island

ESTELLE: In the High Street, the island in the High
Street

BOB: What nature strip, there is no nature strip

ESTELLE: It was said that nothing would be able to
survive on that island. But they created
plantings there and they did survive

BOB: Those things, those evil monstrosities

ESTELLE: They weren't beautiful but a plant is a plant

BOB: They weren't plants

ESTELLE: They were plants, they were architectural
                plants, people these days like the architectural
                plants, things with leaves

BOB: Those things had evil leaves

ESTELLE: They were pollution-friendly plants, I think it's
                a wonderful thing, a plant like that, that can
                take away our pollution

JENNY: They dug them all up again, didn't they, they
                planted them, then they dug them all up again,
                that was incredibly stupid

CHAIR: Jenny thank you, if we could return to the

                (Internal.)

                Some people are born to live in the world by
                offering up their physical or mental or business
                energies, others are born to live in the world by
                tracking and monitoring what's being done by
                the others, putting things into words and not just
                things but shifts, even slight ones; plans, even
                doomed ones; intentions firm or otherwise;
                strategies brilliant or pedestrian; and sometimes
                I might even stray beyond all these to the gulfs
                of hidden interest and deliberately left-out
                knowledge, and shine the light of words on to
                what lies heaped in the darkness. I deal with
                local issues generally

                (To the room at large.)
                If we could return to the letter

ESTELLE: It wasn't their fault what happened, the road
                people came and said architectural plants like
                that were blocking the sight of the road

CHAIR: The letter, if we could just try to keep our
                minds on the

BOB: That nature strip is dirt and fag-ends now,
        that's all they've achieved with their nature
        strip, dirt and fag-ends

        (Internal.)

CHAIR: I don't like this carpet, this brown exhausted
        carpet. I used to like this carpet. I used to like
        it, this matted brown exhausted pressed-down
        carpet, shag pile carpet as it was called in
        those days, there used to be a time when this
        carpet lived up to its name

        (To the room at large.)

ESTELLE: They did such a lot of research, to find out the
            species that take away all our pollution, they
            were trying to save Greenland

CHAIR: All right then Bob, so you say you're not
        puzzled

BOB: No not puzzled

CAROLINE: Chair instead of puzzled what shall I say

CHAIR: Thank you, Caroline, I quite like concerned,
        are we concerned?

BOB: It's a bit of a beardy word

CHAIR: I quite like it

BOB: Concerned, as if they cared, as if they cared if
        we're

CHAIR: Yes concerned at their

BOB: Then you see, chair, the word inaction, what
        does that mean, inaction, see I don't think
        they're inactive

ESTELLE: No well that's what I said

BOB: I think they're active, I think they're evilly
        active in ways we frankly don't even know and
        aren't being told, I wouldn't say inaction, oh
        no, I'd say lack of transparency, that's what it

is, it's their patent lack of transparency, that's
what I'm concerned about, because everyone
knows, they're not about to inform us, and
why, because we're here to be informed, that's
precisely the reason we're here, it makes it too
easy for them, doesn't it, the fact that we're
here, it means when they've got something
they don't want anyone informed of, they
know just who not to inform of it, which is us

CAROLINE: So what are we saying, concerned- at- their-
lack- of- transparency, jolly good, tremendous,
bollocks

CHAIR: Thank you Caroline

(Internal.)

CHAIR: I used to like this brown shag pile carpet and
this big solid smoked glass table, it's thick
and substantial but at the same time, you
can see through it, that really seemed like a
revelation, back in those days when she and I
went to Chelsea and bought this table, it was
something of a technological leap forward,
something of a technological new dawn, this
table, charcoal tinted smoked glass, magical,
like smoke made into glass, as if you could
look into it and maybe you'd see the future,
ephemeral smoke made solid and at the same
time transparent in a perfect gleaming squared
off piece of glass

(To the room at large.)

BOB: Of course they're not about to inform us,
when they're all of them busily inventing
jobs for themselves, all these wonderful cosy
non-jobs for themselves, making wonderful
non-existent nature strips full of non-existent
life-enhancing plants, of course we're

CHAIR:	So we're saying in the letter, we're concerned at their lack of transparency and we feel we're not inf
BOB:	Course we're not informed
CHAIR:	Everyone?
BOB:	Course we're not, of course they don't inform us what they're doing with our property for instance, with our property which has been entrusted to them, they treat our property, which was given over to them to hold in trust, as if it were simply theirs to do what they like with, they consider themselves entitled to liquidate our property or break it all up into pieces or do whatever they like with it
CAROLINE:	Bob, must they be blamed for everything?
BOB:	Yes, Caroline, I think we know who to blame for absolutely everything
CAROLINE:	Must they always be blamed?
BOB:	Yes they must, they're selling our buildings
	(Internal.)
CHAIR:	We didn't want to be cluttered, and we frequently used the word uncluttered, the word uncluttered seemed high praise to us, we halved the size of the skirting boards in this room, I think we wanted streamlined skirting boards, aerodynamic skirting boards, not that they move about much, skirting boards, but if they had, they would have moved fast, we bought Swedish cutlery all in one piece no handles, like surgical instruments and we had our first taste of chilled soup
	(To the room at large.)
BOB:	They're selling our buildings

CAROLINE: They have to sell our buildings, they can't prevent themselves

BOB: Oh what a dreadful affliction

CAROLINE: Don't you understand, they're helpless

BOB: That's the kind of helpless I'd like to be, selling other people's buildings

CHAIR: Chilled soup. The perfectibility of the human condition was something we had a sense of then, and my wife took an evening class, in the polishing of semi-precious stones, she even at one time bought a small portable machine for the purpose, small, but it made a noise like a concrete-mixer when it stamped on the kitchen surfaces with a furious little metal foot, it used to shake the house when she was at the height of the craze

CAROLINE: The buildings are dangerous

BOB: It's not the buildings that are dangerous, it's them

CAROLINE: They can't afford the repairs

BOB: Minor repairs, that's all those buildings need, they talk about those buildings as if they were utterly beyond redemption, those buildings need minor repairs, that's all, but they're not going to carry out any repairs, because it's not in their interest to do so, they'd rather see those buildings go to rack and ruin, and sell them off, for profit

CAROLINE: They have to have the money for special needs

BOB: Their special needs, funding little jobs for all their

(Internal.)

CHAIR: Purity was our aim in furnishing this room, purity, simplicity, and of course, ease of cleaning

(To the room at large.)

BOB: Little jobs for all their

(Internal.)

CHAIR: Ease of cleaning, that was some years ago now

[(To the room at large.)

BOB: Funding little jobs for all their friends

CHAIR: Bob, I'm not sure how much of this we can really put in the letter

(Internal.)

CHAIR: That was some years ago now, there was this thing that somehow got into my mind in 1962 about ease, about painting rooms white and reading poems without any capital letters, and Mondriaan and moccasins and Visconti and wine, I wanted to marry a woman who looked like Monica Vitti and up to a point I did, she's in the kitchen, and we obtained this smoked glass table which went some way to resolving a childhood cluttered with Airfix and wellingtons and hot water bottles and brussels sprouts, and around that time the world all at once began to seem infinitely improvable, and we bought this glossy, as it then was, this glossy, furry brown carpet such as a naked Monica Vitti might be taken on, the glossy furry brown carpet and the smoked glass table and let's not forget the table legs are made of chrome, we aimed at a certain spaciousness, even a certain outer spaceness, we aimed at a smoky glassy floaty misty Italian sort of spaciousness through which a negligently pantherene sort of moccasined man, or Monica Vitti, could drift, and I felt in those days a new sort of confidence that most of the complexities in life could be resolved, of course it's just a maisonette

(To the room at large.)

CHAIR: I'm not sure how much of this we can really put in the letter

BOB: Course not, they'd have us, I know them

CAROLINE: Bob, you don't know them at all, the reality of it is

(Internal.)

CHAIR: The thing about Caroline, she will take her shoes off, like Janis Joplin or Marie Antoinette, the difference is, Caroline's still with us

(To the room at large.)

CAROLINE: The reality is, they have very little power at all, they can't just do as they please, you have to understand they're virtually helpless, they're prisoners, trapped in the toils of their own history

BOB: They should be trapped behind bars

(Internal.)

CHAIR: Still with us, taking the minutes, her hand is round heavy purple and bold, so is Caroline

(To the room at large.)

CAROLINE: They're very little more than figureheads, of course they get everything thrown at them but they're actually bound hand and foot by a whole set of obligations, yes we can draft a letter, by all means chair, draft all the letters you like, but at the end of the day, there's very very little they can

(Internal.)

CHAIR: Still with us, a long way down in a bean bag, taking the minutes. I'm not sure why she does it. As far as I'm aware, it's not for pleasure. In fact it seems to plunge her into gloom and despair, and grand doom-laden gestures

(To the room at large.)

CAROLINE: Very very little they can do, they have no budget

ESTELLE: How can you say that Caroline, we all contribute, we all make sacrifices

CAROLINE: Their budget has completely disappeared, there is no budget, where their budget should be is nothing but an enormous all-engulfing debt, and all contributions are swallowed up in it

(Internal.)

CHAIR: Grand doom-laden gestures, whereas others in this room refuse to be discouraged, others in this room have fortunately been aware that, in dealing with the various complexities of life, it's only thanks to reason, and patience, and a much-needed clarity that anything can ever hope to be resolved

(To the room at large.)

CAROLINE: All contributions are swallowed up in their enormous all-engulfing debt, they're labouring under a debt which was incurred on their behalf a great many years ago but which now they can't shake off, whatever futile efforts they may make

CHAIR: They still have a very large presence, Caroline

CAROLINE: A very large futile presence, and all because a great many years ago, huge amounts were borrowed in order to shore up and maintain the institution, if not, they wouldn't have had a very large futile presence, they'd have simply disappeared, but the result of it is, they still have this enormous engulfing debt on which they're paying interest to this day, that's why they're so helpless, because they're bound hand and foot by unfortunate undertakings made at an earlier time and it's all they can do to keep themselves from simply falling into the abyss

(Internal.)

CHAIR: Patience, and a much needed clarity...She sometimes strokes men's legs with her feet, at local parties

(To the room at large.)

CHAIR: Thank you for those comments Caroline

CAROLINE: Am I not supposed to comment

CHAIR: Thank you for those comments, very um

CAROLINE: Do shut me up

CHAIR: Very, um

CAROLINE: Please do

CHAIR: Very um, challenging

CAROLINE: Chair, if someone cut off your head and threw it out the window, it would roll down the road still murmuring 'very um, challenging', I'm sorry chair, do shut me up, after all, who am I to

RAY: Why are we making excuses? Why don't we just simply get them to

CAROLINE: Sorry chair, I'll shut up

RAY: Just simply get them to target my neighbour, seventeen skips, seventeen skips

(Internal.)

CHAIR: Yes, a much needed clarity, a much needed

(To the room at large.)

RAY: Seventeen skips, she's asking to be targeted,
            seventeen skips my neighbour's dug out
            of there, seventeen skips of rubble, she's
            digging a hole immediately under the
            house, extending I don't know where, my
            neighbour's tunnelling

(Internal.)

CHAIR: Clarity

(To the room at large.)

RAY: What's she want to be tunnelling for?
            Tunnelling back where she came from

(Internal.)

CHAIR: A much needed

(To the room at large.)

RAY: Wherever that is, the woman's not English,
            what is she, a cave dweller? Is she down there
            digging a cave? How far will it spread? The
            street was never meant to accommodate a
            complex of caves

(Internal.)

CHAIR: Clarity

(To the room at large.)

RAY: There's going to be room for a lot of people
            down there, who's she planning to put down
            there? She'll be filling it up with asylum
            seekers, filling it up with asylum seekers
            bringing all their wives, there'll be numerous
            growing families under there, because she's
            burrowing, she's digging a great big hole down

under the house, we're all going to wake up one day and her house will have fallen down the hole and not just her house, my house, the whole street will all just fall in, it wouldn't surprise me, it's all those poor people, that's who I'm thinking of, all those poor people that shouldn't be there

JENNY: Don't be stupid, Ray, they'd have come from somewhere else that's even worse

RAY: I'd see about that, I'd personally see about that

CHAIR: I think the letter should avoid conjecture

RAY: I'll see about it, that isn't conjecture

CHAIR: Ray I'm simply wondering, how these concerns of yours could best be phrased

RAY: Nuke her, that's how, I want the woman nuked

ESTELLE: But does she speak the language?

RAY: She'd understand the language

ESTELLE: Ray, do be serious

RAY: I'm serious

ESTELLE: Does she speak our language?

RAY: Of course she doesn't speak our language, nuke her, she has no respect

ESTELLE: They might be able to give the woman some help with speaking the language

RAY: What's she want to speak the language for, all those people moving in down there won't be speaking the language, I'll be the only one that's left speaking the language

CHAIR: It's really just a planning matter

JENNY: No, it isn't

CHAIR: It's a simple, straightforward planning matter

JENNY:	No, it isn't
RAY:	Jenny's right, chair
JENNY:	Ray you're incredibly stupid, the reason I come to these meetings is to put a stop to people like you
CHAIR:	It's a simple, straightforward planning matter, I suggest we write and ask them to inspect
RAY:	I said to them come, I said to them, come and inspect down in her cellar, you know they wouldn't come? I said to them she's digging in her cellar, I said to them come and see for themselves what she's getting up to down there in her cellar, they said they wouldn't come because she's got permission to be carrying out construction works
CHAIR:	So Ray, you managed to speak to them
RAY:	I speak to them often
CHAIR:	Really
RAY:	I speak to them often, I said to them, what construction works, has she got permission for carrying out destruction works, I said, I could use that
CHAIR:	You really managed to speak to them
RAY:	I'm talking to them all the time
CHAIR:	Oh, really
BOB:	It doesn't seem to be doing you much good, Ray
RAY:	I got them to come in the end, I said there were rats and schoolchildren, I got truancy along and extermination, and the planning inspector came, he looked at the house and said where are the construction works, I can't see any works. I said you can't see any works because the works are invisible from the

	surface, the works are underground. I can't see any works, he says, if there are no construction works, he says, I'm afraid then I can't inspect them
ESTELLE:	I think it's very good they're so meticulous
RAY:	I asked him, does she own the ground beneath her house, and he said she owns the ground all the way to the centre of the earth
CHAIR:	Yes, a fairly straightforward planning matter
BOB:	It doesn't seem to have done you very much good, it's no use asking them, not unless you make it worth their while, she's obviously made it worth their while, help with the language, I don't think she needs any help with the language, I think she understands all about their language
CHAIR:	It just needs a straightforward letter, a well reasoned letter
RAY:	Get the woman nuked
CHAIR:	Straightforward and
RAY:	They can't turn a blind eye forever, they're going to have to hear me eventually
CHAIR:	Reasoned
RAY:	And when they do, it's going to be judgment day
CHAIR:	Yes thank you Ray
RAY:	Judgment day
CHAIR:	Thank you
	(Internal.)
CHAIR:	Ray has tight clothes with ticks on them
	(To the room at large.)
RAY:	Judgment day

CHAIR: Thank you

(Internal.)

Of course it's just a maisonette, there's only
so much drifting you can do, in a maisonette,
before your clothes start catching on the
shelving, before your softly casual clothes
start catching on the shelving, we never were
keen on shelving, we didn't plan to have
much shelving in this room, just one shelf
of glass with some marble eggs and a book
by Nabokov, then I got some temporary
planking, I needed temporary planking for my
files, and the files proved not to be temporary,
my files of correspondence, my files of
correspondence with them, I enjoy a very full
and reasoned correspondence, with them,
a very full and reasoned correspondence
ranging through everything from conservation
to regeneration to waste disposal, only once
you let the folders and the papers and the
clipboards on to the shelving, more things
follow, my wife says I've messed up this room

(To the room at large.)

JENNY: How do they ever think of these stupid
regulations, it shows the utter stupidity of
thinking, I try to do my best not to think

(Internal.)

CHAIR: Being young's not as easy as it used to be,
of course it's even worse if you are, Jenny's
a younger sort of woman with the delicate
frame of a bicycle, and a furrowed brow, like
handlebars

(To the room at large.)

JENNY: They can't see what's in front of them, all
they can see is their stupid pieces of paper,

that stupid diagram, you know the diagram,
you know the diagram drawn up by them, to
show us how much they'd all changed and
how much they were going to be consulting
us. One page, one page, and it looked like a
page from an infants' geometry book, nothing
but pastel coloured squares and rectangles and
circles all joined to each other with arrows,
omnipresent arrows like Y chromosomes
gone mad fertilising everything in sight, and
each pastel coloured box or circle had the
label assembly, cabinet, liaison members,
consultative groups etcetera, and all of the
boxes and circles had arrows coming and
going, showing influence flowing everywhere
from one to the other

(Internal.)

CHAIR: I doubt she'd even know what was meant by a
shag pile carpet

(To the room at large.)

JENNY: And that woman, the explaining woman, the
woman who couldn't make the light box work,
the woman in the peacock coloured evening
jacket who couldn't make the light box work,
and she'd had her hair done specially cause
she's doing a presentation, they should go and
have their brain done, not their hair, and she's
explaining to us how we're all going to be
consulted thanks to them, and she's pointing
with her pointer at the boxes and the circles
and the other randomly chosen geometrical
figures, and reading out all the labels, because
this is what is known as making a presentation,
reading out the labels and the bullet points
which we've all got in front of us, and she's
tracing with her pointer the directions of the
arrows, and talking to us all about the flowing

of the influence and the taking, passing on
and implementation of the influence and
she's proudly showing us where each arrow's
coming from and where it's going, and then
she comes to the box that's representing us
in this group here and it hasn't got an arrow
coming out of it. Not the tiniest little arrow
coming out of it connecting it to anywhere

ESTELLE: Jenny, it's only a diagram

JENNY: That's all they see is their diagrams and their
            stupid pieces of paper

ESTELLE: It's only just an idea, they don't mean it

JENNY: If it hadn't been for us, that diagram would
            have remained like that, and this group would
            have been left forever totally without influence

BOB: This group is totally without influence

JENNY: This group would have had no say in anything

BOB: This group doesn't have any say in anything

JENNY: We had a say in the diagram

RAY: So Jenny

JENNY: Yes Ray

RAY: If you think it's all so incredibly stupid

JENNY: I do, I do think it's all incredibly stupid

RAY: Why are you here

JENNY: I don't know, Ray

RAY: Why is she

JENNY: I don't know, Ray, I think I must be stupid

            (Internal.)

CHAIR: My wife says I've messed up this room, it
            starts with the shelves and then the papers
            get on to them, papers more papers and
            duplicates of papers, and worse is to follow,

rubber bands, pottery, paperclips, brown
paper and shopping bags and the bit of foam
rubber I wore that time I broke my wrist in
the deep freeze and several broken angle
poise lamps that reach out and stroke you like
preying mantises, as my wife says, she's right,
I've messed up this room storing paperwork
etcetera, there's nowhere else for the boxes
to go, the boxes of the various reports and
inquiries, which can be very bulky, and she
can't get round and she barks her shins on the
smoked glass table and the shag pile carpet is
definitely not what it was

(To the room at large.)

RAY: None of which assists me with my problem,
which is quite simply, I want the woman
nuked, I want them to target that woman and
come down on her with a vengeance

ESTELLE: I don't think vengeance is what this should be
about, I think it should be more about sharing

RAY: Vengeance is sharing, nuke her, I've spent
a small fortune on my house and she's
hollowing it away from under my feet, I've got
valuables, a valuable collection, my collection
won't be safe when she's got asylum seekers
coming and going and sending things out
of the country in diplomats' luggage, she's
already started costing me money, I'm having
metal grilles put in

BOB: What do you collect Ray

RAY: Weapons of war, I've got valuable antique
weapons, coshes, cutlasses, handguns, Persian
warrior chain mail, samurai swords, I've
got weapons in my house that date back to
Biblical times and all still in working order

BOB: Yes Ray, I can see it's quite a worry

RAY: That's why I want her out, because she's a menace

(Internal.)

CHAIR: Lampshades, where do lampshades come from? Lampshades with gashes, lampshades with vertigo, as for the stained glass tulip, I don't know how to explain it, and then of course seating, seating often proves hard to predict or control, as is the case here, somehow the bean bags got in and never left, the leather chair was my contribution and we bought the three piece suite when her parents were coming to stay, it used to be orange, yes there's lots of seating I'm afraid, lots of seating, lots of like-minded people to sit in it, that was the hope, that's the... My wife tends to stay in the kitchen

(To the room at large.)

RAY: A menace, that's what she is, a menace to civilised life, she has to be eliminated out of there, they've got the powers

CAROLINE: What powers? Their powers are totally vestigial

RAY: Don't you start

CAROLINE: Their powers are totally inadequate for accomplishing anything at all

RAY: I don't want excuses

CAROLINE: The puny powers they have, they're deprived of the means to enforce

RAY: You'll tell me next they're impotent

CAROLINE: I will. Quite so. They're impotent

RAY: And who exactly are you to tell me this?

CAROLINE: Me, I'm just an observer, just an observer

RAY: You're an observer, I don't think that's nice, observing people, as far as I'm concerned, the line between being an observer and being an out-and-out traitor is a very fine line indeed, personally, I would never trust anything said to me by an observer

CAROLINE: It seems I've not yet earned the right to speak within this room, despite years of devoted service taking the minutes, it seems that all I've done has still not been enough to overcome the legacy of

CHAIR: Caroline, no-one's background means anything to us here, we can all just speak

CAROLINE: To overcome the legacy of having had a decent education, I've paid but it's never enough and I'm never supposed to speak, because my perspective

CHAIR: We can all of us speak, and it doesn't even matter what we say

BOB: That's right, it doesn't, it really, really doesn't

CAROLINE: My perspective isn't popular, my perspective is not the popular one, I know too much, and those who know are always in the minority

RAY: That's why those who know are always wrong

CHAIR: How else can we expect to arrive at a

RAY: That's democracy

CHAIR: At a consensus

(Internal.)

I really enjoy the quiet before the meeting, when people are here deliberately not

350

starting, in the room hardly speaking, because whatever is said might accidentally trigger the meeting into starting before it should, so people sit modestly saving themselves for the meeting, and if anyone moves, it's a small modest movement, and everyone looks really quite composed

(To the room at large.)

Yes, arrive at a consensus

CAROLINE: What consensus, a popular consensus, there's no place for someone like me in a popular consensus

RAY: That's true, that's true

CHAIR: How else can we arrive at a consensus and write them a letter

CAROLINE: A letter that expresses the popular view, oh please

CHAIR: An enlightened letter, a careful letter, a letter which is carefully distilled, a crystal letter, a letter naming everything that is and everything that should be, a letter we can send to their office

CAROLINE: Never to be read

CHAIR: It will be read! The letter will be read, by them, because I know them, it's possible I'm the only one that does, I know they're reasonable, I know it because I'm reasonable, if I can be reasonable, it follows, so can they. Not everyone may understand this

CAROLINE: Understand it, how can I understand it, with my perspective, my perspective leads me to understand something quite different

CHAIR: Caroline, I didn't mean

CAROLINE: But please, forget about me, nothing I say is ever to be taken seriously, it's all to be dismissed

RAY: I'll second that

CHAIR: Of course it's not, Caroline

BOB: Chair, if we're going to be spending the meeting holding Caroline's hand

CAROLINE: Chair I don't want you being martyred on my account

CHAIR: No Caroline, that's all right

CAROLINE: So you do feel martyred

CHAIR: No, no, I

CAROLINE: Oh don't apologise, it's rather too late for that

BOB: If we're going to be spending the meeting holding Caroline's hand, then my nights are not what they should be

CHAIR: I just want to write them a letter!

CAROLINE: Yes write to them, do, it won't have any effect, but don't take my word for it, write, you'll never know how bereft they are, you never listen to me, you never will, you'll never believe what I say no matter how hard I try and how much work I do on behalf of the group, nothing I can do will ever be enough

JENNY: Caroline, put your shoes on, you'll feel better, we'll all feel better

CAROLINE: You're saying I should conform

JENNY: Can't you leave not conforming to those that have to?

CAROLINE: I wish I'd never had such a good education, I wish I could simply throw off the shackles of having such an excellent education, it's all so humiliating and debilitating

ESTELLE: I could take over the minutes if you like

CAROLINE: No, I'll do it, I'm paying my debt to society

ESTELLE: I wouldn't mind

CAROLINE: Estelle, do you have a debt to society?

ESTELLE: No, it's just I'd quite enjoy doing the minutes

CAROLINE: Well, if you don't have a debt to society, you don't need to do the minutes, do you

ESTELLE: If you're sure

CAROLINE: Estelle, please, I'll do the minutes

CHAIR: Thank you Estelle. Thank you Caroline

CAROLINE: Not that it will do any good

CHAIR: Yes thank you

(Internal.)

CHAIR: As for the smoked glass table, it's currently littered with the following: Ray's half doughnut in a brown paper bag; a pile of ignored agendas; Caroline's foot; a copy of the Unitary Development Plan; orange squash; glasses for orange squash; rings left by glasses of orange squash; rings left on the Unitary Development Plan by glasses of orange squash

(To the room at large.)

BOB: I've been thinking, chair, about the word 'concerned', it isn't much of a word, I think it's a beardy sort of word, it's a kindly, therapeutic, feebly patronising sort of word

CHAIR: What a shame, I quite like it

(Internal.)

CHAIR: Rings left on the Unitary Development Plan by glasses of orange squash; a ball of human hair; half a marble egg; scratch marks left by

Caroline's heavy-duty briefcase; purple spots of ink

(To the room at large.)

BOB: I prefer the word 'disgusted', a word that takes no prisoners

ESTELLE: Bob, I'm not disgusted

BOB: You're a disgrace, Estelle, the fact is, we ought to be disgusted at the sale of public buildings

ESTELLE: I'm against it, only not in a negative way

BOB: We're disgusted at the sale, aren't we? Everyone?

SEVERAL: Yes, etc

BOB: Does everyone agree we have to be strong on this?

SEVERAL: Definitely, etc

BOB: Do I have a consensus?

SEVERAL: Yes, etc

BOB: Chair?

CHAIR: What, Bob? Oh, yes, yes...

BOB: We have to be strong on this, because it's quite disgusting, would you agree with me, chair, I hope we stand together on this

CHAIR: Of course we stand together, of course we [do]

BOB: No need to be testy, chair

CHAIR: I'm not -

BOB: So long as we all grasp the importance of a unified attitude, because you only have to look at the morality of the thing to feel disgusted, really disgusted, it's evil and as such we oppose it, chair am I right? Everyone? Am I right?

SEVERAL: Oppose it, definitely, etc

BOB:	We should threaten to oppose it by means of a public campaign
SEVERAL:	Hear hear
BOB:	By a public campaign if necessary
SEVERAL:	Hear hear
BOB:	A public campaign, it's bound to worry them, I think they should be seriously worried, if we flatly refuse to have our buildings sold to fatten up the pay-cheques of their friends, we have to really threaten them, and show them we mean business
CHAIR:	These are bold words, Bob, bold words
BOB:	Yes and then they'll have to make it worth our while
CHAIR:	But that's not right
BOB:	We'll threaten them and find out what they'll give us, to make us go away
CHAIR:	Bob you've just lived down to everything I ever thought about you
BOB:	Really, as bad as that
CHAIR:	Yes, fairly close

(Internal.)

CHAIR:	Purple spots of ink; Bob's flashy mobile that throbs in a black leather holster; Bob's flashy mobile nudging Jenny's white angelic bicycle helmet; undrunk coffee; unwiped stains; a dreadful clotted pair of someone's gloves; Estelle's multicoloured raffia bag from which peep dark corners of tumult; and a plate of biscuits

(To the room at large.)

BOB:	I didn't mean for us, I mean a community fund, I'm sure you see what I mean, I mean

	funding for the community, and wouldn't that be desirable? And wouldn't we all like to get our hands on that? So that if they sell the buildings, we get funding for the community administered by the community, I've actually got a brother who's an accountant
CHAIR:	Mind the sofa

(Sofa breaks.)
Oh dear, Bob, are you all right?

BOB:	I mean it could be used for public projects. Projects for the public. Research into the public's needs
JENNY:	Am I missing something here, I thought the public needs the buildings, I thought that's what the public needs
BOB:	A very interesting idea, Jenny, we could pay you to research it
SEVERAL:	[Sounds of disgust]
BOB:	Only joking
ESTELLE:	I don't think we're here to be making jokes about them, if ever I start thinking badly about them I only have to remember the Christmas lights

(Internal.)

CHAIR:	A plate of biscuits, my wife won't actually come in here

(To the room at large.)

RAY:	Christmas lights, I don't want Christmas lights, I want some fireworks
ESTELLE:	And they do the fireworks
RAY:	I want some fireworks targeting that woman
ESTELLE:	The High Street looks so welcoming when they switch on the Christmas lights, and

they're on every lamp post, none has been left
out, of course there's the occasional one

RAY: Nuclear fireworks

ESTELLE: There are the occasional lampposts that are
faulty and have always refused to light up so
of course when the Christmas lights are on,
those lampposts are plunged in darkness

BOB: It's true what I say though, I've got this
brother who's an accountant, I'm hoping to
find something for him, he's driving a taxi

ESTELLE: But they are a tiny minority in among all the
wonderful sparkling lights all the way up the
hill along the High Street, and the crowning
glory I think is the big coloured stars, I love
them all, the red, the blue, the gold and
especially the green, the green are actually my
favourite of them all, and do you know I think
somebody must have heard me

CAROLINE: Yes, they'd hear you, they'd hear you

ESTELLE: Because just where my road joins the High
Street, I'm low down, you see, so I'm looking
all the way up the starry High Street going up
the hill, well just at that junction there, well
perhaps someone knew that junction was mine

JENNY: I think I must have joined this group to try
and end it all

ESTELLE: Because the star at that junction is a green one,
the brightest most beautiful green

BOB: You know they put a fence round the
Christmas tree, they put a metal crash barrier
round the actual Christmas tree in the High
Street, at Christmas

CHAIR: I expect it keeps the dogs off

(Internal.)

CHAIR: I've messed up this room

(To the room at large.)
Well Bob, the word disgusted, the word disgusted

BOB: Yes, you said it

ESTELLE: I don't want to say disgusted, I want to say encouraged, encouraged by their, what was it?

CAROLINE: Inaction

ESTELLE: Oh, was it really

RAY: I'm not encouraged, I'm not discouraged, they just have to nuke her

JENNY: So long as it's words of one syllable, they're so

CHAIR: And we're asking them to

ESTELLE: Well, thanking them, I thought

BOB: Or else chastising them with all the means at our disposal

CAROLINE: Feeling very very sorry for them really

RAY: Calling upon them calling them to exercise their

JENNY: Showing our contempt for their incredible

CHAIR: So I'll write to them incorporating all the – yes? Incorporating all the? Yes

(Internal.)

CHAIR: I don't think my wife actually believes in their existence. She's out there in the kitchen with a bottle of wine

THE END

WWW.OBERONBOOKS.COM